Modernism's Visible Hand

Buell Center Books in the History and Theory of American Architecture
Reinhold Martin, Series Editor

The Temple Hoyne Buell Center for the Study of American Architecture at
Columbia University was founded in 1982. Its mission is to advance the
interdisciplinary study of American architecture, urbanism, and landscape.

The Temple Hoyne
Buell Center
for the Study of
American Architecture

Modernism's Visible Hand

ARCHITECTURE AND REGULATION IN AMERICA

MICHAEL OSMAN

University of Minnesota Press   Minneapolis London

A different version of chapter 2 was previously published as "Preserved Assets" in *Governing by Design: Architecture, Economy, and Politics in the Twentieth Century*, ed. Aggregate (Architectural History Collaborative) (Pittsburgh: University of Pittsburgh Press, 2012), 1–20.

Every effort was made to obtain permission to reproduce material in this book. If any proper acknowledgment has not been included here, we encourage copyright holders to notify the publisher.

Published by the University of Minnesota Press
111 Third Avenue South, Suite 290
Minneapolis, MN 55401-2520
http://www.upress.umn.edu

Printed in the United States of America on acid-free paper

The University of Minnesota is an equal-opportunity educator and employer.

25 24 23 22 21 20 19 18   10 9 8 7 6 5 4 3 2 1

Library of Congress Cataloging-in-Publication Data
Names: Osman, Michael, author.
Title: Modernism's visible hand : architecture and regulation in America / Michael Osman.
Description: Minneapolis : University of Minnesota Press, 2018. | Series: Buell Center books in the history and theory of American architecture | Includes bibliographical references and index. |
Identifiers: LCCN 2017056774 (print) | ISBN 978-1-5179-0097-7 (hc) | ISBN 978-1-5179-0098-4 (pb)
Subjects: LCSH: Architecture and technology–United States–History. | Architecture and society–United States–History. | Buildings–Environmental engineering–United States–History. | Technological innovations–Economic aspects–United States–History. | Risk management–United States–History. | BISAC: ARCHITECTURE / History / Modern (late 19th Century to 1945). | ARCHITECTURE / Criticism. | SOCIAL SCIENCE / Sociology / Urban.
Classification: LCC NA2543.T43 O86 2018 (print) DDC 720.1/03–dc23
LC record available at https://lccn.loc.gov/2017056774

Contents

The planning room in the Watertown Arsenal. Carl G. Barth Collection, Baker Library, Harvard Business School.

Preface

The taking of a modern steamship about the world (though one would not minimize its responsibilities) has not the same quality of intimacy with nature, which, after all, is an indispensable condition to the building up of an art. It is less personal and a more exact calling; less arduous, but also less gratifying in the lack of close communion between the artist and the medium of his art. It is, in short, less a matter of love. Its effects are measured exactly in time and space as no effect of an art can be. It is an occupation which a man not desperately subject to sea-sickness can be imagined to follow with content, without enthusiasm, with industry, without affection. Punctuality is its watchword. The incertitude which attends closely every artistic endeavour is absent from its regulated enterprise.

Joseph Conrad, *The Mirror of the Sea* (1906)

At the end of the nineteenth century, life in America increasingly relied on infrastructures that delivered electrical power, water, and other amenities to buildings. Among the newly developed mechanical systems within these buildings, some circulated artificially controlled air at a uniform temperature, and others were used to integrate various processes involved in industrial production.

My purpose is to describe the conceptual terrain from which these systems emerged and their adaptation to buildings. As a point of entry, mechanical control of the environment in homes, public buildings, and storage warehouses begins my exploration of a range of techniques developed in this large nation to govern its infrastructure and the lives that it helped support. These systems were coordinated from an array of divergent components, a process of integration that was piecemeal and never unified. Therefore, no single economic theory, technological change, scientific discovery, or political upheaval can fully explain the heterogeneous forces that organized life in the decades between the Civil War and the end of the First World War.

In lieu of a historical event that sets these transformations into motion, *regulation* provides a unifying term for understanding the technologies, reforms, and principles that emerged at that time. This term describes a practical mode of living, working, and thinking; it refers to an assemblage of techniques—mechanical, legal, administrative, and scientific—that defined a range of deviations from normal in which modern life could retain both the appearance of order and the functionality of organization. Common to all these techniques was the assumption that no system could be described as ideal, self-correcting, or inherently ordered. To mark the difference between these techniques and the naturalized theories of the self-regulating "invisible hand" offered by classical political economists, I use the business historian Alfred D. Chandler Jr.'s concept of the "visible hand." Modernism did not materialize in buildings as the embodiment of an idea about a new society; rather it was constructed through intersections of management with technology and physical infrastructure that operated on the environment and the economy to constrain the errors and deviations endemic to a society invested in growth.

The history of regulation in the United States undergirds the history of modernism. Its protagonists include architects, engineers, entrepreneurs, scientists, and industrialists. And although monumental images of the American metropolis filled the pages of European journals, producing the appearance of a society unified around distinctly modern values, the society represented in those images was in fact built up from an accumulation of numerous changes to the mundane routines of daily life. Architecture reflects these minute shifts. Buildings housed much of the machinery and the activities that made American life modern. This is not to say that this machinery was exclusively American; in fact, techniques of regulation tended to pass from one context to another rather easily. I have constrained the geography of this study to make specific connections between regulation and the development of political, social, and economic institutions in the United States after the Civil War. Indeed, against the historiographical tendency to view this New World nation as uninhibited by history, modern architecture arose no more naturally in America than in Europe, with conflicts and unpredictable shifts in the purposes served by technologies used in buildings. While some of these buildings immediately lent themselves to a photographic image of modernity, such as the skyscrapers built during this period, the buildings that are the focus of this study enacted and represented processes that governed the nation in less obvious ways.

This is not a history of enthusiastic people doing interesting things; instead, it is an investigation of the kinds of activities that Joseph Conrad understood to be involved in "taking a modern steamship about the world": the gradual and measured restructuring of American society through techniques related to regulation. Changes in the definitions of home, market, nature, and labor can be traced to what have become canonical modernist images of great machinery—dynamos, giant ventilators, and refrigeration machines—but also in the bureaucratic systems and buried infrastructure that integrated these technologies into the fabric of modern life.

Introduction

After the American Civil War, a set of legal, technical, and economic in-struments formed the visible hand of management. These instruments, systems of communication, distribution, and production, integrated the operations of large corporations. Rather than allow the dynamics of booms and busts to affect the interests of a large firm, as laissez-faire eco-nomic doctrine dictated, Alfred Chandler showed how corporate manag-ers sought to develop tools to secure the company's interests and maxi-mize its profits by balancing the rate and volume of output with market demand.[1] Establishing this balance relied, in part, on the company's ability to control productivity by regulating the activities and conditions inside industrial buildings. Factories and warehouses as well as other building types were managed with the aid of instruments of regulation, which in turn contributed to a vast infrastructure of control—a new basis for gov-ernance in this rapidly modernizing nation.[2]

Many historians have written about the turn of the twentieth century as a period of great transformation in American capitalism. The general term they used to describe broad shifts in social institutions, political economy, and culture was *modernization*, but all these changes depended on innumer-able specific alterations to the inner workings of industry, commerce, sci-ence, and domestic life.[3] The history of regulation that I will address can be found in the techniques and concepts that resulted from these subtle revisions to daily life, many of which have become so fundamental by our modern standards that they appear rather mundane. As an architectural history of regulation and not an economic history of capitalism or manage-rial culture, this book begins with the premise that paying close attention to the changes made to buildings and their operations offers a unique form of evidence for understanding some aspects of regulatory thinking in this period. To further specify the great contributions in the historiography of American modernization with a range of physical artifacts—including machines, record-keeping instruments, and buildings—this book makes concrete history from the infrastructures that subtended the problem of control.[4]

A significant gap existed between techniques of control and the imperatives that drove the decisions of practicing architects, revealing a misalignment between regulatory thinking and architectural discourse. Designs for buildings were never directly determined by calculations made by mechanical engineers or by criteria guiding the decisions of businessmen. This is evident in the responses of architects to the problem of accommodating various new technical demands in their designs. Their discussions can be generally grouped into two topics: first, the effect of machine-made building components on developing new architectural forms, and second, the stylistic impact of adding mechanical plants for managing the interior environment. American architects who claimed their work to be modern found it necessary to take a position on the increasingly pervasive presence of mechanical technology on one or both topics.

As an example of one architect's response to both topics, I will focus briefly on the canonical figure of Frank Lloyd Wright. His notoriety also offers a rich historiographical context of modern American architecture in this period, a fitting case for an introduction. In his lecture on "The Art and Craft of the Machine," delivered in 1901, Wright focused on the first topic, the machine manufacture of building components. Speaking thirty-eight years after Emancipation, he argued that as much as slavery could not coexist with the values of democracy, the classical art of Ancient Greece could never be reestablished in the United States. He linked modern aesthetics to new forms of labor and celebrated the potential offered by an industrialized society to expand the capacity of human expression with the work of machines:

> Every age has done its work, produced its art with . . . the tools most successful in saving the most precious thing in the world—human effort. Greece used the chattel slave as the essential tool of its art and civilization. This tool we have discarded, and we would refuse the return of Greek art upon the terms of its restoration, because we insist now upon a basis of democracy. . . . A distinction made by the tool which frees human labor, lengthens and broadens the life of the simplest man, thereby the basis of the democracy upon which we insist.[5]

Wright believed that the changes brought about by machines in the relations between man and his tools would lead to changes in the forms of art
and architecture. As William Morris, leader of the British Arts and Crafts
movement, had done, Wright observed that the machine distanced the
laborer from handicraft, but he deviated from Morris's moralistic criticism. Hoping to see architects fully incorporate machine-made elements
into the development of new forms of artistic expression, he noted that
industrialization allowed for the mass production of new ornament such
as machine-molded terra cotta tiles that encased the industrially fabricated steel members of skyscrapers' skeletal structure. Wright saw in the
tall office buildings designed by his mentor, Louis Sullivan, a path toward
a fuller integration of the machine into artistic expression. Sullivan's contribution, in Wright's view, was the identification of the skyscraper as an
object for developing the art of architecture according to methods made
available by machines.[6]

In his design for the Larkin Administration Building (1903–6), Wright
also engaged in the second topic, expressing his views on an architectural style that responded to the presence of the mechanical technologies housed in modern buildings (Figure I.1). Compared to Sullivan's skyscrapers, in which the facade expressed the use of machined parts, Wright
claimed that the Larkin Building's solid forms resulted from making room
for new machinery. The building's basement housed numerous mechanical systems: electrical lines for artificial lighting, a plumbing system, and
the most advanced air-handling system then available. Ventilators circulated air from the outside that had been rinsed with water, through vertical ducts built into the monumental shafts at each corner of the building.
Wright explained that this hermetically sealed system protected the office
employees from "poisonous gases" produced by locomotives on the surrounding rail yards, then active in Buffalo. Yet beyond their function as
airshafts, the piers clearly served the architect's aesthetic interests. The
blank masses' dramatic vertical thrust gave the building an iconic exterior form, satisfying the client's desire to present a powerful image of the
Larkin Company. In his *Autobiography*, Wright explained that his design
process was driven by a "principle of articulation," a stylistic interpretation of the building's incorporation of machinery. Wright's retrospective
tale, then, positioned his design between the function of mechanical systems on the one hand and his approach to modern architectural aesthetics
on the other.[7]

FIGURE I.1. The Larkin Administration Building, Seneca Street View. FLLW FDN FA#0403.0030.
Copyright 2016 Frank Lloyd Wright Foundation, Scottsdale, AZ / Artists Rights Society (ARS), NY.

Nevertheless, the form of the monumental masses did not directly correlate with their technical functions. Architectural historian Vincent Scully recognized that the Larkin Building's design extended Wright's integration of space and structure from his earlier house projects. In residences of 1903–5 for William Martin in Oak Park and his brother, Darwin Martin, who worked for the Larkin Company in Buffalo, Scully located similar expressions in piers used in domestic space.[8] Not only were the Larkin Building's piers not determined by advanced mechanical functions of ducts and plumbing, their continued use by Wright helped articulate corners in other buildings, such as Unity Temple in Oak Park (1905–8), that lacked advanced mechanical systems. In his design for the Larkin Building, then, Wright had developed a stylistic device that sublimated the function of the mechanical system. This device helped him produce a building that retained modern formal unity while providing an alternative to Sullivan's language of machined parts, integrated into a gridded facade. The systematic coordination of industrial elements in Sullivan's skyscrapers—tile, steel, and plate glass—directly expressed modern production in architectural form, while Wright's exterior forms suppressed the image of the machines housed in the basement.

A different approach from Scully's stylistic approach to the Larkin Building is found in the writings of the architectural critic and historian Reyner Banham. In the late 1960s, Banham, initially trained in engineering, aimed to construct a technological interpretation of the modern movement in architecture. For him, Wright's design of the Larkin Building extended beyond the corner piers and architectural space inside to the arrangement of the mechanical systems that produced the interior environment. Extracts and exhausts in the balustrades of the balconies that wrapped the atrium, Banham argued, illustrated a need to closely analyze these mechanical details as they related to the ventilation system to understand the building's form.

More generally, Banham believed that the history of architecture ought to be subsumed into the study of methods for shaping environmental conditions, methods that he called "environmental management." Seeing a persistent and troublesome "time-lag—sometimes of decades . . . between a mechanical device becoming available, and its full-blooded exploitation," he advocated knowledge of environmental technologies to be an essential driver for the continued modernization of architecture.[9] When analyzing the buildings profiled in his seminal book, *The Architecture of the*

Well-Tempered Environment (1969), any forces—even political or economic ones—that were not immediately evident at the interface of design with technology, Banham relegated to passing comments, as a way to promote the dominance of technology in determining historical change.[10]

It is not a disengagement of architects from technological action, however, that causes a belated architectural reaction. Rather, there are differences in the methods used by these professions to produce knowledge. In aiming to synchronize architecture with engineering, Banham needed to dissolve any specific forms of architectural knowledge into the expanded field of environmental management.[11] His history of this enlarged domain of knowledge hinged on the belief that mechanical systems were developed primarily to create well-tempered environments for humans. This approach immediately narrowed the range of possible conclusions of his study to one of perpetual improvement, evaluated according to the accommodation of human biological needs. He proposed that the processes of modernization tended to produce an ever-tighter fit between architecture and its user, with the astronaut's space suit as the apotheosis of this tendency. But if environmental technologies, like all other technologies, serve many overlapping purposes, then they cannot be reduced to the determinations of a single naturalized essence like human biology.

Consider again Wright's statement that the machines in the Larkin Building were installed to extract the toxic by-products of industrialized transport. This reveals that the expansion of the rail networks of coal-powered locomotives used to deliver Larkin's soap products and every other commodity they offered in the company's catalog throughout the nation was the cause for sealing the interior of the administration building from the exterior. The machinery in the basement was therefore not merely a technical improvement for the benefit of office work; it represented the reciprocal relation between the consequences of industrialization outside the building and the technologies that helped mediate their effect inside. Moreover, the choice to erect an administration building in this polluted location reveals the company's strategy to centralize different and complementary forms of regulation. The Larkin Building was both the public face of the company as well as its brain, its control center. The large office staff housed inside coordinated the rate of production and distribution with the volume of inventory for this mail-order company according to shifts in demand among their vast lists of customers. The employees seated at the office furniture that Wright designed for the building—desks equipped with graphophones, walls with built-in filing cabinets, and distinctive swivel chairs—were data managers whose work protected the company's interests in the face of a potentially unstable market.[12]

Poisonous gases and economic fluctuations were two immediate risks brought under regulation in the Larkin Company's administrative centralization. As the chapters that follow will demonstrate, regulatory systems addressed uncertainties in many other contexts as well. Advertising for domestic machinery predicted that a more stable household economy would depend upon replacing erratic and expensive servant labor with investments in reliable machinery. In facilities for food storage, cooled space preserved perishables to stabilize prices and thereby manage the persistent threat of economic crisis due to overproduction. Within these spaces, potential changes in the environment could be measured and controlled to produce at least some predictable outcomes. In contrast to a determined path toward mechanization, this book situates technological change as one consequence of the competing motivations for organizing infrastructures to ensure some sort of security. These motivations addressed real risks to industrial profit and human health as well as perceived risks to more abstract concepts such as the preservation of nature or the value of labor.[13]

While Banham's proposed shift of historiography toward environmental management responded to a broader cultural movement of environmentalism of the 1960s, the sociologist of science Bruno Latour provides a recent vantage point from which Banham's formulations can be revised.[14] By redefining technological objects as "collective things" rather than a set of progressively improved innovations, Latour has sought to describe the many mediating elements that compose what we perceive to be technical changes. According to him, understanding the role of a technological object would require including the motivations of its users, makers, and maintenance workers and each of their ties to a collective, that is, an assembly of humans and the nonhuman elements that represent their interests.[15] The history of collective things cannot be translated into ticks on a time line or a definitive narrative of historical progress motivated by innovation. Once we see the machines that were added to buildings with this alternative formulation, we realize that their presence registers the inclusion of all the competing interests that compose Latour's notion of a collective. When a regulatory system is understood as a product of these multiple motivations, it cannot appear as a mere technological improvement in the fitness of buildings to their inhabitants but as a nexus for the multiple interdependencies that exist between humans and their nonhuman instruments.[16]

These interdependencies are not exclusively technical or architectural or always intended to promote human comfort. Latour has shown that considering the often-contradictory values represented by modern infrastructure is fundamental to a realistic understanding of how society operates and that no distinction should be made between objective material constraints and symbolic human, subjective ones. He invokes the example of environmental technologies to illustrate the way we have formed our dependencies on technology in general: "There is no outside: outside is another inside with another climate control, another thermostat, another air-conditioning system. . . . To define humans is to define the envelopes, the life support systems, the *Umwelt* that make it possible for them to breathe."[17] Latour's metaphorical treatment of technology—both intimate and global—replaces the idealization of progress with an idea about mundane and pragmatic actions that he identifies with the most general definition of design.[18]

An undifferentiated and unified mode of thought and action called design, however, potentially destroys the institutional and disciplinary norms that surround cultural objects that are associated with architecture. Architects produce their own history and institutions to sustain and dispute collective values. Like Latour's generalized rubric of design, Banham's notion of environmental management also dissolved this differentiation, leaving the definition of knowledge produced by architectural labor rather vague. In addition, Latour's metaphor of "life support," to describe environmental systems, helps identify certain dependencies but also implies that regulatory systems developed out of the primordial and continuous process of accommodating biological needs.[19] In the chapters that follow, I present historical instances that dislocate human biology from its assumed centrality to regulation in both Banham's techno-architectural history and Latour's theory of collective dependency. I find that competing claims made by diverse actors—corporate managers, technicians, architects—illustrate multiple historically specific causes for adding these systems to buildings that only occasionally were framed to accommodate humans' biological needs. Recognizing the heterogeneous motivations that positioned architects in the development and application of regulatory systems both expands and differentiates the processes associated with modernization. More importantly, architectural discourse retains an identifiable position among others in these changes, one that ultimately helps bring new light to the historiography of modernism.

This book is organized around specific historical effects of regulatory thinking. Each of the five chapters addresses a combination of mechanical systems, buildings, and representations of control that characterize several domains of American culture: family, commerce, science, and industry. In these contexts, the meaning of the terms *home, market, nature,* and *labor* shifted over time. We see this in the first two chapters that deal with certain physical technologies—although not intended to be exhaustive accounts of every such system—developed to control environmental conditions central to the economies of private life and the public markets. While these technical systems were substantial and often occupied entire rooms or basements, they had sporadic and indirect impacts on architectural design. The third and fourth chapters focus on representational techniques that evolved with regulatory thinking in science and industry. These techniques—and they are not always related to mechanisms—brought the objects of regulation into a broad cultural discourse and also became part of modernist visual culture. One consistent theme in the chapters is the conflicted and occasional role of architecture in applying mechanical systems or in representing regulation.

Chapter 1 traces the development of the mechanically controlled interior environment. It begins by identifying the use of thermostats in British industry in the early nineteenth century. The potential application of this instrument became part of a wide-ranging discourse on ventilating air in industrial settings and public sites. Debate was most prominent during the planning for the new Houses of Parliament in London in which the problem of priority between architectural form and systematic ventilation was unresolved. The Englishman David Boswell Reid worked on the ventilation system in that contested project before moving to the United States in the middle of the century to document the simple systems used in American houses. Traditionally, upper-class households required servants to handle heat production and distribution, but in households that could not afford servants, the tasks of ventilating and heating fell to the homemaker. In this context Reid's research on the efficiency and hygiene of simple systems for domestic ventilation influenced the feminist reformer Catharine Beecher. Her transformation of the homemaker's labor refashioned housework into a form of modern labor that was at once separate from and analogous to that of industry. Just as the mechanized production of factories was being formed into systems, domestic environmental machinery was gradually collected into a household system around the economic unit of the modern American family. It was in houses and not in factories that automated thermostatic control was first fully realized. Under the influence of later domestic reformers Christine Frederick and Mary Pattison, these automated technologies became part of a field called the "household sciences." Tracing the development of thermostatic control from the industrial to the domestic context, this chapter examines shifts in the definition of housework from traditional homemaking to the technical knowledge of household management.

Chapter 2 focuses on a larger scale and complexity of mechanical systems in the design and construction of cold storage warehouses. Large commercial buildings that stored commodities for commission merchants required cooling systems that could preserve dairy, fruit, vegetables, and other perishables from decay. While in storage, these commodities were not only protected from bacteria by the cooled interior environment, but also sheltered from the fluctuations of their price caused by unstable economic demand. Investors in these buildings aimed to expand the speculative market in grain to perishables by issuing futures contracts for these commodities, held in cold storage facilities. In designing warehouse buildings, some clients asked architects to develop a visual language that was appropriate for both these buildings' new functions and their urban context. Two significant investments in warehouse design, the Chicago Cold Storage Exchange designed by the partnership of Louis Sullivan and Dankmar Adler and the Quincy Market Cold Storage Company in Boston designed by William Gibbons Preston, show instructive results. These architects worked with their clients and engineers to accommodate an increasingly complex combination of advanced environmental technologies and governmental regulations. Each project aimed to address the public, the first through its monumental form, and the second as a public utility. The diverging definition of "public" in each case reveals that the function of environmental control tested assumptions of traditional architectural practice and required a new level of engagement with the technical and legal infrastructure of the emerging regulatory state.

At both the domestic and commercial scales, then, the process of integrating mechanical systems into buildings required architects to work in unexpected ways. The first two chapters both indicate a growing historical divergence in the types of services offered by the practice of architecture from those offered by the practice of mechanical engineering. Given this divergence, no distinct architectural language was formed to communicate to the public the value of environmental control. The functions of mechanical systems remained largely inaccessible to a broader audience. Indeed, giving an image to the technical functions of these systems may even have run counter to the logic of environmental control. By keeping regulatory infrastructures largely hidden from view, in basements, above ceilings, and inside walls, a semblance of order was produced by concealing the apparatus from an occupant's immediate attention.

But if the book were to remain focused on the complex and occasional relation of architecture to the technologically regulated economies of household and market, or other domains, it would only deliver a narrow history of hidden systems that produced an apparent order. The final chapters, by contrast, broaden the definition of regulation to include methods of regulatory thinking primarily related to *representing* control. These techniques were not rendered in the conventions used for architectural communication, but in instruments, systems of display, and tabulations of data that would greatly affect architectural culture after the First World War. These chapters turn to representations of the systems that managed environmental and economic dynamics in museums, laboratories, factories, and offices. Although mechanical systems are present in these cases, I describe the emergence of regulation through the techniques of visualization used in each. These techniques, developed around describing the idea of control in the science of ecology and industrial management, ranged from life-size panoramic photography to abstract diagrammatic illustration. The images described dynamic systems that focused on differentiating inside from outside, life from death, and profit from loss. This visual language rendered natural and industrial processes as dynamic and time-based and, within a few years of their formulation, became important antecedents to theories of urban expansion and a few architectural functionalist tools of modern design such as circulation diagrams.

Chapter 3 focuses on the representational tools used by ecologists to visualize biological systems of regulation in natural environments. I examine a few buildings that housed instruments for early ecologists to portray their understanding of the interaction between organisms and their surroundings. The chapter examines two exemplary cases: the habitat dioramas at the Chicago Academy of Sciences and an experimental laboratory at the Illinois Vivarium in Urbana. In the habitat diorama, "nature's economy" was represented to a public that was becoming increasingly concerned with preserving nature from industrial expansion. An entire floor in the academy's museum hosted a photographic panorama that formed the backdrop to a diorama: a timeless image of the dynamic changes in the Indiana sand dunes and greater Chicago region. Collapsing time into one continuous three-dimensional representation brought the competing ecological forces in the dunes into a unified spatial experience. In laboratories built for ecology, by contrast, biological specimens were transferred into a mechanically controlled interior to represent their behavior according to the practices of modern experimental research: data collection and interpretation. At the core of this chapter is an analysis of a broad shift in the cultural definition of nature in both scientific display and experimentation. The term *ecology*, conceived through economic metaphors, led scientists to think of organisms with terms borrowed from political economy. Ecologists such as Henry Chandler Cowles and Victor Shelford believed that their object of study was a naturally occurring economic system in which organisms regulated their habitats to preserve life. The term *regulation*, as it was used by these scientists, extended its meaning from the governance of machines and human exchange to the behaviors of organisms that managed environmental change. This use of the term can be traced through the display of the struggle for life in habitat dioramas as well as in the interpretations of data produced in laboratory experiments on living specimens.

While scientists used managerial concepts to represent natural systems, industrial managers used scientific methods of data collection to measure, observe, and alter processes of production in the factory. From this exchange, they developed new techniques to pursue the function of management that Frederick Winslow Taylor called brainwork. This term identified the character of a manager's work with the nonphysical labor of a clerical mind. The processes of brainwork produced representations of physical labor through data as well as through diagrams that explained the clerical apparatus of production control. The contribution of these objects to regulatory thinking is the topic of chapter 4. The chapter begins with Taylor's analyses of the tasks in machine shops during the 1880s and traces their evolution into a bureaucratic system for planning the distribution and flow of work through factory buildings. His disciples, Carl G. Barth and Horace K. Hathaway, refined instruments to identify potential sources of disruption to continuous production. The clerks whom they oversaw organized the work in various machine shops by regulating the speed and volume of production with slide rules, bulletin boards, and instruction cards. Their tools visualized the data that clerks collected from the shop floor to normalize and order the factory's daily tasks. Such methods could speed up output, but also allowed the so-called planning department to restrict production if demand diminished. Visualizing the factory with a dynamic time-based plan allowed managers to organize tasks through distributed time allotments to the machine-shop workers. The planning of these activities occurred in the absence of architects and architectural drawing conventions. Managers formed their own techniques of diagrammatic notation and produced distinctive drawings that prioritized time as the organizing variable over space. In the 1920s, functionalist architects who adopted managerial imagery in their designs explained its value with a vocabulary of flow and continuity.

Although architectural circulation diagrams, based on Taylor-inspired graphic notations, served as rhetorical devices in the design of modernist architecture, the more immediate impact of industrial management on architectural production was the reorganization of the architectural office. The application of management to the labor of architectural offices, addressed in chapter 5, indicates a crucial set of differences that emerged in the twentieth century between the professional labor of modern architects and the product-driven production processes of large-scale industry. This chapter considers the formation of the modern architectural office through innovations in office management and instruments for regulating the services, schedules, and budgets of twentieth-century practice.

Canonical images of mass production—photographs of ocean liners and ball bearings or paintings of glass bottles and factories—have become fundamental to the historiography of modernism. To link this visual language to a broader set of discourses, beyond those internal to modernist artists, architects, and their critics, I pair that canon with other image cultures that have been less explicitly aestheticized. Such images comprise a substantial form of evidence for this book, and many have not yet entered the visual history of architectural modernism. Perhaps this is the result of the difficulty of picturing the mechanical systems that regulated architectural interiors and the disciplinary distance between the visual language of regulation and that common to architectural history. To overcome these challenges has required collecting visual documents that were not intended for artists, architects, or critics of modern culture, but for a host of other audiences. In this book, these image types include advertisements in journals of home economics, cartoons in the popular press, photographs of construction sites, drawings published in technical journals, scientific photography, and diagrams from textbooks on production control. With a close reading of these cultural products, often finding symbolism where it is least expected, it is possible to observe the development of a complex nexus and occasional rift between the purposes served by systems of regulation and the services offered by professional architectural firms at that time.

Modernist representations of industry like those mentioned above therefore do not reflect a victorious image of modernism as it formed into a unified architectural language during the twentieth century. Rather, these idealized images of machines should serve as allegories that reflect an emerging role that architects inherited during the so-called machine age: to interpret the products and functions of industry that might have otherwise escaped visual attention. The appropriation of managerial tools, diagrams, and office furniture by architects of the 1920s was not only the result of the desire for cultural synchrony between architecture and industry but also an indication of the acknowledged distance that had formed between modernist architectural thought on the one hand and the wide-ranging forces of industry on the other. The fetish of the machine and the liberation from historical reference that it allowed was, then, also the image of a growing gap between architecture and industry. Machines gained greater aesthetic attention from architects at the very moment that the avant-garde became conscious of the distance between their intellectual domain and the power of regulatory systems to govern so many aspects of modern life.

CHAPTER 1

The Thermostatic Interior and Household Management

Early nineteenth-century efforts to uncover the electrical regulation of the body, in both scientific experiments and the lore surrounding them, reveal a principle of regulation that extended from methods for controlling industrial machinery to those used to manage environments in public and domestic buildings. One example of the principle's translation from physiological experimentation to practical application was the thermostat, a mechanical apparatus designed to control temperature. From the fifty years after the thermostatic mechanism was patented to its eventual integration into the electrical networks of buildings, a diverse set of agents contributed to forming the thermostatic interior. The history of this regulatory instrument begins with the work of the Scottish doctor and chemist Andrew Ure (1778–1854). Although he never directly tied his physiological interest in electricity to thermostatic control, both his examination of the electrical regulation of bodily movement and his design of this regulatory device positioned his thinking at the center of a metaphorical exchange between organisms and machines.

In 1818, when Mary Shelley published her gothic novel about Dr. Victor Frankenstein, Ure led an experiment that brought into motion the corpse of the murderer Matthew Clydesdale by stimulating it with an electric shock.[1] In applying artificial electrical current to nerves, medical scientists such as Ure and the fictional characters based on them were trying to reveal the forces that guided an organism's physical movement. In one experiment, Ure showed that electrifying the phrenic nerve and the top of the diaphragm could induce a breath. According to the classical definition of life as a "current of breath," the experiment could have been viewed as

1

an attempt to wake the dead.[2] Yet for Ure the aim was not to project a primary relationship between electricity and life but to investigate the internal control of bodily movement, a study initiated by the Paduan physicist Giovanni Aldini (1762–1834), for whom electrical signals were an essential part of the "animal machine." At the end of the eighteenth century, Aldini had already shown the presence of animal electricity in dogs and horses. In 1803, he experimented on the body of a "malefactor executed at Newgate," prompting the corpse's facial muscles to contort into a grimace, but failed to produce any motion in the heart.[3] Fifteen years later, Ure believed that a closer view of nervous action was still possible, that the lungs and heart could equally be stimulated by electrical current.

At stake in these experiments was Ure's hypothesis that electrical impulses coordinated the movements of the body, an idea that drew upon the mechanistic theories of René Descartes. Before scientists understood the physiology of nerves or anything about animal electricity, Descartes believed that an animating fluid induced the movements of the body. He illustrated this automated action with the example of a boy whose foot exchanged signals with the pineal gland when stimulated by the heat of a flame, a stimulus that was then translated back into his body's sudden movement.

In the nineteenth century, the development of the reflex concept revised this explanation of an organism's reactions to external stimuli. The reflex synthesized Aldini's, Ure's, and other researchers' work on electrical nervous impulses with seventeenth-century descriptions, including those of Descartes, in which bodily movements were compared to those of pulleys and levers.[4] The reflex concept differed from earlier theories, however, partly because experiments had shown that this bioelectrical circuit regulated numerous bodily functions. Nineteenth-century researchers therefore understood that certain movements were involuntary and not controlled by a central organ, as Descartes had believed. The electrical signal that constituted a reflex justified an interpretation of the organism's movement as controlled by a set of sensitive mechanisms dispersed throughout the body. The network of nerves that provided the electrical pathways for a reflex offered physiologists an alternative to Descartes's view that the central organization of peripheral movement derived from the heart, as inspired by the soul.[5] Although Ure did not directly participate in formalizing the reflex concept, his research on electrical regulation of movement was essential to the experimental background that gave scientists the tools to explain environmental change as the stimulus for the involuntary behaviors of organisms.

Ure's interest in regulation was not limited to understanding the system of electrical impulses that organized the physical functions of life. While his physiological experiments gained the attention of the medical community and of the popular imagination, when he shifted his research to develop an organizational system for large-scale factory production, his theories became central to early forms of industrial management. He envisioned a parallel organizational system to that in the nerves of animals for the machinery found in increasingly complex production facilities, especially those developed for the textile industry. In 1830, he moved from Glasgow to London, abandoning his medical research to concentrate on systematizing the processes of industrial production.[6]

Ure viewed the labor in a factory objectively as a whole, as Karl Marx later wrote, without regard to its execution by human hands. He came to this conclusion from descriptions of mechanically automated processes in production. Reversing his earlier explanations of involuntary bodily motion, where Ure used a metaphorical explanation of biology through machines, in his writings on the factory he used biological metaphors that explained the regulation of certain mechanical systems. What Ure called the "factory system" was an agglomeration of machines that he hoped to unify into an intricate, unified self-acting machine. His anticipation of a fully automated factory was full of metaphorical reversals—explaining the machine through organic language and vice versa. In several instances Ure described the factory as an artificial living subject guided by mechanical forces, but he also claimed that it was an object from which the mass laborer would learn to embrace a more collective subjectivity.[7]

The reversibility of comparisons between machine and organism was fundamental to Ure's thinking. Consider his description in *The Philosophy of Manufactures* of an automatic cotton-spinning machine designed by Richard Roberts, known as the "self-acting mule":

> [It is a] machine apparently instinct with the thought, feeling, and tact of the experienced workman—which even in its infancy displayed a new principle of regulation, ready in its mature state to fulfill the functions of a finished spinner. Thus, the Iron Man, as the operatives fitly call it, sprung out of the hands of our modern Prometheus at the

bidding of Minerva—a creation destined to restore order among the industrious classes, and to confirm to Great Britain the empire of art.[8]

With this explicit reference to Shelley's *Frankenstein,* Ure established a figural relationship between the factory and her "modern Prometheus." The modernity of this industrial setting was defined by its capacity literally to give birth to mechanical infants, intelligent machines that behaved with a surprisingly well-developed gestural elegance. The instinct that Ure called a "principle of regulation" guided the Roberts machine mechanically and not through electrical impulses. Nonetheless, when this principle was applied to an intricate assembly of moving parts for spinning cotton it presented a level of craft comparable to that of a skilled worker. In addition, its capacity came without the problems associated with managing a human worker such as their exhaustion, forgetfulness, or sickness. The analogy between bodies and machines hinged on the apparent intelligence of the automatic apparatus. Ure's physiological experiments on Clydesdale's body had sought the regulatory principle in the electrical organization of the human nervous system, while Roberts's invention represented a mechanical analogue to a biological network—an intelligence that appeared to be built into the self-acting spinning movements of the mule.[9] Ure concluded that the mechanical instinct of the Roberts cotton-spinning machine would initiate a new sense of order in the working class: it was an example of efficiency, obedience, and technical mastery that would establish a model of well-regulated work for the mass laborer.

Ure's interest in mechanical regulation was already evident in his 1830 report to the Royal Society regarding an invention that he called a thermostat, or heat-governor (Figure 1.1). The sensitive action of a "bimetal strip," he explained, would make it possible for machines to respond to changes in the environmental conditions of heat.[10] Layering zinc and steel into a single strip either by soldering or riveting produced a form of dynamic bending movement in the object. Different rates of expansion of each metal, when exposed to the surrounding heat, produced a "flexure" that translated a temperature change into a mechanical movement. The descriptive term chosen by Ure has the root "flex," or a bend, in common with the nervous *reflex.* Both the bimetallic strip and the bioelectrical impulse produced changes—either by a mechanical bending or bodily movement—that resulted from an environmental shift. Grafted onto other machines, Ure's thermostat became a technological reflex that could modulate the behavior of these mechanisms in response to changes in the temperature of their surroundings. He wrote: "the metallic bars must possess such force of flexure in heating or cooling, as to enable their working rods or levers to open or shut valves, stopcocks, and ventilating orifices."[11] The sensitivity of the thermostat could thus invest nearly any type of machine with a capacity to react to environmental change. Like the electrical impulse of a biological reflex, which acted without a central guiding force, integrating Ure's thermostat into the factory by attaching it to various machines would produce multiple local instances of regulation.

More directly, the potential application of the device that Ure proposed was for regulating the temperature of air within the factory interior so that such a building could maintain an acceptable range of heat for the labor process. Yet the action of a single small strip would not be powerful enough for such a large task. Thus, Ure explained that multiplying the number of bimetallic strips could amplify the subtle movement of a single thermostat. Combining the strips' movement could activate an expanded system of chains and pulleys either to open a ventilation system for hot air exhaust or, if the temperature dipped too low, open a hot air register fed by the furnace. To ensure predictable interior conditions throughout the year the thermostat needed to become part of a generalized automated mechanical system that operated on the ventilation machinery for an industrial building. While small drawings illustrated some applications in his *Dictionary of Arts, Manufactures and Mines*, Ure did not precisely describe any instance in which the device was physically integrated into a factory to govern its interior temperature. He only hinted that in the near future the instrument would give factory proprietors "a self-acting means of regulating the temperature of their apartments, and of promoting their ventilation."[12] By integrating the thermostat into the methods of heat delivery already widely in use, he believed, working conditions in many of Britain's factories could be immediately improved. His hope was to use this system to replace the existing horizontal steam-pipes suspended below the factory ceiling for heat delivery, like those used by Matthew Boulton and James Watt, for example, that could ensure neither that the air temperature was carefully regulated nor that the distribution of heat was uniform.[13]

Even though the thermostat's place in regulating the temperature of factory buildings remained unresolved, its function for specific industrial purposes such as "pharmacy, dyeing, or any other chemical art" was more

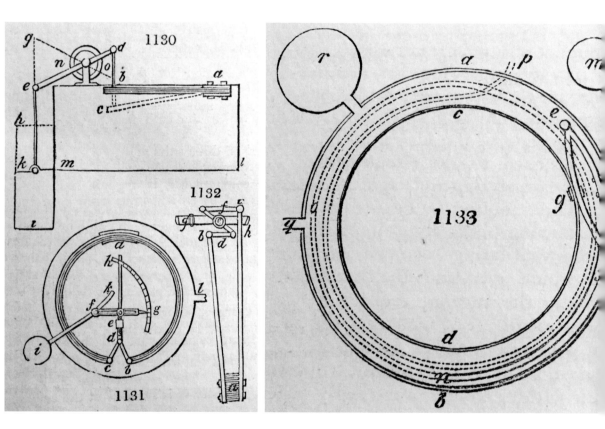

FIGURE 1.1. Ure's diagrams showing the bending produced by the bimetallic strip activating a lever system in his figure 1130, a "thermostatic hoop" in 1131 and 1133, a "circular turning register, such as is used for a stove, or stovegrate, or for ventilating apartments" in 1135; 1134, Ure writes, "represents another arrangement of my thermostatic apparatus applied to a circular turning register, like the preceding", and 1137 "represents a chimney, furnished with a pyrostat." Andrew Ure, *A Dictionary of Arts, Manufactures and Mines* (London: Longman, Brown, Green, and Longmans, 1853), 843–44.

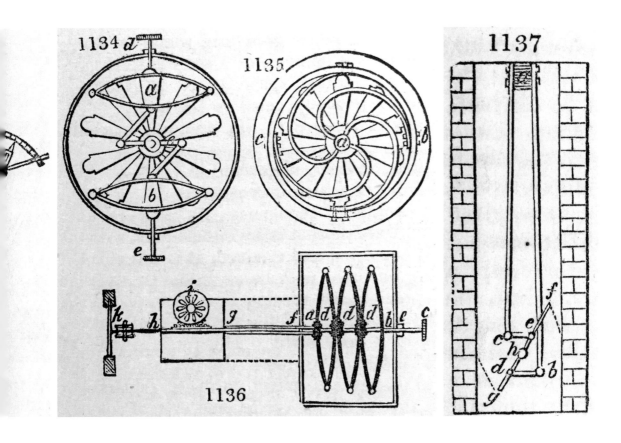

clearly elaborated. The more specific the purpose of the machine, the more directly the thermostatic device could be applied. A thermostatic hoop, for example, immersed in a pool of liquid, could maintain a stable temperature by regulating the inflow and outflow of water of different temperatures into a common chamber. Similar operations regulated a distilling apparatus.[14] In all these cases, the thermostat could not, by itself, regulate the temperature of either a liquid or a gas. It relied on other mechanisms to produce an action that altered the conditions of the medium. Furthermore, a thermostatic device could only be employed on one machine at a time. As a result, no relationship could be produced between two variables such as the temperature and movement of air because each machine that controlled one of the variables—the furnace and the ventilator—would require its own independent sensory mechanism.

Although he aspired to establish the factory as a giant automated machine made of numerous smaller interrelated machines, Ure did not successfully integrate a thermostatic device into that context. Based on his more theoretical writing, such as the above passage on the Roberts machine, it would be possible to situate this sensitive mechanism among those that he believed would integrate the British factory. There were three categories of industrial processes he described in *The Philosophy of Manufactures*: those that produced power, those that applied it to modify the forms of matter into objects of commerce, and those that regulated the conditions of production. The thermostat would fit into the third category.[15] As an instrument of regulation, it mediated between the origin of power and the output of products in the industrial process, performing a function akin to the apparent intelligence that Ure observed guiding the movements in the self-acting mule and the electrical impulses in the human body. If the effect of this instrument could eventually be distributed throughout the factory building, he believed, its guiding intelligence would play an essential role in the factory's unification into a system.

The inability to fulfill this intention made explicit a fundamental difference between machines and organisms that Ure could not have understood based on the knowledge of biological regulation available at his time. For while an organism responds to a stimulus from a relay of signals that pass through its nervous network, as Georges Canguilhem has described, that system produces slightly different responses each time.[16] The mechanism of the thermostatic device, by contrast, was capable of initiating only one kind of change on an individual machine. Although the addition of electricity to this system would have better approximated the analogy between a mechanical system and the vital force of an organism, linking multiple machines to form a thermostatically controlled system, the ensemble would still lack the flexibility that remains uniquely tied to an organism's internal forms of regulation.

AIR BECOMES A SYSTEM

Along with his interest in physiology and industrial machinery, Ure also engaged in discussions about techniques for heating and ventilating public buildings. The topic found a prominent forum in a committee charged with identifying the best methods for warming and moving air through the new Houses of Parliament. Although he was not involved in that deliberation, Ure felt that the practical knowledge he derived from working on factory mechanics and his interest in the environmental conditions of industrial processes could add greatly to applying these technologies in such a context.[17]

The existing knowledge on ventilating public buildings had been summarized in 1825 by the civil engineer and encyclopedist of architecture R. S. Meikleham. His preface invoked the value of methods of ventilation:

> As Great Britain is proverbially allowed to be more subject to vicissitudes of temperature than any other country in Europe; and as the only means of counteracting the effects of these rapid atmospheric changes, in the interior of our dwelling-houses, is by a judicious application of artificial heat, on [the] one hand, and by an adequate degree of ventilation on the other—it is presumed that any attempt to facilitate these important objects, will meet with a favourable reception.[18]

Meikleham thus identified the two variables—heat and ventilation—that required equal attention of the engineer. Finding a way to regulate both in one building would require treating air as a unified system. While his well-illustrated treatise showed that these variables were still managed independently, the technical attention given to air's qualities in the plates illustrates Meikleham's challenge to the invisibility of atmosphere, an extension of numerous efforts in early modern Britain. Jayne Elizabeth Lewis rightly begins her survey of this tendency at the moment that air received its modern scientific definition: the experiments that Robert Boyle performed with his air pump around 1660.[19]

In the time between Boyle's experiments and Meikleham's publication, scientific studies of pneumatics became particularly important for those who sought to regulate the conditions of air in social institutions established around the late eighteenth and early nineteenth centuries such as prisons, theaters, and hospitals. These were spaces in which every aspect of the inhabitants' conditions—both social and environmental—was brought under extreme scrutiny.[20] The development of central heating and forced ventilation in this period has been traced by the architectural historian Robert Bruegmann as a determining factor in many designs of such buildings, especially in Britain.[21] But one limitation of focusing on buildings—public or otherwise—as Ure was amply aware, was the role of ventilation in industries, especially those existing outside of the building interior, such as coal mining. Circulating fresh air through mines could preserve the health of coal workers while also helping to prevent explosions of coal dust.[22] Thus while many studies of air quality in buildings focused on their use for human purposes such as heath and comfort, the industrial context of a mine shows one example of research that was also dedicated to describing the airborne risk to the value of fixed capital.

The mechanical fan was one primary technology used to alleviate such risks in mines, and it was equally essential to the inner workings of steamships. In both cases, the issue of human comfort was not under consideration. For example, in 1832 Ure measured the power of Captain John Ericsson's fan aboard the *Corsair* to compare the efficiency of its fan with other configurations. Ure proved that the *Corsair*'s fan, with its eccentric radial geometry, made it considerably more efficient than the concentric fan designed by the French physicist Claude Pouillet.[23] He then aimed to understand and formalize the physics that described a machine's internal efficiency to apply this knowledge for ventilating architectural interiors.

One immediate application of Ure's interest in mechanical ventilators was a request made by the directors of the Customs Fund of Life Assurance and did concern human biology. The company was housed in the Long Room of the Custom House in London where the directors noticed a "state of indisposition and disease" plaguing their nearly two hundred employees. In studying the air movement at the Custom House, Ure deduced that these maladies were directly attributable to the way in which the space was heated and ventilated. The symptoms of the employees whom he examined were "tension or fullness in the head with occasional flushings of the countenance, throbbing of the temples, and vertigo, followed, not infrequently, with a confusion of ideas."[24] Combining his knowledge of medicine with his interest in mechanically regulating interior conditions in factories, Ure made direct correlations between human physiology, which he called "the animal economy," and the movement, temperature, and relative humidity of the air.[25] Each symptom, he believed, could be attributed to a particular fault in the mechanics of the ventilation system. For example, he explained that the propagation of an electrical current through the overly dry air caused the employees' mental confusion. He proposed the installation of a system of hot steam pipes and "self-acting register valves"—referring to his own thermostatic devices—at the ceilings to "regulate the discharge of foul air, and maintain a wholesome ventilation in the air below."[26]

As we have seen, for Ure, the regulation of the body's mechanical movements served as a model for an automated factory system made up of interrelated mechanical operations. This reciprocity between organisms and machines, in turn, allowed him to interpret a system that mechanically ventilated air according to a set of physiological responses. The function or dysfunction of a system, by his logic, transcended all the obvious differences that existed between a mechanism and an organism. Physiological response, coordinated through the regulatory action of the nervous system, made the human organism into a diagnostic device for identifying the flaws in the mechanical ventilation of the Custom House. The electrical current that had induced the breath of a dead body could now be understood as a misplaced current that induced a mental pathology of a live body. The only kind of system that could properly regulate the movement of air inside an architectural interior would be one that responded to changes in the environment more like an organism does. Thus, the interdependence of mechanical and living systems found in any modern building housing machines would participate in a perpetual loop of metaphorical reversals.

To regulate the specific effects of spoiled or vitiated air on the bodies inside the Long Room, Ure sought to isolate the variables that governed its movement: heat, pressure, and velocity. Relationships among these variables were central to an ongoing scientific effort to describe the so-called heat engine, a theory developed by Sadi Carnot to explain the conversion of heat energy into mechanical energy.[27] Even before Carnot, however, experiments had already been conducted to find a mathematical correspondence among these variables in buildings; one example was the work of chemist Charles Sylvester who had run air through differently heated iron tubes to observe the change in its velocity. Sylvester proposed that the velocity of air could be calculated in proportion to its density and, with William Strutt, tested his mechanical formulae on a heating system for the Derbyshire infirmary starting in 1807.[28] Thus, by the time that Ure began work on the Custom House, experiments on the dynamics of air were well underway as were ideas regarding their application to buildings. Yet the direct correlation between the conditions of the interior environment and the physiological response of the human body were unique to Ure's study. For the directors of the Customs Fund to have involved Ure shows that his combined knowledge in industrial production and medical science was useful to their immediate needs. Ure's recommendations were not applied to the Custom House, but treating air as a system guided by physical and chemical laws that affected human bodies would soon be applied to numerous buildings of various size and function.[29]

The Long Room case was an essential step in developing criteria to evaluate a building's design according to the management and delivery of heat and humidity through treated air. Correlating the forces that guided ventilation and architectural design became the project of another Scottish physician and chemist, David Boswell Reid (1805–63). Unlike Ure, whose approach to ventilation originated from his consultancy with various industries, Reid's views on ventilation were based in his scientific study of chemistry. The design of his laboratory in 1833 presented an early experiment from which he developed a few core principles for ventilating systems. In his chemistry textbook, published three years after he established his laboratory, he tested these concepts as they related to the dynamics of gases in a domestic context. For example, he explained how the heat produced by fireplaces established several specific types of interior air currents.[30]

Contemporaneous with Ure's work at the Long Room, Reid's interest in ventilation expanded to become one of the major contributions to formalizing its application to buildings: this was his widely publicized system for treating and circulating air through the temporary House of Commons (Figure 1.2). After the fire of 1834 in the Houses of Parliament, a committee hired Reid to build a ventilation system for the former House of Lords as part of its appropriation for the House of Commons. Several men of science had already addressed the quality of the air in the previous chamber. Christopher Wren had attempted to improve it in the 1660s but only made the conditions worse. Exhaust ventilators, designed by the

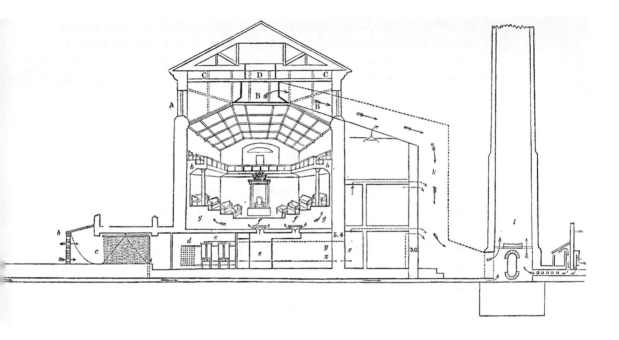

FIGURE 1.2. Cross-section showing the plenum system installed at the temporary House of Commons, 1836. Here is the detailed description of the drawing given by Reid: "*a* the vitiated air from the drain in Old Palace Yard, controlled by the underground ventiduct, and conveyed directly to the shaft; *b* the fresh air entrance when the air is taken from Old Palace Yard, with the suspended fibrous veil, 42 feet by 18 feet, for excluding mechanical impurities; *c* temporary apparatus for moistening or washing the air; *d e* the hot air chamber communicating with *e*, the lower air chamber, which receives warm, cold, or mixed air, according to the temperature required; deflectors for diffusing the air in the equalizing chamber *g g*; *b b* the supply for the galleries conveyed from *g*, by the channels between *b* and *g*; the dotted lines above *y*, and below *z*, shew the flow and return-pipes from the hot water boiler, which is placed at *x*, and supplies the hot water apparatus in *d e*. The large arrows from the ventilating chamber *B*, indicate the progress of the air to the ventilating shaft, while small arrows indicate the discharge of vitiated air from the libraries and various other places in the vicinity of the shaft. *A* indicates the external windows; *C C* the original altitude of the ceiling; and *D* the vitiated air channel from the House of Peers, communicating ultimately with the shaft that ventilates the House of Commons." David Boswell Reid, *Illustrations of the Theory and Practice of Ventilation, with Remarks on Warming, Exclusive Lighting, and the Communication of Sound* (London: Longman, Brown, Green, and Longmans, 1844), 282–83.

chemist and inventor Sir Humphry Davy in 1811, also hardly ameliorated the air there.[31] Unlike these piecemeal alterations, the approach Reid took to systematize ventilation considered the entire building. His technique soon became comparable in its value to future mechanical engineers as the value of Ure's work to factory automation would be to industrial managers.

Reid aimed to manage the air quality within this large enclosed space by heating, cooling, and conditioning it in what he referred to as a "plenum," a space located under the floor. After air drawn from the outside passed through a filter that extracted dust and other particulate matter, it was heated, moistened, and mixed with unheated air to regulate its temperature and humidity. The treated air was released into the main space through hundreds of thousands of holes that had been drilled into the floor, while the vitiated air was released through an exhaust chamber located above the ceiling. Plenum ventilation generally relies on establishing a positive difference in pressure between the interior of a building and its exterior. Fresh heated air from the plenum pushes into the occupied spaces to produce higher pressure that is released by directing the cooler vitiated air to blow outward through an exhaust usually high in or above the room. To control the speed of the air moving through the House chamber, Reid situated a valve between the extract duct and the downcast shaft connected to the furnace and chimney.[32]

The air that entered the plenum was the medium around which Reid's system operated: it was trapped, funneled, treated, circulated, and then released. In the sectional drawing through the building that illustrated his system, arrows represent the direction of the air as it moved through the structure. The controlled air inside had changed its status and no longer belonged to the free and unregulated exterior: it had become regulated "fresh" air. Outside the confines of the building, where no artificial control could be exerted over the air, Reid did not represent its movement. The boundary defined between inside and outside air was not mediated by an architectural element—like a window or a door—but by the entry and exhaust of air into the system. Even the architectural drawing convention of lines that represent a cut through the walls of a physical building here act as a mere backdrop to the action of arrows that bend through ducts, merge in collection chambers, and split around obstructions. It is clear from the drawing that in Reid's mind the entire building had become a giant automated pneumatic machine. The elements that had formerly been organized around the political functions of the chamber had become secondary to the unity of the apparatus, organized around the technicalities of ventilation.

Members of Parliament admired Reid's ventilation system and decided to have him apply it to the new building that Charles Barry was designing. Yet in the process of translating his system into the new context, Reid's increasingly rigid views on ventilation came into conflict with Barry's plans. The differences between the two men became the most notable public display of a rift between the symbolic value of architectural form and the technical imperatives of systematic ventilation.[33] One sign of this rift was Barry's reference to his more mechanically minded counterpart as "the Ventilator." In response to the architect's apathy toward his recommendations, Reid insisted that his system ought to be given as much attention as the architectural forms. In a treatise on the topic that he published in 1844, he wrote of the efficiency in ventilating buildings, a result made possible by developing an informed approach to planning those systems rather than the ad hoc approach taken by architects such as Barry:

> This subject can never, indeed, be placed on the most desirable footing till the architect shall always design in unison with the principles of ventilation, and make them a primary, instead of a mere secondary, consideration, in his structural arrangements. When this principle is not adopted, the means of economic ventilation may too often be considered as superseded, before any attention has been bestowed upon them. . . . The mobility of air is such, that it can be made to move in any direction that may be required, but the economy or facility of executing such movements form very different questions.[34]

Although air was a highly flexible medium and could be pushed nearly anywhere, Reid believed a systematic understanding of ventilation could bring architectural form into direct correspondence with what could be its preferred movement. His criticism of Barry's inattention to the new Parliament building's ventilation became more direct and soon spilled into the public realm. In response, the press ridiculed Reid as "the great atmospheric philosopher" who had proposed to build a "refreshment-room" at the Parliament "for brewing draughts of different kind of atmosphere."[35] Under the pressure of such public ridicule, aimed directly at his expertise, Reid could no longer convince the members of Parliament of his value to the project. By 1846 his role had become marginal, and he was officially dismissed from his post in 1852.

Reid was far more successful in his application of a ventilating system in St. George's Hall, in Liverpool. The plenum system applied to that public building, completed in 1854, ventilated law courts and a concert hall and served as an exemplary instance of Reid's thinking for years to come.[36] In 1855, Reid moved to the United States and abandoned his consulting practice in England. He was invited to deliver three lectures at the Smithsonian Institution in Washington, D.C., in 1857. Among those assembled was Montgomery Meigs, the engineer of the U.S. Senate chambers, who repeatedly noted the influence of Reid's theories on the design for his proposed ventilation system there.[37]

Reid's primary employment was as a medical inspector for the U.S. government, causing him to shift his interest in scale from public buildings to private dwellings. For two years he studied and documented the methods of ventilation and their impact on the hygienic conditions of various American houses. He published his findings to illustrate his belief that even the simplest forms of ventilation could manage the effects of extreme temperature and, in the aggregate, could contribute to maintaining the sanitary condition of cities. The diagrams that he used to illustrate his book were intended to "assist the non-professional reader in selecting the system that may be especially applicable to his own wants, and the circumstances of individual rooms and large habitations." Imagining that his readers would not only include architects, but also city officials and builders, he chose examples that would most directly instruct this broad audience on the simplest methods for properly ventilating air. Brightly colored diagrams clarified these explanations: "red, purple, and blue, to indicate respectively a pure, a mixed, and a vitiated atmosphere . . . as well as describe the movement of the aerial currents which are, under ordinary circumstances, entirely invisible."[38] Aiming to package his knowledge in a few direct and demonstrable principles, the drawings showed how simple modifications to the interior of a building could improve the movement and quality of air in several different types of spaces.

The first two diagrams in the book represent Reid's thinking most directly (Figure 1.3). They compare a badly ventilated room to one in which a few additions have significantly improved the distribution and purity of the interior air. The top drawing illustrates a room without a discharge above the level of a fireplace in which blue vitiated air accumulates in large circular clouds at the ceiling. Most of the room is painted blue to indicate that the proportion of pure heated air is low and badly located. A cold current

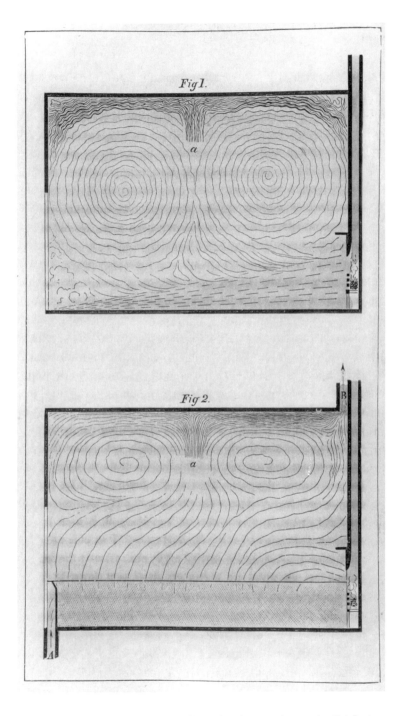

FIGURE 1.3. A comparison between a badly ventilated room and a room in which fresh heated air is pushed through a plenum in the floor. David Boswell Reid, *Ventilation in American Dwellings: With a Series of Diagrams, Presenting Examples in Different Classes of Habitations* (New York: Wiley and Halsted, 1858).

developing along the floor at the opposite end of the room from the fire-place adds another negative consequence to this configuration. In the bottom figure, by contrast, a steady supply of fresh warm red-colored air rises from the plenum through holes in the floor—much like the system he designed for the temporary House of Commons and St. George's Hall—and is evenly distributed through the room while the vitiated air escapes through a gap in the ceiling. Not only is the proportion of pure to vitiated air changed, but also the orderliness of its distribution is inscribed into the line work on the page. The lines' form differentiates the air currents in the two rooms: in the top figure they appear frenzied and unevenly distrib-uted while in the bottom figure they become ordered as an illustration of a generally predictable movement of air from a space below the floor to one above the ceiling. In both cases, the air held within the boundaries of the room is made visually explicit, illustrated as a physical medium through its qualities: movement expressed by lines, and purity rendered by color.

Reid's replacement of arrows, drawn in the diagrammatic section of the temporary House of Commons, with lines and colors that filled the diagrams drawn for his book on American dwellings made visible more as-pects of the dynamics of air. Directly corresponding to the refinement of his representation of the atmosphere, Reid reduced the surrounding architec-ture to a few rudimentary lines. He extracted each room from its context, removed the furniture, and indicated no programmatic use for the space. In these diagrams, the opening in a wall for a doorway did not indicate the presence of a door, and after a new floor was added to establish a plenum for the heated air, the opening remained in the same place. To serve a human purpose, the opening would need to be moved in order to make entry pos-sible. This fundamental architectural element could be overlooked because Reid considered the improvements to the room's ventilation primary and everything else secondary. In reducing the size of the structures in which he studied ventilation from monumental public buildings to modest do-mestic interiors, he replaced the complexity of the large interior space with a simpler model of air dynamics. The household interior allowed Reid to abstract his system to its essential parameters. The transformations he pro-posed established the room as the elemental device for its systematic con-trol. His drawings allow no worthwhile distinction between the design of a house's interior space and the management of the air that it contained.

The simplicity of this model led Reid to declare that "the practice of ventilation requires to be brought home to the habitations of masses of the population, and their sympathies enlisted in its principles, and extended to all classes of buildings and sanitary improvements."[39] Modifications to every habitable unit of space, he believed, could become a means for governing the health of the modern urban dweller. Each home represented one more opportunity to apply the system. Reid went further, claiming that the principles of domestic ventilation outlined in his book would transform the definition of architectural work. The deliberate and scientific control of air, he explained, could produce "a complete system of architecture, where beauty, utility, and economy shall each have their legitimate influence."[40] From his point of view, once the design of architecture was fully committed to the principles of proper ventilation, it could unify social and aesthetic aspirations into a system that was legitimated by the sanitary reform of modern cities.

The work of transforming air into a system—even an architectural system—turned on a reduction in the size and complexity of the enclosure. Simple mechanisms of control were not immediately aligned with complex purposes: neither the varied functions of industrial production nor the chambers of government provided the elemental simplicity of a domestic interior. The economic unity of the family, housed in the isolated private dwelling, became the setting in which air could be most clearly formed into a system.

THE THERMOSTATIC INTERIOR

While Reid's interest in the air within dwellings was primarily related to his concern for managing public health at the scale of the city, the feminist reformer Catharine Beecher addressed the techniques of heating and ventilation to redefine the domestic interior as the domain for the modern mother. In a book written with her sister Harriet Beecher Stowe, *The American Woman's Home* (1869), she offered a thorough approach to integrating ventilation as a tool that maintained the family's hygienic environment. Beecher had already revealed the depth of her technical knowledge about ventilation a few years earlier, in her design of a Gothic-revival cottage that she illustrated in *Harper's*. Every aspect of the house's physical organization was essential to her argument that the social role of the American woman was split into three: training the child's mind, nursing the child or the sick, and managing the domestic economy. All these functions were evidence of Beecher's doubling of the mother's identity: on the one hand, she would need to act morally as a "home minister," and on the other, she would need to acquire the expertise of a skilled "professional."[41] To become the minister of the home, Beecher advocated that a woman embody the virtue of self-sacrifice. At the same time, and perhaps paradoxically, a woman's contributions to the household had to be valued at the same level as those of a man's profession.[42] Beecher viewed the household as the center of moral value rather than economic value, and yet it was also the site of skilled labor that required proper training: the product of this expertise was a healthy living environment. While the home minister aimed to construct a moral distance between the household and the prevailing demands of industrialization, the professional saw her work as transforming that isolated environment into a place that sustained the economy by means of the family's continued capacity for biological reproduction.[43]

Many of Beecher's recommendations regarding ventilation stemmed from her view that the technical matters related to operating the household interior were central to professionalizing woman's work. For her knowledge of ventilation, she acknowledged a debt to Lewis W. Leeds who worked alongside David Boswell Reid for the Sanitary Commission, ventilating government hospitals during the Civil War. Leeds's lectures on ventilation were delivered at the Franklin Institute in 1866 and published two years later. The book included colorful sectional diagrams that relied on Reid's illustrations to describe the effects of ventilation on the conditions of the air within a room.[44] Yet unlike the rooms described in both Leeds's and Reid's drawings of architecture shaped by the purposes of ventilation, Beecher's organization of a healthy household carefully treated the house as an architectural form that also responded to the various economic functions it was intended to perform. Anticipating her later work, in 1841 she enumerated the various aspects of house construction in which women should be involved: "There is no matter of domestic economy, which more seriously involves the health and daily comfort of American women, than the proper construction of houses. There are five particulars, to which attention should be given, in building a house; namely, economy of labor, economy of money, economy of health, economy of comfort, and good taste."[45] In this list, only good taste escaped the organizing power of an economy. While prescriptions could be made to help guide household decisions regarding labor, money, health, and comfort, taste remained an open category to integrate the competing demands of these various economies into a unified architectural composition.

Reyner Banham observed that Beecher's integration of ventilation into the plans she included in her book laid the groundwork for the twentieth-century free plan organization and its capacity to absorb technical functions. He pointed out that her "conception of an unified central core of services, around which the floors of the house are . . . open in layout but differentiated functionally by specialised built-in furniture and equipment," anticipated R. Buckminster Fuller's Dymaxion house of 1927.[46] Based on the plans published in Beecher's book, Mary Banham drew an axonometric cutaway view of the "American Woman's Home" and identified most of the functional elements in the house as if they were mechanical parts that composed a single patent: the stove, the flue, the system of ducts, the cooking range, and a moveable wardrobe (Figure 1.4). Stripping this building down to its carcass of studs and rafters revealed the house to be a sophisticated assembly of various modern technologies. The visual language of parts assembled into a technological whole in the axonometric did not address the architecture of the house as primary but described the building as a complex and unified machine. This representation buttressed the broad historiographical position that aimed to shift the focus of architectural history from style and structure to technical transformations of environmental management. Banham's alternative genealogy of the modern house traced Fuller back to Beecher, assembling the houses into a process of technologically improved planning strategies. The knowledge developed of the technical systems in Beecher's proposal positioned it as an essential contribution to the history of environmental control. Yet Banham's historical analysis did not address the changing role of women in the household at this time. By contrast, the feminist scholarship by such historians as Dolores Hayden and others has emphasized the social impact of Beecher's designs. Integrating these interpretations, it is now possible to also reveal the role that technologies of heating and ventilation played in redefining women's modern social role: as elements in a domestic sphere defined to be complementary in its technicality to that of industrial production.

Beecher understood the mechanics of ventilation to be part of the domestic "economy of labor." Her thoughtful location of the Franklin stove, the efficient arrangement of the ductwork running through the floors, the collapsible partitions and moveable wardrobes were all elements that she used to refashion the middle-class house into a testing ground for the reform of homemaking. Her aim was to establish this form of work

FIGURE 1.4. Catharine Beecher's American Woman's Home. Cut-away axonometric drawing by Mary Banham. The numbered elements are labeled as: 1. Hot air stove, 2. Franklin stove, 3. Cooking range, 4. Fresh air intake, 5. Hot air outlet, 6. Foul air extracts, 7. Central flue, 8. Foul air chimney, 9. Movable wardrobe. Reyner Banham, *The Architecture of the Well-Tempered Environment* (Chicago: University of Chicago Press, 1969), 99. Reproduced by kind permission of Mrs. Mary Banham, first published in 1969 by the Architectural Press, London.

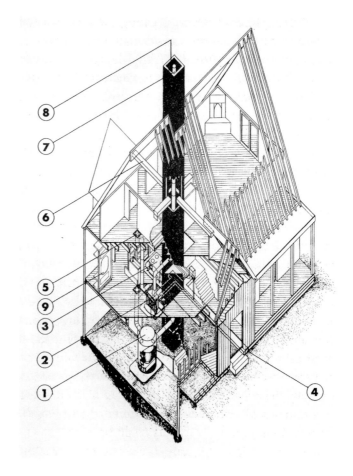

as an expert knowledge that also included the ability to maintain a well-ventilated house. The technical specificity of that arrangement would eventually prove to be one of the "the conveniences of domestic labor," as she called it, that would not only save time but also "render such work less repulsive than it is made by common methods."[47] By positioning the mother as interface between modern industry and the home, Beecher believed that technologies such as ventilation and heating could displace the work of servants whose "common methods" lowered the general value of household labor. Under the influence of her domestic reforms, the home became an inward-looking place that was at once distinct in its values from the industrial outside and, at the same time, similar to industry in its endless capacity to integrate technological functions into the internal economy.

With the furnace directly heating the air running through the ducts in Beecher's house design, large deviations in interior temperature would have been common. Beecher acknowledged the difficulty of combining proper ventilation with temperature control. The various elements of environmental machinery were only assembled into a unified automatic system a few years after her death, with the introduction of electrical power into domestic life.

Once electricity became available, beginning in the 1880s, the first amenities included artificial lighting, mechanical fans, phonographs, and sewing machines.[48] As more electrical wiring became available to the American homeowner, interdependent circuits of power allowed one machine to influence the action of others. In an essay published in 1890 on electricity in the household by Arthur E. Kennelly, chief electrician at the Edison Laboratory, the author observed that electrically motivated machines were still "essentially of mechanical nature."[49] Electricity did not alter the way mechanical devices operated but organized their interrelations around a network of power. Thus fifty years after Ure's invention of the thermostat, this sensitive device could finally be integrated into an existing network of electrical mechanisms. Manipulating the circuitry that bound the house to a source of power could regulate the temperature inside buildings. Kennelly described the electrical instruments developed by the Edison Laboratory individually and also included a wiring diagram to indicate the way household instruments could be connected to a central main of power supply (Figure 1.5). The core services would split off from the main to power an "Illuminating System," a "Burglar Alarm System" and various domestic tools. While the diagram did not specifically use the term "thermostat," in the lower right corner a place had been reserved for its function in the overall network, a "Heat regulation & Fire Alarm System."

The first application of the electrical thermostat was not to the circuitry of a house, and therefore not for human use, but to incubators by chicken farmers seeking to automate the hatching of eggs. A great deal of attention was given to the display of one electrically regulated incubator during the 1884 International Electrical Exhibition held in Philadelphia. Manufactured by the Perfect Hatcher Company of Elmira in New York, the electrical thermostat was described as "exceedingly delicate and sensitive." The catalog of the exhibition documented the method used by the inventor, Frank Rosebrook, to translate the bending movement of the bimetallic strip into an electrical signal. By simulating the biologically regulated

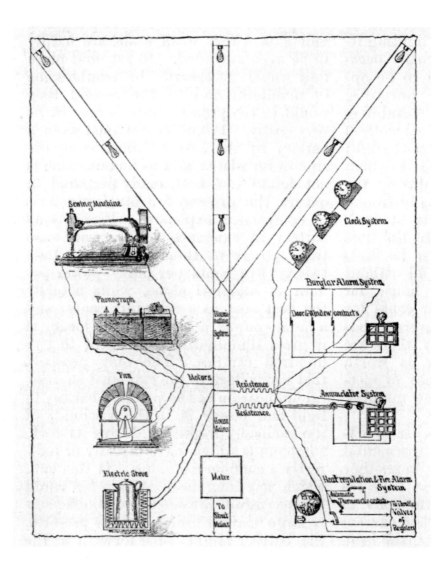

FIGURE 1.5. A diagram of the wiring for a generic house, connected to the "Street Mains" by the two long vertical lines that run down the center of the image. On the left are the amenities of the household interior: sewing machines, phonograph, fan, and electric stove. One the right are various systems connected to the power source, including a synchronized clock system, a burglar alarm, an annunciator system, presumably for communication before telephones, and a heat regulation and fire alarm system including "Thermometer contacts" connected to "Throttle Valves of Registers." Perhaps the electrical bulbs in the "Illuminating System" that branches at the top of the diagram into three parts are illustrated in this way as both an amenity and a system. Arthur E. Kennelly, "Plan of Wiring a House for Its Various Electrical Appliances." *Scribner's Magazine* 7 (January 1890): 114.

temperature of a hen, the incubator demonstrated the relationships that had already been observed between environmental controls and physiological response. Now the system had extended its value to the mass production of poultry. The same catalog also showed how the apparatus might be applied to regulate the temperature of a domestic interior.[50] If temperature regulation could work in the context of a small incubating machine, then control over heat in the rooms of a household would require only a change in scale and the exchange of humans for chicken eggs.

In 1886 Albert M. Butz (1849–1905), an inventor of fire extinguishers, patented an electrical thermostat that was specifically designed for domestic interiors. He quickly pitched the product as an electrical amenity for the modern home.[51] Conductive wires allowed a physical distance between the thermostat hung on a wall and the furnace in the basement. His invention came to be described as the "the damper flapper" because it controlled the damper that regulated the heat produced by the furnace.[52] The electrical signal sent by the thermostat coordinated its movement into a responsive mechanical system. When the temperature rose above the mark designated by the inhabitant, the bimetallic strip was positioned to bend and complete a circuit, thereby sending an electrical impulse to the basement. There, a second circuit would be activated to propel a battery-powered motor to close the damper, reducing the amount of heat produced by the furnace. If the strip bent in the other direction as the room temperature dropped, it would close another circuit to reverse the process, raising the amount of heat produced by the furnace. One of the drawings included in Butz's patent shows part of a house in cross-section, revealing the electrical connection between the basement and the occupied areas (Figure 1.6). Wires attached to the walls passed beside the furnace, rendering the ancient technology of an open hearth unnecessary, a nostalgic luxury for the first floor. On the second floor, the same wires connected to an alarm that would alert the servant living there if fuel needed to be added to the furnace. The alarm was hung beside a shut window; the windows of the house could remain closed, or were better closed, because the interior temperature inside was under the continuous control of the thermostat.

After two years of production, Butz sold his company and patent to the Consolidated Temperature Controlling Company.[53] A popular builders' magazine reviewed the company's electric thermostat in its "Home" pages to enumerate the advantages that the device held for domestic interiors. Criticizing the older mechanical systems of temperature control, the

A. M. BUTZ.
THERMO ELECTRIC DAMPER REGULATOR AND ALARM.

No. 347,866.   Patented Aug. 24, 1886.

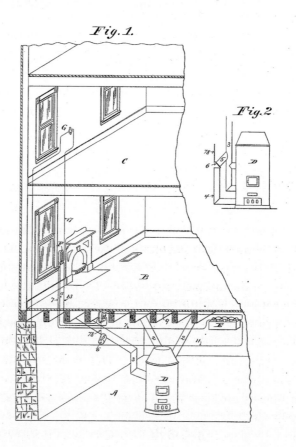

Fig. 1.

Fig. 2

Witnesses   Inventor

R. H. Sanford.   Albert M. Butz

FIGURE 1.6. A "sectional elevation" of Albert M. Butz's patented electric thermostat system. The thermostat is hung on the wall at point F, on the first floor, and the alarm at point G, on the second. The damper is at point 6 in the basement. Between the thermostat, alarm, and the furnace are the wires that run along the wall and under the floor joist in the basement. They connect to a battery at point E. A. M. Butz, Thermo Electric Damper Regulator and Alarm, U.S. Patent 347,866 (issued August 24, 1886).

writers explained the advantage of the distance produced by an electrical system that connected the regulator in the rooms to the furnace with conductive wires:

> the principle of regulating the temperature of the living rooms of a house by means of devices actuated from the furnace heater is radically wrong, since the temperature of the hot-air chamber of a furnace ... bears no relation to the temperature prevailing in those apartments which are situated some distance from the source of heat. The draught opening of a furnace controlled mechanically may be closed before the temperature in these apartments has been brought to the point of comfort, or *vice versa*, by reason of irregular conditions prevailing in the apartments themselves, of which the mechanical regulator at the furnace or heater can have no cognizance, and to which it cannot therefore respond.[54]

A sensitive electrical instrument, by contrast, would give the furnace "cognizance" of the temperature surrounding the occupant in its vicinity. Such terms recall the mechanical intelligence that Ure believed his apparatus could bring to the mechanical systems of the automatic factory, an extension of what he called the "principle of regulation" that guided the self-acting cotton-spinning machine. Once a revised version of Ure's mechanical apparatus was connected to an electrical signal, the reading of a temperature in the room could be automatically transmitted through conductive wires to a furnace in the basement. This implied that the entire household environment had been brought under guidance of that same principle of regulation.

While the Butz system controlled the temperature of interior air, the thermostat was not designed to control the speed of its movement or its quality. Machines for moving and cleaning air could have been integrated into the circuit, but the only elements that Butz included were the furnace dampers. In Beecher's view, the ventilation of air was critical to improving the hygienic conditions of the middle-class home, but Butz's patent did not address that aspect of the interior environment. His innovation was strictly an extension of the electrical circuit that connected the thermostatic device to the furnace, and this did not account for any of the broader household dynamics that were emphasized in the discourse of domestic reform. An indication of the difference between the technical limits of this system and the ideological imperatives of Beecher's reforms can be

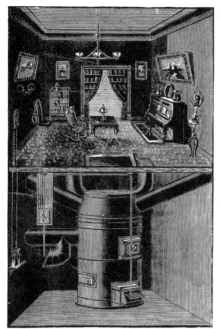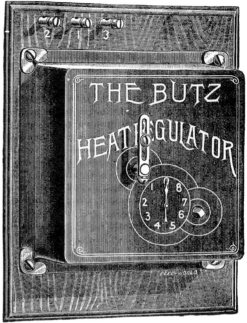

FIGURE 1.7. This version of the Butz system is taken from his 1888 patent, Automatic Temperature Controller, U.S. Patent 390,281 (issued October 2, 1888). It did not include an alarm, but instead of one, there are two dampers on the furnace. "Automatic Heat Regulation by Electric Means," *Manufacturer and Builder* 20.11 (November 1888): 259.

identified in an image published of the Butz system in the review cited above, from 1888 (Figure 1.7). In a sectional perspective through a house, somewhat like the one pictured in his earlier patent drawing, only with more illustrative detail and less technical specificity, the living room of the house was filled with upholstered furniture, decorative objects, and drapery. These accouterments remained unaffected by the presence of a grating in the floor, connected to the furnace ductwork, or a thermostat hanging on the living room wall. Unlike Beecher's interiors, in which the plan was coordinated around the furnace and ductwork for the efficient delivery of sanitary heat and fresh air, Butz's electrical thermostat was a relatively modest technical improvement to an existing set of domestic amenities.

Competing systems for managing the household environment quickly overcame the limitation of the Butz system. In 1901, the Powers Regulator Company published drawings of a thermostatic control system with a mechanically ventilated plenum chamber that pushed heated and conditioned air through the household interior (Figure 1.8).[55] The path from a thermostat at point A, in the interior elevation, to a relay in the basement at point B was notated by a line that then extended to point C, where a damper mixed hot and tempered air in a plenum chamber. The circuit was completed by a connection to another thermostat at point D that regulated the temperature of incoming tempered air so that it would remain below sixty degrees. A damper at E regulated the amount of air brought into the plenum chamber by the mechanical ventilator. While Butz's network was only based on a direct signal from the sensor to the furnace, the Powers system regulated the furnace heat as well as the quality of the air inside a plenum, a mechanized version of Reid's earlier proposals with an updated version of Ure's regulatory apparatus. To integrate the plenum into the mechanical system, the Powers engineers contained it within a chamber and metal ducts rather than in leftover spaces under floors, inside walls, and above ceilings. In the box labeled "plenum chamber," air at several temperatures could be mixed to an exact heat under the guidance of a few thermostats. The air was then pushed through the network of ducts and into the rooms of the house. A drawing of the system's plan shows that the ducts moved sideward in all directions from the chamber. Contained within well-defined ducts and chambers, the air of the entire domestic milieu had been mechanized and automated. It could be fixed at a desired temperature while being continuously refreshed with air from the outside. The concept for moving air and maintaining its freshness extended Reid's proposals into a network of domestically scaled mechanical parts. Even a similar use of arrows in the representation of air movement suggests a common assumption that air was a medium that traveled through a system of pneumatic machinery.

By packaging regulatory technology as one component in the communicative circuitry of modern houses, the thermostatic interior was gradually made available for middle-class consumption.[56] Producers of temperature control systems sought to develop language that would relate the function of their products to these families' concerns so as to make householders into future customers. With her approach to defining the economy of labor in the home, Beecher had already anticipated that instruments for asserting environmental control were essential for reforming the domain of the homemaker. As we have seen, in the decades after she published *The American Woman's Home*, the environment that surrounded the family

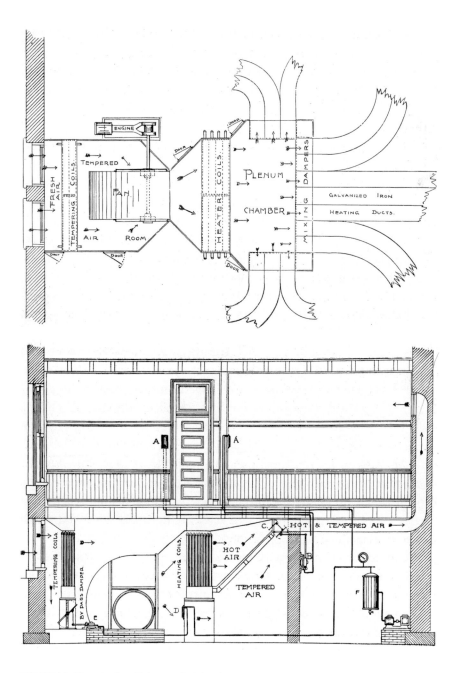

FIGURE 1.8. "Plan view" and "elevation" of the plenum system. Powers Regulator Company, *The Powers Systems of Automatic Temperature Control* (Chicago: Powers Regulator Co., 1901), 9–10.

became increasingly mechanized. Ruth Schwartz Cowan has argued that the proliferation of domestic technologies displacing skilled housework services paradoxically multiplied the number of tasks to be overseen by the mother. As these tasks multiplied and became centralized, the problem of housework also became a problem of organizing the labor into a manageable day's work.[57]

At the same time as these transformations were occurring in the home, factory owners sought to produce a flexible workforce by replacing skilled machinists with systems for managing unskilled industrial laborers. New tools for industrial management led to a striking asymmetry between home and factory: while industrial mechanization arrived in tandem with managerial systems that maintained the unity of production, no corresponding structure existed in the domestic sphere. Thus, at the end of the nineteenth century, reformers who followed Beecher sought to develop systems for managing housework. Their goal was to bring domestic tasks into correspondence with the emerging managerial systems designed for industry. The coordination of technologies developed by Butz, Powers, and others helped these reformers make the case that housework was work as long as it could be understood through the distinctly modern tools of industrial management.[58]

THE POLITICAL ECONOMY OF HOUSEHOLD MANAGEMENT

In his history of the work ethic in industrial America, Daniel Rodgers explained that the definition of women's labor was a touchstone for the development of the feminist movement. Reforming the status of women hinged on the value that was given to their work, but not all feminists agreed that the household could even be considered a legitimate domain for their labor.[59] For the feminist reformer Charlotte Perkins Gilman (1860–1935), domestic chores were not work because they remained isolated from the social interactions that she believed to be an essential aspect of all modern labor. Contrary to Beecher's interest in the internalization of the household, Gilman held that the establishment of communal kitchens and nurseries would be required in order to preserve the human race from what she observed to be a slow degradation produced by the social isolation of women.[60] Influenced by the writings of the novelist Edward Bellamy (1850–98), Gilman believed that women should be paid for their labor and no longer be bound to the domestic setting, disconnected from society at large for which they apparently produced nothing. Bellamy had already proposed similar changes to the home in an essay on the "domestic problem" that he published in 1889. He also claimed that a truly democratic society could not sustain a stratified caste system produced by the presence of a servant class in the household.[61] Gilman, capturing the literary power of the mechanical utopia from Bellamy's novel *Looking Backward* (1887), poignantly observed that there was a moral cause for replacing the labor of domestic service with the labor of machines. To "demand celibacy of our domestic servants," she argued, made them into a temporary and unskilled labor force; only machines could be forced to accept their celibate fate. The diffusion of sexual tension between a wife and a servant, she held, would be made possible with the growing capacities of automatic machinery.[62]

Replacing servants with services was a persistent theme in the literature on thermostatic systems. For mechanical engineer John H. Kinealy, an inventor of numerous instruments for air purification and ventilation, automating thermostatic control of the interior was a means for middle-class homeowners to overcome the lapses of their employees. Thermostatic regulation, he explained, employed "a watchful device which takes notice of changes of temperature [that] is ever alert and ready to turn on or shut off the supply of heat as may be necessary . . . [substituting] the negligent or forgetful, or busy individual [by] an automatic device which is never negligent, never forgetful, and never too busy to note the changes in temperature and regulate the supply of heat as the conditions demand."[63] Thermostatic regulation represented the interface between supply and demand of heat. The invisible hand of the household environment was in fact the product of a mechanical system and its artificial intervention in the interior environment. Once the homemaker replaced the servant's negligence with obedient machines, she no longer needed to experience fluctuations in heat due to a misalignment between the supply of hot air and the family's demand. A uniform temperature was made possible by an automated environmental system that, if well maintained, would only need to be given occasional directions as it continued to work. With a mechanized household, in an updated version of Beecher's proposals, the housewife would not be required to find additional work outside the household or revert to executing domestic chores manually to be considered employed. Advocates for technological change diffused Gilman's critique by arguing that a mother's expert knowledge of household management would become her own domain of industrialized automation. By 1913 Mary Pattison, aiming to formalize household management through Frederick Winslow Taylor's methods for production control, predicted that this new vocation for women would "eliminate the servant problem by eliminating the servant class."[64] In her application of Taylor's principles to the home, Pattison described the domestic economy as a system of objects of varied sizes and purposes, each fitting certain standards of organization.

Under the homemaker's command, the administration of the family's health could be controlled with techniques for preserving food, filtering dust, and managing the molecular mixture of air. In her *Chemistry of the Household* (1907), Margaret Dodd, a graduate of MIT and a teacher of science at the Woodward Institute for Girls, instructed her readers that air molecules were material objects that could be subjected to precise governance. She wrote about the constant passage of air through the bodies of those inhabiting a home: "Air is a real substance. It can be weighed. The air in a room 15 feet by 20 feet by 10 feet high weighs 210 pounds, and would fill ten ordinary water pails if liquefied. . . . . It requires considerable force to move it. When a bottle is full of air, no more can be poured in. Our houses are full of air all the time. It pervades all things, the cells and tissues of our bodies are full of air."[65] The chemistry of domestic air could extend from the correct proportional mixture of gases to physiological standards regarding the preferred temperature range for the interior of a home. "At 66° or 68° the blood is properly distributed between the skin and the internal organs," wrote the authors of *The Human Mechanism* (1906), Theodore Hough and William Sedgwick, "and there is no excess in either. At 60° or 61°, on the other hand, the blood is forced back upon the internal organs, thus threatening serious congestions and other unhealthful conditions."[66] Despite their belief that the cell was a "living machine," they explained that the human sense of environmental temperature was not as trustworthy as that of a mechanical device. Biological systems did not reliably follow protocols and could mistakenly allow the temperature of a room to fall into the "Danger Zone," below seventy degrees and above sixty degrees (Figure 1.9). To avoid the fallibility of the human senses, the thermostat, a watchful mechanism, eliminated that risk by protecting the body from the threat of unregulated heat.

The concept of room temperature that implies a normative range for the heat of the interior emerged at the moment that air in a room, through the action of automatic mechanisms, could be brought to a uniform and

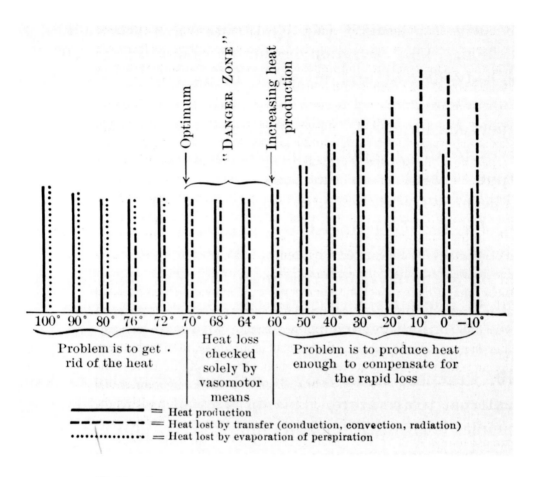

FIGURE 1.9. The physiological response to room temperature. Theodore Hough and William T. Sedgwick, *The Human Mechanism: Its Physiology and Hygiene and the Sanitation of Its Surroundings* (Boston: Ginn and Company, 1906), 202.

stable heat. Hough and Sedgwick's proposal that seventy degrees was the optimum temperature for a room was not their attempt to accommodate an idealized view of human comfort but conformed to their study of the internal regulation of the body's physiological response. In keeping with Ure's mechanistic view of the body, this was the temperature, they claimed, that would result in neither precipitous heat loss nor heat gain. The conceptual association of comfort with room temperature is the historical consequence of the mass-marketing strategies of companies that sought to promote their regulatory systems to potential customers. The persistence of this naturalized concept of room temperature, one that was equated with a universal sense of comfort, is indicative of the influence that their advertisements had in positioning the thermostatic system as essential to any healthy modern household.[67]

An advertisement for the Minneapolis Heat Regulator from 1906 provides evidence that the disparate cultural interests regarding technology, health, economy, and society could be assembled into a single gesture (Figure 1.10). The first line of text advises readers that sanitary heating "is impossible without an automatic heat regulator to maintain a uniform temperature." Uniform, or even, temperature was described as desirable for both comfort and health. The word "sanitary" implies the machinery would maintain a clean environment for a hygienic home.[68] The advertisement also explains that the instrument can contribute to saving on coal bills and to balancing the household's finances. A photograph illustrating the advertisement shows a female hand reaching toward a knob affixed to the bottom of a thermostat; both the hand and the instrument have been extracted from their context—presumably a home—and surrounded instead with text. The thermostat hangs as the interface between the circuitry of a home, which could belong to anyone, and the hand of the anonymous household manager whose ring finger boasts engagement and wedding bands indicating both her class and social position within the family. Below the thermostat, the words "Adjust Here" establish the purpose of her gesture. Under her wrist, the words "IT'S AUTOMATIC" refer to the exchange between her will and the instrument's dial: the thought of fixing the temperature required no labor beyond the turn of a knob. It is almost by reflex, then, that the mechanisms of the house respond to the movement of the manicured finger. The thermometer above measures the temperature in the room, just below seventy. The knob is also at seventy, implying that the machine has already acted upon the household manager's desire. Perhaps we are watching the hand slowly withdraw from the instrument after all the machines have already done their work.

The advertisement presented the thermostatic interior as an investment on which the family could receive a consistent return. A free trial of thirty days would prove to the household manager that the initial outlay could quickly pay for itself. In a technical manual for cutting and folding sheet metal for ventilation ductwork, Alfred G. King made a similar argument to instruct his readers on "how to sell thermostats." A new class of experts in domestic ventilation, he believed, should educate homemakers

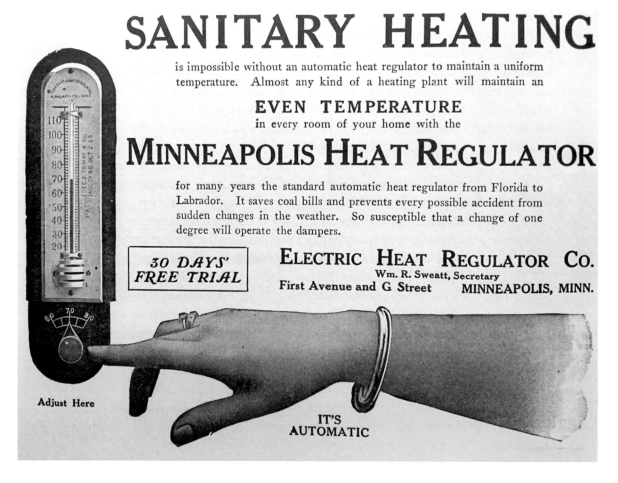

FIGURE 1.10. An advertisement for a thermostat produced by the Electric Heat Regulator Company. *American Homes and Gardens* 3 (1906): 262.

about the healthfulness and comfort that could be brought about by a thermostatic device. He also proposed that his readers could recite the following calculation to potential customers: "the thermostat really costs the house owner nothing, for it saves many times the interest on the investment each season until the saving made pays the cost of the installation, after which it earns money for the owner at a greater rate than any ordinary business investment he may have."[69] Just as Frederick Winslow Taylor had argued in his *Principles of Scientific Management* that investing in a managerial system would give an owner greater control over his investment, installing a system for thermostatic control would make the family's expenditure on heat into a predictable expense in the management of household finances.

Advertisements consistently separated images of the systems of environmental control from the physical form of the houses they would occupy. The generality of their imagery presents a stark contrast to that of Frank Lloyd Wright's early domestic architecture, particularly the Robie House (1909) in Chicago, in which Reyner Banham showed that the environmental systems were fully integrated into the greater organic whole.[70] Abstracting the systems from their context mirrored the abstraction of Taylor's systems that his disciples represented in diagrams, routing sheets, and other forms of paperwork so that they could apply them equally to any configuration of industrial labor. In following Taylor's method, household management also shifted the attitude toward domestic reform from the early proposals of Catharine Beecher that were far more specific about the relationship of architecture to the labor of housekeeping. This distinction between the management of household mechanics and the physical configuration of a house is immediately evident in Mary Pattison's exclusion of domestic images from any publication produced from her Housekeeping Experiment Station in Colonia, New Jersey. Her intention in not representing the particularities of physical layout was to allow any homemaker to apply the lessons of "domestic engineering" that she had developed in Colonia to the specificities of her own context.[71] Similarly, "a household efficiency engineer and kitchen architect," Christine Frederick, published photographs of the tools she tested in her Applecroft Home Experiment Station but never presented a complete image of the physical building that stood in Greenlawn, Long Island.[72] In their effort to mix science with household labor, these protagonists established what they considered scientific "stations" for domestic experiments, sites in buildings that no longer functioned as the homes they once housed. The stations had become laboratories in which the abstract techniques of household management could be researched, refined to a method, and taught to an audience of interested homemakers.

Domestic engineers sought to maintain a clear distance between the emotional role played by the mother as the moral center of her family and her professional role as a manager who followed standard practices. In fact, Pattison explained that to implement her managerial techniques, the concept of "home" needed to be redefined as "the constant production of an atmosphere, or state of organized existence."[73] The central object of household management was not the house itself, but the objective treatment of the atmosphere it enclosed and the processes that organized life there. And just as the scientific study of factory labor required perpetual coordination of machines, tasks, power, and the economy, so did the labor of managing the household. Frederick proposed that if the homemaker studied the manner in which she performed her household tasks, certain movements could be standardized and made into habits. They could thus be performed as if by reflex, "every day in an identical manner without much mental attention."[74] The labor of constantly producing and reproducing an organized domestic atmosphere, under proper management, would eventually become automatic as if it were one of the mechanical elements that regulated the temperature, movement, and quality of the interior air.

The role of these experiment stations was to test new domestic technologies and offer instruction on the best method of their integration into the home. An unpublished photograph of the Applecroft kitchen reveals that Frederick preferred to use moveable furniture elements rather than built-in appliances because they could be constantly reconfigured and updated (Figure 1.11). With two arrangements of the same kitchen she compared two movement diagrams of a woman's path through the space as she worked (Figure 1.12). In one, the stove, cabinet, table, sink, china closet, and icebox were distributed so that the tasks associated with preparation and clearing required numerous changes of direction.[75] The other arrangement, pictured in the photograph, positioned the equipment to economize the "chain of steps" taken by the homemaker. In drawing the diagrams, Frederick borrowed notational systems from Frank Gilbreth, a follower of Taylor and a contractor. Like the motion study that Gilbreth used to direct the correct method for laying bricks, for instance, Frederick

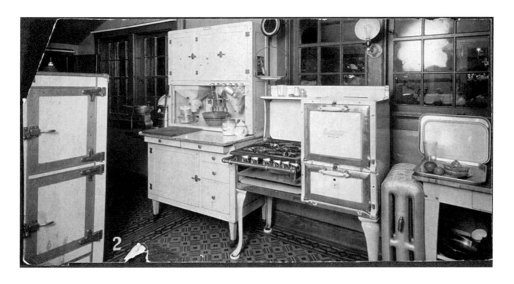

FIGURE 1.11. Interior view of the Applecroft Home Experiment Station kitchen, ca. 1920–25 [20021590_1]
Schlesinger Library on the History of Women in America, Radcliffe Institute, Harvard University.

documented lines of movement to translate the visual language of industrial management into the domain of housework.[76] One difference between
Gilbreth's and Frederick's objects is significant: while industrial managers were not manual laborers, each of Frederick's diagrams represented
the homemaker as both laborer and manager simultaneously, the subject and object of managerial control. As a laborer, walking according to
her general habits, she was the object of management, regulating those
movements according to her own analysis. But the homemaker was responsible for recording the lines that traced her existing habits and then
also revising those lines into mechanically rationalized instructions. Thus
the goal of the home economics movement was to train the homemaker
with methods for transforming her identity from a laborer to a manager
and back again to a laborer—she was the ideal object of self-regulation.
Viewing her own labor from an objective vantage point would allow her to
bring its process into harmony with the mechanical systems that constituted her modern home.

    We see, then, that household management was not intended to liber-
ate the woman from the burden of household chores. Rather, it presumed
that modeling her productivity after the ordered space of industry would

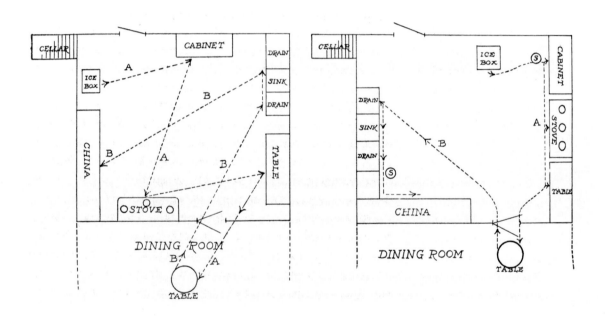

FIGURE 1.12. Comparative diagrams for preparing or clearing a meal in a kitchen. The diagram on the left shows a kitchen with "badly arranged equipment, which makes confused intersecting chains of steps, in either preparing or clearing away a meal." On the right is the arrangement seen in Figure 1.11. It shows a "proper arrangement of equipment, which makes a simple chain of steps, in either preparing or clearing away a meal." In both diagrams the line labeled "A" indicates "preparing," and the line labeled "B" indicates "clearing." Christine Frederick, *The New Housekeeping: Efficiency Studies in Home Management* (Garden City: Doubleday, Page, 1913), 52.

infuse the home with an analogous set of positive values: domestic productivity and efficiency. Yet the negative consequence of blending the home and the factory was that, as a manager of one's own production, the woman internalized the often-fraught relationship in industry between labor and management. According to Thorstein Veblen, this internalized tension, in which she played two contradictory roles at once, could not produce a unified subject who could be identified as the modern mother as Beecher had hoped. Instead, that tension pushed the homemaker into the background where she increasingly took on the automated character of the silent mechanisms she was meant to control.[77]

The frontispiece for a brochure produced by the Barber-Coleman Company, a temperature control maker, is an emblem of a new kind of domestic space guided by the combination of technological and managerial power (Figure 1.13).[78] The room pictured in the photograph looks empty: there is no human body in this domestic interior, and the only objects that appear at first glance are a radiator and a chair. Perhaps the chair is simply there to give a sense of scale, but it is more likely that it indicates the absence of a human servant who has been replaced by the technologies of control that hang on the wall beside it. Plywood veneer clads the walls. Its grain produces a nearly symmetrical pattern at approximately eye level, forming an implied artificial horizon inside the room. The cladding protrudes at the corner, perhaps to make way for a column. This detail, where the wood remains continuous despite the irregularities of the room, reminds the reader of the brochure that the cladding is there for another reason: to hide the technical complexity of the electromechanical systems. Invisible in the photograph, but fully explained in the diagrams that fill the pages that follow, are wires that connect the thermostat to valves on the boiler in the basement, steam pipes from the boiler to the radiator in the room, and more wires that connect the light switch to both the power source and the bulb. While the reflex describes the fundamental unit of control for bodily movement, the electrical thermostat hanging on the wall gives mechanical life to this wood-clad interior. Thus despite the appearance that nothing is happening, the room contains moving air that is heated by the steam circulating through the radiator; valves are clicking as a sensitive device is sending electrical messages to the boiler to retain the room's uniform temperature. This interior environment is managed by circuitry that has made it both dynamic and controllable, the appearance of technical order in the absence of human guidance is granted by

FIGURE 1.13. Frontispiece of the catalog for the Barber-Colman Company, *An Electrical System of Temperature Control* (Rockford: Barber-Coleman Company, 1931).

the principle of regulation that guides these systems. The household managers' abstract diagrams do not remove the physical aspects of existence from domestic space. Instead, the regulatory apparatus on the wall that is an extension of that managerial power fills the interior of the house with another set of environmental qualities that define what would come to be viewed as a modern interior.

In the transition from Beecher's proposal for a house shaped around the technical needs of the mother to the methods developed by writers on household management, both the architectural context for regulation and the homemaker's labor required standardization. To achieve this new standard, the pages of brochures and those of the managerial studies reflect a purposeful erasure of differences between individual houses; this normalization also applied to the women who lived in those houses. Household managers described a generic domain for a woman's labor, a modern unit of domestic production, that made it possible to compare the work of a woman in the home to the work of a man in the factory because both were overseen by industrial systems of control.

Ure's principle of regulation, captured by the action of the thermostat, had extended from the mechanics of industrial production to the biological reproduction of a household. With this extension, elements of his theory of industrial management, based in the value of automation, were also applied to the private sphere. The electrified thermostat, analogous in its function to the biological reflex, helped form a domain of managerial control over that domestic milieu as a political economic unit. But we cannot conclude that the technical regulation of the enclosed household environment was determined by the economic reform of homemaking; rather, both the technical and managerial aspects of the modern interior were forms of practical knowledge that clarified how the family was situated as an organizational element in the infrastructure of modern life. The technical knowledge that pertained to regulation was thus given a distinct form: a collection of thermostats, ventilators, ductwork, and electrical circuitry that produced an internalized network of control. This "state of organized existence" helped transform the conceptual boundaries that structure modern life—interior versus exterior, work versus home, labor versus management, and mechanism versus organism—into the physical environment of a managed household.

CHAPTER 2

Cold Storage and the Speculative Market of Preserved Assets

Edward Bellamy's novel *Looking Backward*, written in 1887, begins with a description of the main character, Julian West, refurbishing the basement of his home. Controlling the environment in this underground space, he believed, would make it possible to maintain the vitality of his body through an extended period of uninterrupted sleep. After inviting a professor of animal magnetism to entrance him into a deep slumber, West awoke more than a century later in the year 2000, perfectly preserved. This death-defying feat was made possible by the combination of an extraordinary hypnotic method and well-regulated domestic architecture. In West's basement, cool fresh air entered regularly while stale air was exhausted. In the new millennium, West gradually discovered that all the economic and political problems plaguing the nation in 1887 had been resolved. Technological progress in all domains of life had made it possible to regulate an uncertain future into a perfectly coordinated mechanical utopia.[1]

The success of *Looking Backward* is well known; it sold nearly half a million copies in the first year of its publication. The fully mechanized world that Bellamy introduced in the novel also involved the state ownership of industry, based on his rejection of the laissez-faire ideology that structured much of the economic thought during the Gilded Age.[2] As an image of a new world in which the state played a dominant role in daily life, the novel attracted the audience of those that criticized the rampant individualism and unequal distribution of wealth in late nineteenth-century American society.[3] Bellamy's trope of hypnotized time travel reappeared in *Equality*, a sequel that he published in 1897. One reviewer of it referred to the already-famous sleeping chamber as Julian West's "cold storage house."[4] This was no ordinary technical description. In the ten years that had passed between Bellamy's first and second novels, cold storage had become a topic addressed in every major American newspaper and was the professed solution to the constant economic crises of the 1890s.

Cold storage warehouses were created to preserve perishable things over time and were powered by the types of machines that Bellamy's futuristic novels celebrated. Unlike the apparatus found in a domestic basement, these buildings were massive industrial structures that involved significant investments in urban real estate and technically advanced systems for cooling their interior environment. These were not utopian machines. Controlling the environmental conditions around commodities such as fruit, vegetables, meat, and dairy protected them from bacterial decay as well as from unstable economic demand. Whereas the technologies used to manage the household environment circulated widely through the pages of journals for domestic engineering, the design of cold storage warehouses concerned only a few experts whose knowledge circulated in specialized trade journals. But the anticipated effect of cold storage extended well beyond its capacity to serve as an amenity for cities. The proliferation of these buildings at the end of the nineteenth century was driven by the investment of entrepreneurs who aimed to extend to perishables the speculative futures market that had developed at midcentury in grain.

This chapter examines the role of these buildings in a broad shift in economic thinking in the United States—from laissez-faire ideas based in classic political economy to proposals for greater governmental regulation. Speculation and regulation were not at odds in this case. Rather, the mechanical regulation of the environment within cold storage, the expansion of the futures market, and attempts to assert control over the national economy were all bound together. Two significant cold storage facilities, in Chicago and Boston, demonstrate the challenge that this new building type presented to the profession of architecture. They reveal the need to define the scope of an architect's work in relation to new mechanical systems and to the growing power of the regulatory state. Attempts made by architects to address the public through the design of cold storage warehouses also expose the changing role of architecture in representing the value of such an institution to economic regulation as that task gradually shifted from small groups of entrepreneurs to corporations and governmental agencies. Diverging views on the place of architecture in the design of cold storage facilities make visible some competing models within

architectural practice during the period—models based on different proportional combinations of art, service, and expertise.

In Chicago, the construction of a monumental structure for cold storage required the notoriety of the city's most famous architectural partnership, that of Dankmar Adler and Louis Sullivan. In Boston, the less famous
architect William Gibbons Preston was hired to design multiple modest
buildings connected by a subterranean infrastructure that gradually established the nation's largest network of cold storage spaces. Scale and
style were major variables in positioning these institutions within their
cities and in relation to the gradual accumulation of governmental regulatory power. Traditional uses of monumental architectural form and urban
design were needed to accommodate the formation of a new institution
in Chicago; but the role played by architectural design was different in
Boston as technological and legal changes prepared these facilities to become part of a larger economic system. As more investors sought to control and expand American commerce through the cold storage system, the
scope of architectural work shifted to embrace certain types of technical
expertise and the knowledge of governmental guidelines that regulated
the entire system's accountability and predictability.

With the establishment of new agencies for managing the national
economy, the demands for technical and legal knowledge about cold storage exceeded the capacities of classically trained architects. Regulating the
economy through a nationalized system required developing a new type of
architecture, and the practices that could produce it; these were buildings
that accommodated the increasing influence of managerial expertise.

TECHNOLOGY, FUTURES, AND THE MANAGEMENT
OF ECONOMIC CRISES

Until the 1880s, cold storage warehouses were cooled with harvested ice.
Expensive to transport and nearly impossible to obtain reliably during the
summer months, ice was a primitive and unreliable cooling agent.[5] Most
of the large-scale cold storage facilities in cities were built to support the
transport and storage of meat. Refrigerated railroad cars, also cooled with
ice, had been developed in the 1850s by engineers working for Gustavus
Swift and eventually by the rest of the "Big Four" meat companies. The key
benefit offered by these moving iceboxes was the capacity to transport
slaughtered meat rather than live cattle, eliminating both the time delays

associated with feeding during the journey and the investment in terminal slaughterhouses. Ice cars centralized the meat-packing operation through a network of cooled terminal buildings at major distribution centers.[6] Swift insisted that updating his "reefer cars" with the newly available mechanical refrigeration technology would further expand his network.[7] He hired the engineer Andrew J. Chase to develop and manufacture a proprietary insulated refrigerator car that would extend the company's sales to more distant markets.[8] Mechanical refrigeration could produce cold year round and also free valuable space in the railroad car for more meat. Thus, cooling technology moved from ice-cooled buildings to mechanically cooled railroad cars, and finally from reefer cars to machines that were powerful enough to cool entire storage warehouses.

Investors in cold storage facilities that served commission merchants rather than just a private meatpacking company hired the engineers of the reefer cars to develop a variation of Chase's patented technology that would be appropriate for the volume of air held in large warehouse buildings. Their long-term aim was to establish reserves in perishable commodities—fruits, vegetables, dairy, and eggs—that could support the issuing of futures contracts like those used for grain at the Board of Trade. Futures contracts are agreements between a buyer and a seller to exchange a commodity for a set price at some future date stipulated by the contract. Between the issuance of the contract and the date of the commodity's delivery, the contract can be transferred among speculators who bet on changes in the commodity's value.[9] Beyond establishing speculative practices for commodities, futures were also viewed in the late nineteenth century as tools for stabilizing prices through a reserve that could tune supply to demand. The Board of Trade and numerous other trading "pits" promised to exert control over fluctuations in the market.[10] While they had no clear effect on stabilizing the national economy, under their influence prices oscillated less extremely, and by 1890 these institutions made futures the dominant form of commodity exchange in the United States.[11]

Constructing the volume of cooled storage space necessary to preserve perishable commodities for future delivery relied on expanding the process of mechanical refrigeration technologies for this new purpose. Instruments compressed ammonia from a vapor into a liquid that was then pumped through vast assemblies of coiled expansion pipes to absorb heat wherever a warehouse needed to reduce the quantity of heat. Experiments conducted by the emerging profession of refrigeration engineers such as

John Ewald Siebel and his students at the Siebel Institute of Technology revealed that regulating the volume of ammonia to water in the coils could establish exact temperatures in each storeroom based on the unique needs of the commodity stored there.[12] Scientific experiments were conducted to find a temperature range for storing specific commodities—eggs versus apples, for instance. The bacteriological chemist Mary Engle Pennington, for example, calculated how much humidity was tolerable or even desirable to maintain certain foods in cold storage.[13] In the early days of cold storage, there was nearly no data available to assess how long a fruit or vegetable could be held in temporal suspension by mechanical systems. This research, sponsored by the cold storage industry and the federal government, was part of an effort to make the technology of the system reliable and predictable enough for warehouses to become responsive environments that could dependably buttress the market in perishables as seasons changed and demand fluctuated.

The time that commodities would be held in cold storage extended the interval between the farmer's sale and the broker's purchase. This time lag challenged a central axiom of classical political economics: that a necessary equilibrium exists at all times between buyers and sellers.[14] According to Karl Marx, from his *Theories of Surplus Value*, this tenet was based upon the false assumption that buying and selling constituted a single harmonious act. Marx understood buying and selling as two independent and opposite phases in the metamorphosis of commodities; therefore any belief in an inherent harmony between purchase and sale was fundamentally unfounded.[15] Crises, for classical political economists, were signs that the economy had not conformed to the pure rational structure of exchange. From David Ricardo to John Stuart Mill, crises were explained as an error in the natural economic equilibrium and would cease to exist if the processes of production were properly organized; the unity of buying and selling was at the very center of their ideal system. By contrast, Marx claimed that the possibility of crisis was inherent in the very structure of capitalism. After all, the need to convert a commodity into money through its sale was a transformation of something useful (the commodity) into something abstract (money) that the seller was not compelled to use to buy anything else. The independent and opposing steps in this process fundamentally precluded any kind of natural equilibrium between buying and selling.[16] This structural disjuncture within the transformation of the commodity into money defined the origin and necessity of the possibility of crisis. As Marx explained, "The difficulty of the seller . . . only stems from the ease with which the buyer can defer the retransformation of money into commodity."[17] If an economic crisis produced by this deferral were to be managed, it would require storing a commodity in a reserve that held it back from the market for later sale. This was the underlying logic for the development of the grain silo as well as the cold storage warehouse. The trading of futures contracts on commodities was first made possible for grain with its storage in silos and soon thereafter for perishable produce in cold storage.[18]

At the end of the nineteenth century, all industrialized capitalist countries, regardless of the particularities of their social and economic institutions, faced the problem that economists called overproduction, a term already used by Marx. The term described the condition in which there was an overabundance of goods in the market that could not be sold to consumers for profit. Overproduction became a topic of broad public concern in the United States and soon received significant scholarly attention from economists and other social scientists.[19] Martin J. Sklar's study of the transformation of American economic thought in this period has shown that the imagined solution to overproduction was related to the shift from small competitive businesses to significant concentrations of capital in the hands of a few consolidated firms. With this shift, a new theory of the capitalist market emerged in the work of three figures in American economic thought—Charles Arthur Conant, Arthur Twining Hadley, and Jeremiah Whipple Jenks—all of whom independently served as advisors to Theodore Roosevelt and studied the newfound power of the large business enterprise. They sought to resolve the problem of overproduction as part of a regulatory approach to economic crises.[20] For example, like Marx, Conant wrote about the inherent possibility of crisis in capitalist societies as "universal . . . and intimately interwoven with the structure of modern credit and the speculative tendencies of the human mind."[21] It followed from this nonidealized description of credit and speculation that Conant's suggestion for managing the problem of overproduction was pragmatic, rather than dogmatic like his predecessors. Crises, he argued, could be controlled as part of the cyclical nature of the economy, similar to the way that a living organism incorporated regulatory systems to manage environmental change.[22]

Conant knew that the possibility of administering the market was central to the operational logic of the large American corporations that emerged during the second half of the nineteenth century. Their size put them in a position of economic power that could restrict the unpredictable effects of competition and thereby regulate their production to stabilize price and profit.[23] Under this corporate logic, independent dealers of agricultural commodities who were still subject to the risks of the competitive market believed that they too could protect themselves from the risk of crisis. Regulating the interaction of buyers and sellers through a reserve of perishables would allow merchants to shield the price of their commodities from the irregular fluctuations of both seasonal weather and market demand. The size of the large corporation allowed it to internalize the disjunction as a means of escaping the immediate pressures of an unstable market. Sellers of agricultural products, by contrast, would require a collective infrastructure to help regulate the flow of their goods into the market. What had been unregulated in the competitive marketplace became regulated through the large mechanically cooled cold storage house, a place in which commodities would be held for later sale.

THE CHICAGO COLD STORAGE EXCHANGE

A delegation of 150 of Chicago's produce commission merchants met on April 17, 1874, at the Commercial Hotel in Chicago to establish a produce exchange that would be planned on the precedent of the Chicago Board of Trade (Figure 2.1).[24] This new institution would become a central clearinghouse for commodities not yet included under the regulatory capacity of the Board of Trade such as butter, cheese, eggs, fruits, and vegetables.[25] Just as the Board of Trade had developed a system for the grading of grain, the officers and inspectors at the Produce Exchange set the rules that regulated the way perishable commodities were traded by its members. Systems of classification graded them, grouped them by quality and type, and established common methods for packing and shipment.[26]

The main goal for the Produce Exchange was, as their mission read, "to gain the advantages resulting from the centralization of interests by bringing the buyer and seller at once together; thus giving to the buyer a place where he can at all times find property for sale, and the seller a mart for his merchandise."[27] By regulating and centralizing the activities of the produce market, the Exchange formalized the relationship between buyers and sellers. Mediating their interaction in one place, as the officers of the Exchange understood it, would help cure the unremitting state of

FIGURE 2.1. Interior view of the hall in the Chicago Public Produce and Stock Exchange, located at 135, 137, 139, and 141 East Madison Street. The building was entered from Calhoun Place, at the rear of the Board of Trade. Brochure published in 1879. The Chicago History Museum.

crisis that affected the produce market. The very cause of the Exchange, to "bringing the buyer and seller at once together," recognized the inherent opposition within the market between these two parties and justified this mediation.

But the merchants of perishable produce had not considered the facilities that they would need to store commodities for future delivery and, as a result, only offered on "cash" or "spot" trades that required the immediate delivery of goods.[28] In order to establish a speculative market in perishables with futures contracts, the Produce Exchange would require a vast investment in the construction of storage. As the investment was not made near the founding of the Exchange, it folded after only a few years of slow business marked by political infighting. The Chicago Produce Exchange was reorganized in 1898 as the Butter and Egg Board of Chicago, the institution that would eventually become the Chicago Mercantile Exchange, the largest speculative commodities market in the world.[29]

The first significant attempt to establish a cooled warehouse facility of significant scale in Chicago was initiated only in 1888 by the engineer J. Ensign Fuller, president of the New York Consolidated Refrigeration Company. To prove that his apparatus could operate in the expanded enclosure of a warehouse building as well as it did in a refrigerated railroad car, Fuller installed a refrigeration plant in an existing warehouse and invited more than a hundred potential investors to experience the cooling

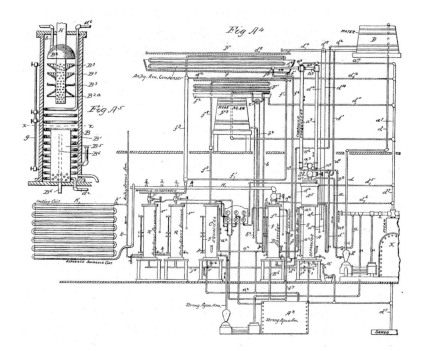

FIGURE 2.2. J. Ensign Fuller's patented Combined Ammonia Distilling and Refrigerating Apparatus that was presumably used for his demonstration in the Chicago warehouse in 1888, the year he applied for the patent. Note the expansion coils on the left and the condensing coils at the top. U.S. Patent 489,897 (issued January 10, 1893), 4.

power and accuracy of his mechanical system for ammonia compression and circulation (Figure 2.2). The *Chicago Daily Tribune* reported that the temperature in each of the storage rooms could be fixed anywhere between forty-five degrees above and thirty-five degrees below zero and would remain stable, thanks to a novel thermostatic mechanism.[30]

With the success of this early experiment, Fuller, together with the real estate magnate Joseph L. Lathrop, began to organize a team of shareholders to found a company they called the Chicago Cold Storage Exchange. Hoping to convince others to invest in "the world's largest cold storage facility," located on the bank of the Chicago River, they published their plans in the summer of 1890. The location was considered a critical factor in the success of the project: the warehouse buildings would straddle numerous railroad tracks beneath and directly abut the proposed West Side elevated railways. The building would thus be accessible by water, rail, and streetcar. By November, they had raised enough capital to begin construction, and a cornerstone-laying ceremony featured speeches by the city's mayor and Colonel R. M. Littler, the secretary of the Produce Exchange. William

Sooy-Smith, the Civil War general and civil engineer, also spoke, calling the planners "a company of wizards." Expressing his fascination with the systems that produced the exact temperatures desired to store any perishable product imaginable, Sooy-Smith interpreted the space of the facility as a location that would allow perishable commodities to overcome the effects of time:

> The active agents of decay are heat and moisture. Control these and you can convert the perishable into the almost imperishable. The temperature in these storerooms is controlled so that it can be made either that of the polar regions or of the burning tropics. The perishable products of the whole earth can be brought together and placed in rooms the temperature of which is reduced below the point at which fermentation and decay can take place, and they can be preserved until needed. This enterprise is based on no more theoretical deduction or untried experiment. In yonder building fish, fruits, and other very perishable things are stored, many of them frozen hard as rock and everlasting.[31]

Having exceeded the earlier experiments of "theoretical deduction," a group of experts had in fact scientifically planned an unprecedented assembly of machinery that would cool the entire building. An instrument devised by Albert M. Butz, the inventor of an electrical thermostat, regulated the temperature in each of the storerooms to the desired range. Butz configured a unique system of "delicate levers and valves," applying an altered version of his domestic system that electrically regulated a furnace to produce heat, to automatically adjust the amount of anhydrous ammonia that was allowed to expand to cool each room of the monumental Chicago facility.[32]

Sooy-Smith reserved his most laudatory comments for the company's selection of the architectural partnership of Dankmar Adler and Louis Sullivan to design the building that housed this new technology. He noted that this famous partnership would "pass from planning and building that superb temple—the Auditorium building—devoted to the culture of our great city, to the design and construction of this eminently useful structure that is destined to contribute much to the health and comfort and employment of life of our whole community, rich and poor."[33]

Why did the investors of the Exchange choose these architects? From newspaper stories that followed the cornerstone-laying ceremony, it is clear that the choice was a large part of the business strategy. Famous architects would give new investors confidence in a scheme that was still far from solvent. Also, Adler and Sullivan had just completed the most provocatively heterogeneous project in the city, also mentioned by Sooy-Smith: the Auditorium Building. Built in 1889, that facility combined a theater, offices, and a hotel in one dense square block.[34] Like the Auditorium Building, the program that the warehouse buildings would hold was also intended to be diverse. The proposed buildings would combine storage and offices with a glass-covered shopping arcade spanning from Lake to Randolph Streets between the two ten-story warehouses (Figure 2.3). This promenade was to hover over the existing railroad tracks that facilitated the delivery of goods for storage and retrieval on demand. The arcade would be lined on either side by thirty-five shop fronts for the produce trade. The entire floor area, one level above the street, was intended to house ninety offices for commission merchants as well as an expansive room for the daily operations of the Produce Exchange.[35]

Finally, beyond the skill and fame of the partnership, the newly founded company hoped to deliver the impression that their facility was a civic monument. With its wide Romanesque arches, a tall dentil cornice, and the enclosed arcade that connected West Water Street to Lake Street, the published proposal was intended to make the structure appear to any Chicagoan as a form of public architecture. For the business venture to be a success, the investment in the operation of the facility would require the general support of the commercial interests in the city. The building's monumental form and urban disposition was thus an attempt to express its value to a broad community of businessmen as well as the general public who could come to shop in this most modern facility.

Carl Condit, the historian of modern building technology, called the warehouses "a study in texture and geometric purism," but failed to mention the novelty of the mechanical systems and the programmatic mixture of storage, shopping, and office space.[36] According to Condit's analysis, Adler and Sullivan took cues regarding their masonry details and the simplicity of wall treatment from H. H. Richardson's influential Marshall Field and Co. Wholesale Store, built in 1885–87. In their 1889 Walker Warehouse, also in Chicago, they had eliminated the Richardsonian rustication and opened large arches onto the street; they carried over both of these choices into the design of the cold storage warehouses. In keeping with their use of steel for the structure of commercial buildings such as the Wainwright Building in St. Louis, completed in 1891, the architects proposed that the

FIGURE 2.3. Adler and Sullivan's rendering of the two warehouses and arcade on West Water Street. "Chicago Cold Storage Exchange," *Inland Architect and News Record* 16:3 (1890).

Cold Storage Exchange be constructed from a mixture of steel frame elements and bearing brick with stone and terra cotta ornaments.

The translation of the steel structure into the gridded facades of the tall office building was the underlying motive for Sullivan's now famous line, "form ever follows function." While the functions served by cold storage had clear implications on the building's form—the size of window openings and the massive amount of space given over to the mechanical systems in the basement and inside the walls—Sullivan's statement from 1896 did not extend to the design of warehouses. Rather, it was the relationship between the practical needs of modern office work, which he viewed as guiding "the economics of the building," and the architectural form that would result from the new forms of office work that would take on "a true normal type." Between the basement and attic of an office building, which held the "tanks, valves, sheaves, and mechanical etcetera," stood the pure simplicity of a constant and standard form: a grid of structure that organized the space within as well as the machined elements that composed the facade of the building.[37]

The organic relationship of function to form that Sullivan sketched out in his essay "The Tall Office Building Artistically Considered" drew on his understanding of that relation in nature. The metaphorical connection between a work of architecture and an organism was nothing new; it had already been central to German aesthetic discourse all through the nineteenth century. Yet while German theories of tectonic expression related the purposive unity of an organism to an aesthetic whole, following Immanuel Kant, Sullivan was an avid reader of Charles Darwin and believed that buildings—and therefore their architects—should respond to their social and economic context as organisms respond to their natural contexts.[38] In *Autobiography of an Idea* (1924), Sullivan later explained that it was the responsibility of the architect to more closely align his "state of mind" to that of the engineer. Replacing the ambiguities of the unstandardized practices of architecture for those of engineering offered architects the rigorous methods of science to see the single essential purpose in things. Engineers "who knew a problem when they saw it," he wrote, were never distracted from the direct and simple facts, their "minds were trained to deal with real things."[39] According to Sullivan, the task of the imagination was to find a certain "stability of truth" as a formal solution to the real problems posed by modern life. This worked well in the case of the steel frame, which already had a distinct gridded form, but no true form of mechanical systems could be privileged in the same way. Sullivan's spiritual belief in the stability of a type—architectural and biological—and the image of essential truth that could be conveyed through form can be read against the views held by Dankmar Adler to reveal disagreement at the center of the partnership, emblematic of two possible positions occupied more generally in the profession at that time.[40]

The partnership had dissolved in 1894, two years before Sullivan published his essay on the tall office building. Adler's response to his former partner's aphorism in that same year came at the thirtieth annual convention of the American Institute of Architects with a corrective. Recognizing that Sullivan had based his "law" on "observations of nature," Adler argued that this scientific perspective had not been taken far enough. Form and function were related indeed, but as evolutionary science had recently shown, it was "an ever changing environment" that produced differences between species. This dynamic and unpredictable combination of natural and historical forces would, Adler noted, continue to affect the development of ever-new forms of life and therefore equally heterogeneous architectural styles.

> Therefore, if "form follows function," it does not follow in a straight line, nor in accordance with a simple mathematical formula, but along the lines of curves whose elements are always changing and never alike; and if the lines of development and growth of vegetable and animal organisms are infinitely differentiated, the processes of untrammeled human thought and human emotions are even more subtle in the differences and shadings of their manifestations, while the natural variations in the conditions of the human environment are as great as those that influence the developments of form in the lower organisms; and human work is further modified by necessary artificial conditions and circumstances.[41]

Replacing Sullivan's direct relation of form to function through "straight lines" with "lines of curves" and then articulating those curves with shades of difference, Adler proposed a more complex relation between changes to architectural style and the ambitions of the building's occupants and makers. Environmental changes—among which he included new technologies, new working habits, new social beliefs—were fundamental to the determination of any emerging architectural style. Adler proposed that Sullivan's dictum be revised to "function and environment determine form." Rather than claim to overcome style with an ideal functional solution that resulted in a "true normal type," Adler proposed that the profession, as part of its natural evolution, should absorb historical discontinuities of any sort. For him, change was inevitable and socially dispersed; it could not be localized in a single artistic idea as Sullivan had proposed. In turn, style was a social force that held form, function, and the environment in a momentary, if fleeting, historical unity.

The design of the Chicago Cold Storage Exchange preceded this discussion by six years but shows the difficulty of embracing stylistic change as a quasi-natural process. The numerous environmental changes housed within the warehouse buildings were fully integrated into a single massive project. Despite the novelty of the program and the technology that controlled the conditions within the storerooms, Adler and Sullivan's architectural response unified the design to give it a strong civic presence; nothing on the exterior indicated the systems that were housed inside. Indeed, a large sign was drawn onto the Water Street facade in the rendering, as an announcement of the building's functions. Trains were routed beneath the arcade, and cargo boats loaded and unloaded along the river dock, keeping the fluctuations of supply and demand almost entirely concealed from public view. The refrigeration systems were fully obscured, buried in the basements with no indication of the massive infrastructure of cooling coils that ran along the walls and ceilings of the storerooms. All the activities of the market, negotiated by the commission merchants at the Exchange, were also hidden. The dynamic and heterogeneous functions that made this place unique were internalized to allow the exterior style to produce a clear monumental image to civic life. Adler's proposal implied that style could absorb historical discontinuities through a process analogous to biological variation, but due to the sheer size and unity of the Chicago Cold Storage Exchange it did not display that variation.

After the global economic downturn of 1893 tested the resilience of the company, the *Tribune* reported that "it was in the hands of a receiver, appointed under a foreclosure proceeding, but the property was released and the company resumed business." Over the next two years of operation neither three hundred thousand cubic feet of cooled reserves nor the investment in the unified image of monumental architecture could counter the corrosive effects of the crisis on the company. In 1895 the Chicago Cold Storage Exchange claimed bankruptcy with its liabilities greatly overwhelming its assets. The company never turned a profit.[42] Only seven years after the company's bankruptcy, the one constructed warehouse building of the two that had been planned was demolished. The pathbreaking technology used to cool the facility was deemed to be "too scientific . . . to be practicable as a working plant."[43] Aside from technological issues, there were several reasons for the company's failure, particularly the misguided effort of the organizers to become, in their words, the "world's largest" facility of its kind—a monument to cold storage. This ambition was the source of their reluctance to consolidate the operation with smaller facilities in the city. The competition that resulted among all the companies in Chicago drove down the price of storage, further mounting the company's debt and exposing the initial investment in the facility to the risks that were endemic to the very market it was designed to regulate.[44]

Over the building's brief life, from its design in 1890 to its demolition in 1902, the ideological divergence between Adler and Sullivan was publicly exposed. Their positions offered two views on the role of the architect in representing social and technical change. On the one hand, Sullivan represented the master architect who viewed his role as an author inspired to give modern reality a true and stable form. On the other hand, Adler was an architect who viewed his professional role as an interface between a process of perpetual change, civic responsibility, and the modulation of historical styles. In the case of the Cold Storage Exchange, the economic fluctuations overwhelmed the stability that the company sought to represent through monumental architectural form. Adler's views were prescient: changes in the technologies used to expand and integrate the service of cold storage for the speculative market as well as changes to the methods of delivering that function in buildings rendered the unique signature of the firm's architectural expression moot and the centralized mechanical systems obsolescent. Although architectural form helped gain public attention, the investment in the civic appearance of the Exchange could not protect against the economic competition that caused the company's failure. To produce a systematic relationship among technology, capital, and law would require reformulating the role of architecture in the design and construction of cold storage facilities. A speculative market in perishables could not be developed on the massive holdings of a colossal building alone. Only an infrastructure of interconnected cold storage facilities operating through cooperative networks, both physical and abstract, could deliver the hoped-for future promised by the Exchange.

THE QUINCY MARKET COLD STORAGE COMPANY

The cold storage network established between 1882 and 1915 by the Quincy Market Cold Storage Company in Boston offers a revealing alternative to the Cold Storage Exchange in Chicago by relating form to function on an occasional basis. In Boston, many of the mechanical systems that had been hidden in the Adler and Sullivan building were housed in buildings that were physically separated from the cooled storage space. Rather than integrating all aspects of cold storage in one place to give it a single monumental urban presence, investments in architecture in the Boston case were linked to incremental expansions in the company's services and capacity.

In 1882, when the Quincy Market Cold Storage Company approached the architect William Gibbons Preston to design a warehouse, Preston was known for the design of numerous bungalows on Cape Cod and the Rogers Building at the Massachusetts Institute of Technology. In Jean Ames Follett-Thompson's study of his professional practice, she referred to her protagonist as "a prolific but by no means brilliant Boston architect who executed over 700 commissions between 1862 and 1910." Along with H. H. Richardson, Preston was a member of the first generation of self-declared architectural professionals in Boston. After returning from the Parisian Atelier Douillard, he formed his office as a partnership with his father who had been an architect-builder. The younger Preston converted the office from a construction-centered operation into a fully professionalized design company that produced drawings and specifications and oversaw building construction.[45] He received the Quincy Market Cold Storage Company commission after having done twenty years of work; the 1882 building was the first of several projects by Preston's office under the company's purview to expand the cold storage space available in the city. The *American Architect and Building News* profiled the building among a number of assorted images that had been reprinted from British and French magazines with only a brief description of its technical specifications (Figure 2.4).[46]

Preston's proposal for the warehouse on Commercial Street in Boston was an understated building when compared with the monumental civic presence of the Chicago Cold Storage Exchange. It was also half the height and a small fraction of the proposed square footage. The short side of each building in the Chicago facility, lined by large arched windows, was the same length as the longer 160-foot-long side of the Boston warehouse, with

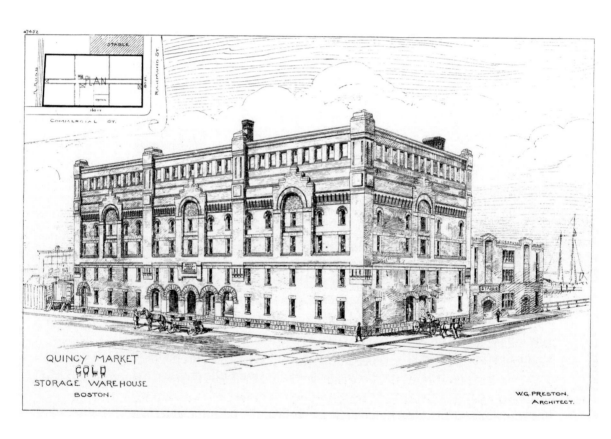

FIGURE 2.4. The original cold storage warehouse designed by William G. Preston. The harbor is visible behind the stable that serviced the warehouse. "Quincy Market Cold Storage Warehouse, Boston, Mass.," *American Architect and Building News* 12 (August 26, 1882).

five modest semicircular entrance arches. There was almost no investment in advertising the project in the newspapers; the building was innovative neither in design nor in its technical fittings. The three main bays expressed on the facade followed the organization of the interior: three sections split in half by a central corridor. The scene surrounding the building in the lone published image shows only a few elements of the busy life in the market district. Its performance as an urban monument was evidently not valued in the same way as it was in the building designed by Adler and Sullivan.

A cross-section through the warehouse reveals that the storerooms were originally cooled with blocks of ice stored in a nineteen-foot-high space on the fifth floor (Figure 2.5). The chilled air from the loft was channeled to the floors below through a system of ducts that ran along the exterior walls and an interior corridor at the center of the structure. Raised floors contained "a very large quantity of one-inch-thick hair-felt" to insulate each floor from those above and below. Without any means for precise temperature regulation, the warehouse could maintain only a roughly graduated interior climate from the top to the bottom, with the highest floor closest to freezing and the bottom floor closest to the outside temperature. The exterior walls were built hollow to insulate the building from changes in exterior temperature, and the window frames were filled with three panes of glass. There were three freight elevators used to raise the perishable goods into the storerooms as well as the ice that was brought to the storage space at the top each winter for the year's supply.[47]

After ten years of inconspicuous operation in this building, a merger with the Faneuil Hall Cooling Company, and a significant increase in demand for cooled storage space in the city, the company set out to acquire land behind the original warehouse, facing an adjacent street. The directors sought to construct a second warehouse there, and approached Preston to design the structure (Figure 2.6). The new building would be cooled by a variation on the compressed ammonia refrigeration technology used in the Chicago warehouse. Rather than sacrifice any space within the warehouse for the large machines, Preston's office attached an engine and boiler house to the rear of the complex that powered a refrigeration machine with enough capacity to cool the combined storage space in both warehouses. At a height of twenty-four feet and a length of forty-five feet, "the largest refrigerating machine ever built" was the company's greatest investment. This two-hundred-ton machine was lit from above by skylights and surrounded by catwalks and ladders so that engineers could

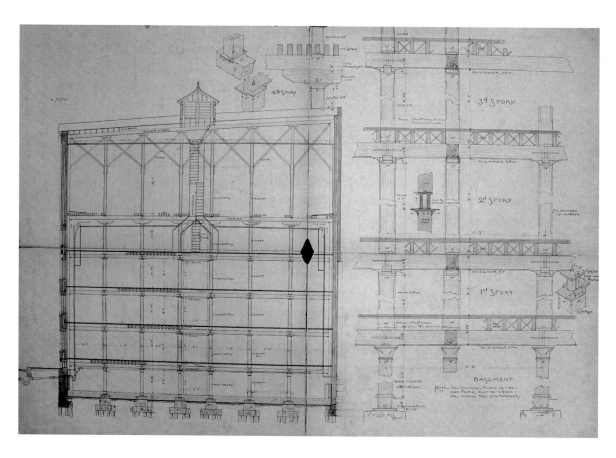

FIGURE 2.5. A section through the cold storage warehouse shows the ice loft on the fifth floor and details of the structural system. The cool-air ducts that run along both sides of the exterior of the building are rendered in red. The floors are raised on blocks with cross bracing. The pipe, rendered in blue in the basement, collects the water, from the ice that melted in the loft, depositing it in the harbor. William G. Preston Collection, Boston Public Library, vol. 22, no. 8. Courtesy of the Boston Public Library, Arts Department.

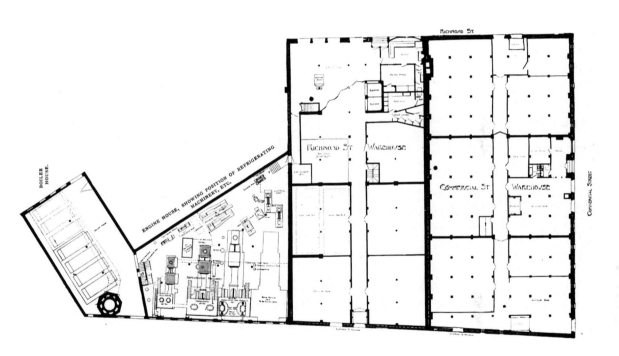

FIGURE 2.6. First-floor plans of the warehouses at Commercial and Richmond Streets. The latter was the structure built in 1892 and contained a new administrative office. The engine and boiler houses were set back from the street. "Boston's Cold Corner," *Ice and Refrigeration* 9.6 (December 1895): 377.

maintain it. An interior rendering of the machine, located in a double-height neoclassical interior, shows two mechanics, one tending to it with an oilcan in his hand (Figure 2.7).[48]

Instead of attempting to build the world's largest warehouse, the company commissioned the construction of this gargantuan compression engine and applied what was known as the "indirect method of mechanical refrigeration" by circulating the expanded ammonia vapor through coils that cooled large tanks of brine.[49] The cooled brine was then pushed through insulated pipes into the company's warehouses, to destinations in the neighboring structures, and then circulated back to the plant to be cooled again. With the application of this new technology, the space that had been used to store ice in the original building was converted into two additional floors for storage. Retrofitted with cooling coils, the storerooms in the old Commercial Street warehouse could now be regulated to a temperature specified according to the type of commodity that would be stored there. Preston's office drew the machines that were to be added to the new structures; in their drawings of the old ice storage space they paid particular attention to the physical transformations that were necessary at the points where the cooling coils would require removing or strengthening structural members.[50]

Within a year the company's head engineer, George H. Stoddard, convinced the directors that a second machine of the same scale, powered by additional steam boilers, should be added so that the company could continue to grow the volume of cooled space it controlled. With two engines in place, Stoddard calculated, the company could produce the equivalent effect of 860 tons of ice melting every twenty-four hours, a quantity that could outmatch the total amount of space that already existed for cooled storage in the entire city. Focused on the task of cooling a network of buildings, Stoddard initiated a project that eventually delivered cooled brine to seventeen nearby warehouses, several market companies, and as many as five hundred independent concerns.[51]

A permit filed in 1895 to lay and operate the pipeline throughout the market district, issued by Boston's municipal agencies, was crucial to pursuing this plan. The company began to install the cooled brine system underground (Figure 2.8). The intimate scale and nature of Boston's market in perishables aided the network's growth. J. V. Fletcher, the president of the cold storage company, had a long-standing relationship with Faneuil Hall, and James C. Melvin, the treasurer, was the director of the Clinton

FIGURE 2.7. "The Largest Refrigerating Machine Ever Built." Designed and built by the Pennsylvania Iron Works Company in Philadelphia for the Quincy Market Cold Storage Company. The compressors were 26 x 48 inches, and the steam cylinders were 24 x 44 x 60 inches. *Ice and Refrigeration* 9.6 (December 1895): 374.

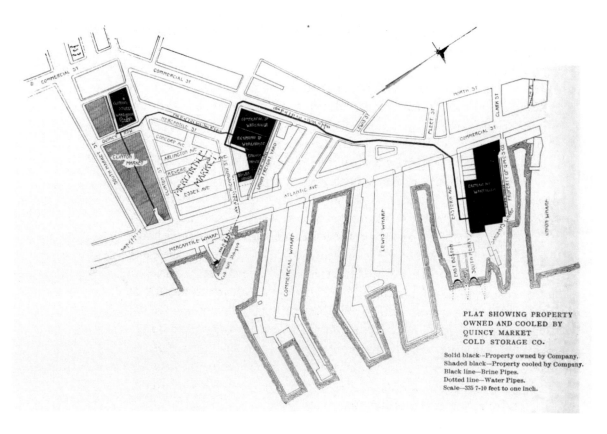

PLAT SHOWING PROPERTY
OWNED AND COOLED BY
QUINCY MARKET
COLD STORAGE CO.

Solid black—Property owned by Company.
Shaded black—Property cooled by Company.
Black line—Brine Pipes.
Dotted line—Water Pipes.
Scale—335 7-10 feet to one inch.

FIGURE 2.8. Plat showing the property owned by the Quincy Market Cold Storage Company in 1895: solid black hatch is owned by the company; the shaded black hatch is cooled by the company; the black line is brine pipe. The buildings to the southwest, hatched, belong to the Clinton Market; the Clinton Warehouse is in black fill. At the center is the plan seen above, and to the northwest is the largest warehouse facility, on Eastern Avenue. "Boston's Cold Corner," *Ice and Refrigeration* 9.6 (December 1895): 376.

Market Company, which owned the nation's largest meat market. These economic interests initiated the first extension of brine pipeline, connecting the cooling apparatus in the engine house to Clinton Market. Running in the opposite direction, up Richmond and along Commercial Streets, another long trench connected the cooled brine network to the company's new million-cubic-foot warehouse on Eastern Avenue, also designed by Preston's office. According to one observer's description, digging for the pipeline exposed the accumulation of utilities that were increasingly being buried beneath the city streets. Like sewers, gas and water pipes, telephone, telegraph, and electric power conduits, cooled brine became another form of utility in the city.[52]

Two photographs taken by Stoddard during construction show the long gash in the market district with three white conduits of brine running along the bottom of the trench under wooden boards and temporary bridges that connected one side of the street to the other (Figure 2.9). As the brine conduit extended farther from the engine house to additional surrounding buildings, it threatened to exceed the engineers' capacity to guarantee a temperature. How would Stoddard know if the storerooms on the third floor of the warehouse on Eastern Avenue, for instance, were properly cooled if he was sitting far away in his office at the engine house on Richmond Street? Even one degree of inaccuracy could be the cause of massive spoilage. It was not enough to install a thermostat in each storeroom that might malfunction; control required the system of thermostats in the various facilities to be brought under the guiding eye of a single trustworthy supervisor. The complexity and diversity of the Quincy Market Cold Storage operation proliferated the number of thermostatic interiors that required constant human supervision, leading the company to supplement their automatic mechanical systems with a mediating device for managerial coordination.

To achieve this purpose an electrical instrument called a "thermophone" was installed on the wall of the engine house (Figure 2.10). The name combined the Greek words for "heat" and "voice," describing the function of the device that had been developed for measuring the temperature in the depths of Boston's water reservoirs. It would be used as follows: While turning a dial, graduated to indicate the temperature in degrees Fahrenheit, the user heard a tone, a buzz from a telephone receiver. When the dial approached a point at which the current was balanced between two leads in a coil each made from a different metal, the tone went

FIGURE 2.9. The brine conduit being laid underground in the market district. "Boston's Cold Corner,"
Ice and Refrigeration 9:6 (December 1895): 386–87.

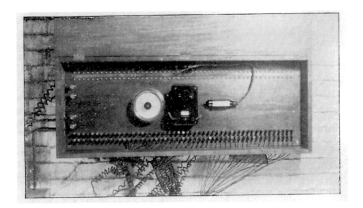

FIGURE 2.10. The thermophone at the Quincy Market Cold Storage Company, hanging on the wall of the engine room. "The Thermophone Installation of the Quincy Market Cold Storage Co.," *Ice and Refrigeration* 12.1 (January 1897): 34.

silent. At this moment, in silence, the instrument offered a temperature reading. Tone was noise, while silence signaled information. The journal *Ice and Refrigeration* described the apparatus: "We illustrate herewith the recently invented Thermophone, an instrument which seems to come into general use in large modern refrigerating plants. For a long time there has been a call for some form of apparatus, which should enable the engineer or manager of a cold storage warehouse to instantly inform himself of the temperature of individual rooms or of circulating pipes and ducts in distant or inaccessible parts of the building."[53] Forty sensitive coils distributed throughout the company's storerooms were all connected to the thermophone at the Quincy Market Cold Storage Company. Each coil was represented by a brass button on a switchboard that hung in the engine room beside the Richmond Street warehouse. To accommodate the further expansion of warehouse space, the switchboard could contain as many as one hundred of these connections. Thus, gathered within arm's length, the instrument brought together "the temperature of air ducts in the seventh story of the building, of pipes under floors and on high ceilings, and of others in deep and dark brine tanks."[54]

Six miles of brine pipeline physically connected the compression engines to the surrounding warehouses while the thermophone centralized the system's management through the electrical surveillance of a supervisor's sensitive instrument. As the company expanded and its facilities became physically dispersed, it required a center from which its system could be overseen. Imagine George Stoddard standing beside this switchboard, occupying the center of the network in which change was constant and the danger of spoilage was always imminent. All the commission merchants in Boston relied on the correct functioning of the massive infrastructure that was under his command: warehouse buildings, refrigeration machines, a brine pipeline, cooling coils, and a thermophone that offered a continuous stream of information on their operation. In their assembly, these elements were intended to ensure that their assets were properly preserved to retain their value for future delivery. The city's market was definitively tied to the coordination of these buildings with their mechanical systems. In fact, not only did the city require the system's technical functioning, but as the Quincy Market Cold Storage Company expanded its network incrementally, the entire nation adopted some of the methods developed by the company to control a vast network of cooled space. In 1911, a volume of 9.5 million cubic feet was under the company's control in Boston. This aggregation of spaces became a critical node in the assembly of a nationally integrated cold storage system. This urban utility, and the huge investment in its management, worked directly against assumptions about the natural equilibrium of supply and demand. While it became a tool for regulating the nation's economy, it also brought new focus to the status of perishable commodities as objects of technical expertise.[55]

EXPERTISE AND THE REGULATED MARKET

The Chicago warehouses were made public through monumental architecture: a glass-enclosed shopping arcade, a prominent location, and the fame of a distinguished firm. By contrast, Boston's system absorbed various buildings and infrastructures into a network of cold storage that was organized in a piecemeal fashion. The Boston company's pragmatic approach to expansion, paradoxically, was a better example of Dankmar Adler's evolutionary metaphor: as each new component of the system was designed—an engine house, a new million-cubic-foot facility, a thermophone—it fulfilled a specific function according to the needs of this dynamically changing industry. In the 1910s, local, state, and even federal regulators added legal stipulations that aimed to produce a uniform code that would integrate a national warehouse system. In the process, these regulations reduced the variability in the architecture of cold storage according to a set of reliable technical formulae, or standards.

Those who considered themselves experts in cold storage design and construction began to advertise in the pages of trade journals such as *Ice and Refrigeration*, selling their specialized knowledge of this building type, its attendant technologies, and government guidelines. One example is Hans Peter Henschien, a packer who worked for Swift and Co. from 1905 to 1909, who then became part of Swift's packinghouse design team, led by David I. Davis.[56] In 1914 he established an independent practice in Chicago and published a reference book in 1915, *Packing House and Cold Storage Construction*, identifying himself as an architect. The content of the book was not based on any education Henschien had received in a school of architecture (his knowledge was not taught in even the most technical school), but on his practical "observation and experience." The viability of his company relied on this expertise, an exemplary instance of a general shift toward specialized practices involved in warehouse design. In his preface, Henschien explained the motivation for publishing his treatise: "That there is a demand for such a work, has been evidenced to the author by numerous inquiries from architects and owners, and also by the fact that there exists no similar work describing modern American methods and materials."[57] Clients and architects turned to this type of specialized practice because of the limited amount of time available to a traditionally oriented office to accumulate the knowledge required in designing buildings that complied with an increasingly regulated domain of modern infrastructure. Henschien's firm eventually joined the American Institute of Architects but, even several decades later, remained primarily involved in producing architectural designs for cold storage and meatpacking.[58]

Claims to expert knowledge in the construction of cold storage warehouses and the installation of refrigeration technology were, in part, responses to the increasingly prominent rejection of the system's expansion. Mass media, including cartoons and muckraking efforts such as Upton Sinclair's *The Jungle* (1906), contributed to the growing skepticism regarding claims made by leaders of the cold storage industry that it served the public interest.[59]

A cartoon published in the magazine *Puck* in 1910 illustrates the suspicions that some Americans held regarding the unspoken ambitions of the cold storage system (Figure 2.11). It depicts a food speculator as a masked bandit holding two loaded guns that are each labeled "cold storage."[60] One gun is aimed at the producer, the farmer carrying butter, milk, eggs, and a slaughtered pig on his back; the other is aimed at the urban consumer, who clenches his money fearing this unanticipated interruption in his trip to the market. The three characters have been assembled on the "road of supply and demand," where they are now trapped at a violent impasse. The

FIGURE 2.11. The food speculator stands on the road of supply and demand. The "hold-up" is double, as the caption of the image announces, because both the farmer and the merchant cannot meet to exchange goods for money. This event is made possible by the bandit's two guns, both labeled "cold storage." "A Double Hold-Up," *Puck*, October 6, 1910, 8–9. Prints and Photographs Division, Library of Congress, LC-DIG-PPMSCA-26416.

cartoon's caption, "A Double Hold-Up," suggests two possible interpretations: the first is that we are witnessing a theft by the imposing bandit, an uninvited third party unwelcome in an otherwise more direct transaction; the second is that the event is a stoppage in time, a delay in the meeting of the buyer and the seller. It was the food speculator who "held-up" the movement of food from its origin to its destination—held food from finding its place in the consumer's empty basket. Critics of the expansion of the cold storage system claimed that through manipulations of time—time banditry—food speculators hoodwinked a naive public, raising prices and delivering spoiled goods. Frederic C. Howe, a member of the Ohio Senate, insisted that "the cold storage evil" was not "an agency of universal service and a means of cheapening the price of food, [but] one of the principal agencies of the speculator." Howe represented a commonly held belief that cold storage would never be properly regulated for the public welfare because, as with many other utilities, it would always exclusively serve private interest.[61]

One advocate of the "pure food movement," a butcher named Herman Hirschauer who had worked as a manager of a cold storage beef house for an unnamed packer, noted a troubling fact that "cases of poultry yet in stock" had been "killed and packed more than two years ago." Within these seemingly forgotten bodies, he described a "nasty, greenish mess" of rotting entrails that could only be cleaned by certain radical measures such as the use of "chemicals and dopes" that further compromised the wholesomeness of the product.[62] Despite such negative views of the way the system was used for the benefit of a few and against the public welfare, the *Puck* cartoon contained a second caption, more positive in tone: "Good Guns in Bad Hands." It was not the cold storage system itself that had caused these problems, but the abuses of the system by greedy speculators.

With rising pressure from an alarmed public, the U.S. Senate held hearings on the foods held in cold storage to assess the effects of speculation on their price and "purity." The chief of the Bureau of Chemistry in the Department of Agriculture, Dr. Harvey W. Wiley, mastermind of the Pure Food and Drugs Act of 1906 known as the Wiley Act, opened the proceedings in April 1910.[63] He communicated his findings on the proper storage time and the range of suitable conditions for holding poultry and eggs. His comments centered almost entirely on the technical definition of terms that had traditionally been qualitative: "wholesomeness" of food and its "adulteration" were transformed into chemically specific conditions. Wiley would soon join the staff of *Good Housekeeping* as the head of the magazine's research institute to advocate on behalf of housekeepers—or, as we have seen in the previous chapter, an emerging group of household managers—in relation to the quality of foods, drugs, and the general conditions of domestic life.[64] Although Wiley viewed the profit drive of industry as the primary culprit for the degradation of food, during the hearing he and many of the senators serving on the committee agreed with representatives of the cold storage industry that establishing strict guidelines to govern the conditions of cold storage warehouses would make the system more reliable and thereby transform consumer suspicion into public trust.[65] In Massachusetts, for example, the House of Representatives appointed five inspectors to collect data about the preserved holdings in the state, to report on the effect that speculative practices were having on food quality, and, more urgently, to calculate if they were the cause of the recent increase in the cost of living.[66]

This, and other inspections like it, found that speculation in futures contracts had coincided with the rising cost of living but, on the whole, had also stabilized prices.[67] Quoting the work of Frank W. Taussig, an economics professor at Harvard University, the Massachusetts Commission explained that the reduced variability of prices was a positive effect of speculation: "The influence of speculation is to lessen fluctuations in price and promote 'the expedient rate of consumption.'" Despite Taussig's great admiration for the principles of classical political economy as defined by Ricardo and Mill, he believed that their theoretical doctrines needed to be amended according to the specific contributions made by modern institutions like cold storage. By extending the field of speculation to include perishable products, he explained, the cold storage system further stabilized the distribution of supply. "Fruit, meat, fish, eggs," wrote Taussig, "no longer come on the market in spasmodic and irregular amounts. Supplies that are heavy at one time are brought by dealers, put in storage, and held for sale at a later period of scantier supply. Prices are more equable, and on the whole the profits of the dealers are probably less. There is less risk to them, and the community gets its supplies at a smaller charge for their services as middlemen."[68] Writing in 1911, Taussig already concluded that cold storage had become so integrated into the economy that it was essential to the operations of a speculative market and to the planned spending of an average modern family. Although this prominent economist might have still fundamentally believed in the eighteenth-century doctrine of equilibrium with only some modifications, his statements were used by public officials in states with large volumes of cold storage space to justify their legal regulation of the industry as a "public utility," just as they did for railroad and telephone companies.[69]

To integrate the warehousing industry, including cold storage, household goods, and general merchandise, the American Warehousemen's Association framed the Uniform Warehouse Receipts Act in 1906.[70] It was quickly enacted by those states with large warehouse holdings as a way of outlining the responsibilities that would be common to all warehousemen, including those working with cold storage.[71] This law protected holders of warehouse receipts by making the liability of the warehouse owner explicit and legally binding. The hope was to make it possible for customers who stored their goods in so-called public warehouses—that is, those that were not used exclusively by the owner—to receive "uniform receipts" that could become nationally recognized instruments of exchange. In his treatise on *Public Warehousing*, a professor of business administration, John H. Fredrick, explained how the law was envisioned:

> the Uniform Warehouse Receipts Act was to increase the integrity of all types of public warehouse receipts in order that they might be more highly regarded by storers as evidence of their ownership of the goods deposited, and by bankers as collateral for loans. Uniformity of rules and regulations governing the issuing of public warehouse receipts and the responsibilities of public warehousemen for the storage and delivery of goods in their custody was necessary in order that the receipts of a warehouse in one state, or section of the country, may be acceptable as collateral or as delivery of the goods in another part of the country.[72]

The uniform receipt became a legally binding negotiable instrument, a contract available for transfer or sale throughout the nation. It allowed a complete separation of the utility of an object held in storage from its abstract value on the market. To guarantee the receipt as negotiable, the warehouseman was required to print a statement on it that he was responsible for the safe delivery of the goods in his custody. The act thereby established the uniform receipt as another regulatory apparatus—of a different variety than the mechanical devices built into warehouses—to protect speculative traders from the unwelcome risks of theft, loss, or damage to the goods they were trading. The mechanical regulation of the interior environment and the abstract regulation over the forms of paperwork operated in tandem in this modern infrastructure. Regulation was both a technical and a legal problem, and in this case the standardization of a physical utility required the legal force of the storage owner's liability.

Deemed safe from any risk to the commodity's value, most assets held in storage could be accounted for by the standardized receipt system and used as collateral or traded for other goods. Yet cold storage warehouses required additional stipulations than those set by the Uniform Warehouse Receipts Act in order to produce receipts that guaranteed the value of refrigerated commodities. Preserved assets such as produce or dairy could not retain their value forever; there was only so much time that apples or butter could be held from the market before they lost their value. To remedy the problem, in 1914 Congress passed a Uniform Cold Storage Act that brought the cold storage industry under a common legal code. Beyond allowing states to set limits to the amount of time that foods could be held in cold storage, the act stipulated that all warehouse owners were required to receive licenses from the Department of Agriculture and annually renew them to ensure that their facilities were sanitary and properly managed. This centralized oversight was also intended to stem the possibility of hoarding by "profiteers." Finally, the law required that all "foods [be] branded, stamped, or marked in some conspicuous place, upon the receipt thereof, with the day, month, and year when the same was received for storage or refrigerating."[73] This was the legal origin of what we know in contemporary life as the "sell-by date."

In hearings considering cold storage legislation held before the Committee on Agriculture of the House of Representatives in 1919, a discussion emerged regarding the effects of refrigeration on the "lives" of apples. The secretary of the National League of Commission Merchants of the United States, R. S. French, offered the following statement: "chilling them, up to a certain time naturally increases the character of their keeping qualities—I mean the value of the apple." W. M. French, the president of the International Apple Shippers' Association, clarified his colleague's equation of preservation and value: "apples coming out of cold storage are presumed to have their natural life preserved." The act of preserving life and thereby preserving value was not without limits, he continued: "the longer the apple remains in storage the shorter its life becomes."[74] Beyond the apple itself, the value of that commodity had a separate "natural life" that was interrupted by its existence in cold storage. While the interruption could increase the physical commodity's so-called keeping qualities, after some time the "qualities" that defined its life and therefore its value as a consumable apple, for example, diminished. The geographer Susanne Freidberg has shown that many cultural values associated with food in modern life are directly tied to technological preservation of a commodity's life, the manipulation of its "state of being," and a general acknowledgment of a distinction between the natural state of the object and its industrialized life expectancy, often referred to as its "freshness."[75]

Until cold storage had become a utility, food was either fresh or spoiled. By the 1920s, most of the food consumed in America had spent some time in cold storage. In this new reality, what could be considered fresh? What did this term mean? Would anything be fresh again? The nationally regulated cold storage system required that representatives of the industry disassociate the concept of freshness from a commodity's origin, replacing its natural life with its preserved value. One warehouseman in the hearings surprised some of the inquiring congressmen with the following statement: "The word 'fresh' is not as an offset against cold storage, but it is as against preserving by other processes. That is the meaning of the word 'fresh,' in my judgment."[76] Freshness was not a quality found in just any form of preserved commodity. Rather, a commodity was fresh as long as it retained its form, some semblance of its flavor, and therefore also its value on the market. Pickled vegetables or canned fruit were clearly not fresh, and in their changed state they helped the industry identify all its products as fresh.

The mechanical control of temperature and humidity allowed the cold storage industry to produce a set of spaces in which commodities stabilized their identity and value over time, a time that was stipulated by a combination of legal limits and viability in the market. After preserved assets—fruits, vegetables, dairy, eggs, and meat—had been separated from their natural origin, they entered a reserve governed by the combination of technological and legal regulations. This reserve was detached from the seasons and available to the demands of a speculative market that sought out more opportunities to wager bets on the future. Yet before these commodities could be reduced to capitalist abstractions, the physical architecture of cold storage was worked out, not only in response to the problem of style, but also as expert knowledge accommodated the exigencies of function. An architectural monument to commerce could not operate as effectively in this context as could the tall office building.

At the very moment that Sullivan related architectural form to the pragmatics of modern office labor, the transformations in mechanical refrigeration and the market in perishables tested the architect's capacity and the client's interest in expressing technological modernity with images of civic monumentality. Instead of the imagination of a genial mind, more technically oriented forms of architectural practice were better suited to design the physical form for the cold storage system. In place of an outward expression of the institution's service to the public, the history of the architecture designed for the cold storage industry offers evidence of a less immediate image of modernism but one that still abided by a set of refined standards for designing the modern regulated interior.

At the center of that controlled interior were perishable objects, some of which were similar in their organic composition to the human body, but different in their requirements. By contrast to the mechanical regulation of the interior environment of the house, organized around the needs of a domestic economy, this industrial system was organized according to the goal of its integration into an economic system that stabilized the market in perishables. Here, the "envelopes, the life support systems," identified by Bruno Latour as the nested interiors of modernization, defined a concept of life for things that circulated through the market, lives that were not defined by a vital force, or by human biology, but by the artificial extension of a commodity's value in time.[77]

CHAPTER 3

Representing Regulation in Nature's Economy

Regulating the temperature of the household interior and preserving the nation's food supply brought new forms of control to both private life and public infrastructure. We have seen that buildings and the environments inside them materially changed with the addition of mechanical systems and electrical circuitry, changes that were integral to the development of new modes for legal and economic governance. The technical issues related to controlling the environment around such things as modern families or perishable produce, however, do not make clear some important applications of regulatory principles in representational mediums. The topics that follow focus on less immediately tangible aspects of regulation than thermostats and warehouse design; they explore the methods of documenting and visualizing the dynamic systems found in nature and industry. Management's visible hand, as Alfred Chandler repeatedly observed of the railroad and other big businesses, depended upon accounting practices for collecting data from the day-to-day operations of the enterprise.

Despite radical differences in their intentions, both early twentieth-century scientists and managers—the agents in this and the following chapter—introduced such accounting practices to describe fluctuations as well as the means of their regulation. While managers developed tools to study the processes of large-scale manufacture that would identify and govern their inherent variability, scientists sought to describe the complex interactions between organisms and their surroundings. Both exemplify forms of reasoning that did not idealize their object of study as self-equilibrated. Rather, much like the cases described in the previous chapters, these protagonists defined the processes found in ecological systems and machine shops by focusing on the potential of crises, errors, or mishaps and the means of their avoidance. These processes were sometimes observed and documented with the sorts of hardware found in modern houses and refrigerated warehouses; even more refined instruments were developed for state-of-the-art laboratories, but equally as often, they were recorded and represented in what appear to us as artful photographs and elegant graphic notations.

This chapter focuses on ecological representations of dynamic systems as evidence of a cultural shift in the definition of nature. In contrast to a view of the natural world as a product of divine order, nineteenth-century scientists secularized their object of study—both living and nonliving—by explaining the behaviors they observed as a system of overlapping cycles. Descriptions of the dynamic interactions between cycles occurring within an organism and those in its surroundings helped illustrate how the biology of the planet operated in this field of continuous change. In studying the responses of organisms to environmental cycles and other stimuli, ecologists translated the "economy of nature," as discussed in Charles Darwin's writings, into images, three-dimensional constructions, and experimental simulations.[1] They used the term *regulation* in all these cases to refer to the ways in which organisms preserved their lives through their responses to changes in the environment. Urban sociologists drew upon the regulatory concepts developed for ecological botany and zoology to explain the dynamics they observed in human settlements.

Common to the words "economy" and "ecology," the Greek root *oikos* means "household." It also means balancing accounts, or household management.[2] Drawing on the house as an economic unit, Darwin viewed nature's economy as a metaphorical extension of a domicile's inside to the interactions occurring outside. If nature had once been understood as ordered by the hands of God, the economic metaphor described that once divine sphere as bound together by an invisible network of exchange. By gathering the elements of the natural world into an economy, a household of nature, Darwin set them into mutual interdependence. But nature's economy was not in fact anything like a domestic arrangement, governed by the managerial power of the mother or anyone else. With limited resources, organisms compete with one another and establish hierarchies as part of the struggle to survive in their respective habitats. While some interactions between living things stabilize the conditions of a habitat, others appear violent and destructive. Due to the intersection of different species' needs, Darwin explained, life is "constantly destroying life."[3] Dependencies and competition determined an organism's place in nature's economy, even if its fate there would be always uncertain. Theories of ecology that followed Darwin's use of economic terminology sought to extract the principles that regulated the transactions in nature's economy by studying the behavior of organisms in their *oikos*. Two forms of visualization reveal their thinking: the diorama and the laboratory.

Housed in different forms of architecture and located in different institutional contexts, these objects of ecological representation were also designed to address different audiences. Habitat dioramas were constructed in natural history museums found in centers of large cities. They presented a timeless image of natural habitats free of human interference. By contrast, on university campuses, the experimental apparatus of research laboratories extracted specimens from the field and situated them in technological simulations of the natural environment. Experimental instruments produced data for an audience of specialist scientists, while dioramas produced a visual analogue of environmental interaction for general spectators. Evidence of ecological thinking can thus be found in both the public art of display and in the more technically explicit apparatus of experiment.[4] Ecological ideas were not determined by their modes of representation, and those visualizations were also not determined by the scientists' methods. Instead, we find that the search for images of regulation by ecologists took at least two remarkably different and robust forms. The protagonists of this chapter, Henry Chandler Cowles and his student Victor Shelford, worked with descriptive and experimental methods in parallel. Cowles's work became the basis for dioramas, the new displays in natural history museums, while Shelford's work adopted experimental machinery to record ecological interactions in his laboratory. Display and experiment produced complementary as well as contradictory representations that were equally important for communicating the image and logic of ecology. Broad public viewing, narrow scientific discourse, as well as their respective methods of description and evidence production gave force to the ecologist's view of nature, one that relied on a metaphorical extension of mechanical regulation to the processes of life on the planet.

The German naturalist Ernst Haeckel coined the term *ecology* in the mid-nineteenth century, but the scientific discipline that we know today was formed a few decades later in the United States.[5] To establish a new kind of thinking about nature, would-be ecologists needed to synthesize two well-developed nineteenth-century sciences: physiology and physiography. The physiologists' object of study was the organism; the physiographers'—or physical geographers'—was the planet. These sciences both relied on descriptions of systems that embraced the flux inherent in nature. To understand the processes that sustained an organism's life, the physiologist theorized that the exterior milieu—the chemical conditions of air and soil, the humidity, and the temperature—changed according to numerous variables while the organism itself constantly worked toward a state of internal equilibrium.[6] Physiographers divided observable changes on the whole planet into systems that affected one another—for example, wind, water, and land—to show how these elements produced dynamic geographic features.[7] The problem for ecology, then, was to bring these two scales of science into one common field of research, bridging the gap in scale between the organism and the planet.

The work of the Danish botanist Eugen Warming represents an early example of this new approach. His book *Plantesamfund* (1895), or "Plant Geography," focused on the regional distribution of plants.[8] Warming replaced the botanical term "plant formation" with "plant society," to shift the discipline's emphasis from the formal characteristics of plants and their groupings to the ways in which they related functionally to their environment—hence the metaphorical use of the term *society*. The water content of the soil in which a plant grew was the primary method for identifying it as part of a plant society. The taxonomic aspect of ecology, in Warming's view, was different from that of botany. Its purpose was to produce categories for defining plants as members of a plant society dictated by the needs it had in common with other plants. He referred to some plants as hydrophytes, for example, because they required consistent exposure to water, while mesophytes required less, and xerophytes could grow with very little access to water. Warming's method introduced a twofold shift in botanical research. First, he expanded the objects of botanical study from a single plant and its organs to the affiliation of plants based on their capacity to live in similar environmental conditions. Second, he privileged the effects of geographic space over the adaptations brought about by evolutionary time.[9]

In 1896 the American botanist John Merle Coulter reviewed Warming's book in the *Botanical Gazette*, the journal that he had founded twenty years earlier. In the same year, Coulter was appointed head of the Botany Department at the newly founded University of Chicago. Relating Warming's work on geographical distribution to the current state of plant physiology, Coulter predicted that the book would have a durable effect on the emerging field of ecology: "With the development of plant physiology it became possible to organize [physiographical] facts upon a scientific basis, and this organization introduces us into the great modern field of ecology, of which geographical distribution is a conspicuous part."[10] Warming's book became one of the core texts in the curriculum Coulter designed for the Chicago Botany Department. With a strong tradition of plant illustration in the nineteenth-century study of botany, incorporating images of geography into plant ecology would prove difficult. Over the following decades, Coulter and his students sought out an appropriate medium for thinking about nature—and representing its dynamics—at the scale of the plant and the planet simultaneously.[11]

ECOLOGICAL IMAGES

The Hull Biological Laboratories were established on the Chicago campus in 1897, in buildings that housed the Departments of Botany, Zoology, Anatomy, and Physiology (Figure 3.1). Among the speakers delivering dedication speeches for the new laboratories was William H. Welch, the first dean of the Johns Hopkins Medical School. He linked the opening of the buildings to a general shift from taxonomy toward experimentation in biological science. In praising the university for its investment in excellent new facilities, he predicted that rigorous modern laboratory methods could be brought to botanical and zoological studies. Close study of the forms and behaviors of organisms in a controlled setting, in his view, would establish the three buildings in the Hull complex as the future model for these fields.[12]

Welch's observations about the experimental trend in the life sciences was visibly confirmed by the greenhouse atop the botany building, announcing the department's commitment to the study of plants as living organisms. The campus architect, Henry Ives Cobb, designed the laboratory complex and collaborated with Coulter on the technical specifications to equip the botany building. Yet neither the greenhouse nor the equipment in the laboratory—including temperature- and humidity-controlled spaces on the fifth floor—immediately established a new direction for plant study.[13] The glass structure symbolized an effort to shift botanical knowledge toward physiology, but no physical building, mechanical

FIGURE 3.1. The east face of the Botany Building, Hull Biological Laboratories, University of Chicago, Chicago, Illinois. The greenhouse was ornamented with neo-Gothic forms in keeping with the rest of the campus architecture. American Environmental Photographs Collection, [APF2-01053], Special Collections Research Center, University of Chicago Library.

system, or architectural style—neo-Gothic or otherwise—could fully embody Coulter's hopes for new forms of research. At the cornerstone ceremony, he proposed that a modern teacher and researcher be a "pioneer and explorer" outside the constraints produced by a campus building.[14] The historians of science Robert Kohler and Sharon Kingsland have shown that new directions in biology at the beginning of the twentieth century—against Welch's expectations—expanded the limit of scientific observation beyond the phenomena made visible under a microscope.[15] As botanists began to study the physical and geographic context of plant life, Coulter proposed finding a method of research to account for the effects of environmental dynamics on plant physiology. His students began to work in places that Kohler has called "field-lab borders," locations in which they could relate the morphology of plant life to its surroundings. This was a relationship based on the plant organism's capacity to regulate its own growth as well as affect the changes in its dynamic environment.[16]

In this vein, Henry Chandler Cowles committed his graduate work to studying the vegetation on Indiana's sand dunes along the southern coast of Lake Michigan.[17] In his dissertation, completed in 1899, Cowles showed how the relationship of the physiographic environment to plant physiology could be understood by investigating dune formations:

> The ecologist employs the methods of physiography, regarding the flora of a pond or swamp or hillside not as a changeless landscape feature, but rather as a panorama, never twice alike: The ecologist, then, must study the order of succession of the plant societies in the development of a region, and he must endeavor to discover the laws which govern the panoramic changes. Ecology, therefore, is a study in dynamics. For its most ready application, plants should be found whose tissues and organs are actually changing at the present time in response to varying conditions. . . . Perhaps no topographic form is more unstable than a dune. Because of this instability plant societies, plant organs, and plant tissues are obliged to adapt themselves to a new mode of life within years rather than centuries.[18]

Changes, constant in the dunes, were neither linear nor predictable. Cowles hoped to understand the dynamics of this landscape by finding the physiographic laws that governed large-scale cycles. Deducing these laws would allow him to explain systematically the reciprocity of the plant–environment interaction by which plant organisms gave shape to the dunes and the movement of the dunes affected their physiology. Cowles believed that a plant's physical adaptations, those that allowed it to avoid death due to environmental changes, could be observed in dune vegetation over short periods of time, even within the time that it would take to collect research for a dissertation. He saw these changes—a root becomes a stem, a stem becomes a root—as responses to the moving topographies of sand, an unstable system but a system guided by rules nonetheless. A plant survived, he believed, because its life depended on internal regulatory systems that managed environmental instability. To be sure, with an excess of flux, the plant would succumb and die.

Cowles's approach to plant morphology was different from that of other contemporary botanists. Lorraine Daston has shown that the "type specimen" collected from the field had become the legitimate form around which botanists built a collective record of each living species. Preserved samples of plant life, bound in herbaria, allowed scientists to produce an exhaustive and accumulative library of botanical knowledge.[19] While most botanists agreed that type specimens would give concrete form to the abstract idea of a species, Cowles viewed the ecologist's work of documentation differently—as the notation of *transformations* from one type specimen into the next. He aimed to link shifts in the concrete form of a plant to the dynamic force of topographic change. To pursue his ecological theory of relations between the dunes and the life they sponsored, he treated topography and vegetation as a single intricate system—what he called a "dune complex." The physiological interaction of plant life with its immediate environment appeared to depend on a few physiographic laws; this combination would allow him to bridge the gap between two scales of scientific observation.

Cowles often used the word "panorama" to describe an ecologist's view of this dynamic landscape. His choice evoked the static backlit images of this popular mid-nineteenth-century spectacle, in which a round or oval room displayed a 360-degree image such as a landscape, a city, or a battle. Like the viewer of the panorama, immersed in an image but denied a focal point, the scientist perceiving the dunes was equally encompassed by the scene and disoriented by its perpetually changing form.[20] To document this landscape, Cowles illustrated his research with photographs rather than type specimens or physiographic maps. William McCallum, another doctoral student in the Chicago Botany Department, made the images on field visits with Cowles. Each photograph recorded a topographic element and the plant formation that lived on it, captured at an instant that would never exist again.[21] In publishing McCallum's images, Cowles demonstrated his aim to visualize moments of inflection in the landscape as a complementary set of documents to his written narrative that outlined the rules of the dynamic environment. Compared to the definition of a botanical type as a specimen taken from the field, these images defined an alternative ecological datum: an image of a topographic element and the plant life that it sponsored. In his study of underwater photography, Edward Eigen has called such images of dynamic environments a "visual milieu."[22] In this case, the image was filled with moving sand, wind, and plants; the one thing that could be fixed was the photographic frame. Cowles's descriptions connected one such frame to the next to compose a visual representation of the panoramic changes he described in the text. Viewing his object—the dune and the plant life on it—through a medium that stopped its movement at an instant allowed the ecologist to concentrate on images that identified a perceptible and concrete moment of regulation.[23]

Compared to the restless activity in nature, the photographs were calm, even passive. Moreover, Cowles's tone communicated an objective view taken from a significant distance, as if he encountered his object of study through laboratory apparatus carried into the field. The communication of distance in his writing style was thus reflected by the visual objectivity offered by McCallum's camera as it transformed the interaction of wind, water, temperature, humidity, and light into a visual code of the dune complex as a regulated system. Cowles did express interest in the physiological effects on the plants that lived in this harsh environment but focused his writing and photographic evidence on the dune physiography, the topographic shape produced by the movement of sand, and the variety of plant life that it sponsored. By contrast to Warming's geographic method centered on the location and quantity of water in the formation of plant societies, Cowles explained changes in plant associations through the dominant effects of topographic change. The dunes changed so rapidly and dramatically that the presence or absence of water would always be secondary to changes in the form of the surrounding landscape. Moreover, unlike Warming's approach to the organs of the plants that he studied, Cowles did not use laboratory equipment to make physiological observations because no plant society—made up of multiple species growing at the same time and in the same place—could be placed under long-term observation outside its living context.

The shift to observations at this scale led Cowles to explain the general dynamics of plant growth throughout the dune region with the term *succession*. As one topographic form replaced the next, he explained, the process of dune succession structured the changes to plant societies through multiple relationships of cause and effect, even if the complexity of that process was imperceptible. While the process of succession was gradual, it could be revealed in the photographs as moments of "tension" in a dune's transformation.[24] The transformations on the dune landscape, in Cowles's description, were progressive, beginning with a grass organism that trapped sand to form an "embryonic dune" (Figure 3.2). As the grass grew its root network, the sand would become further stabilized into a "stationary dune." The plant life growing on such a dune became more diverse as individual organisms formed a plant society and gradually culminated in a deciduous mesophytic forest (a term he borrowed from Warming) that he saw as the "climax type" for the lake region.[25] The wind-swept sand could also become an antiprogressive force. At unpredictable intervals, with a change in direction, the movement of sand on a dune could engulf a forest, killing even decades-old trees, returning the process of succession to its beginning (Figure 3.3).

Reading Darwin may have inspired Cowles's interest in events that worked against the progressive model of succession. As Darwin had described the interplay between heredity and selection, so Cowles described laws that guided the development of dunes and the forces that destroyed them. Changes in dunes were not linear but prone to random events that produced breaks in the process of development. He called these interruptions "retrogressions" (Figure 3.4).[26] The dunes, by this description, formed a landscape in a state of perpetual historical discontinuity, simultaneously moving toward a stable climax while also unpredictably reversing direction. A dune and the life that it sponsored did not form historical layers with meaning and memory. The natural dynamics of the region revealed their form as a system of cycles. While these changes were never predictable, with their repetition they could still be described as a system.

Cowles concentrated on the physiographic laws that explained the effects of wind, the displacement of water, fluctuations in temperature, and changes in sun exposure to understand the dune landscape. Recording the interactions of plants with this environmental dynamic in his observations and in photographs allowed him to produce categories of dune habitats, some more stable than others. An ecological view of the dune

FIGURE 3.2. Cowles's caption for this image is "Embryonic Ammophila dune on the beach at South Chicago. . . . Sinuous trough at the center, where there is no vegetation." [APF8-01687]. University of Chicago Department of Botany Records Repository, Special Collections Research Center, University of Chicago Library.

FIGURE 3.3. "The encroachment of a dune on swamps and forests." [APF8-02319]. University of Chicago Department of Botany Records Repository, Special Collections Research Center, University of Chicago Library.

FIGURE 3.4. After the movement of a dune over a forest, the trees would die. Cowles describes this scene as "a dune graveyard of Pines, Chesterton, Indiana." [APF8-02453]. University of Chicago Department of Botany Records Repository, Special Collections Research Center, University of Chicago Library.

complex thus translated a dynamic topography into a set of regulated processes that Cowles narrated with both words and images. The more visible nature's economy became, the clearer it was that the dune complex was cyclical but aperiodic. Indeed, this landscape would not have been available for ecological observation by the human eye or a camera lens had it not been for the always imminent and apparently random interruptions to its development. While Cowles used photographs to illustrate fleeting stabilities, these moments were exceptional in a dynamic system that was always subject to interruption and change. As an ecological object, then, the dunes tied the adaptations of organisms to topographical instability and positioned the organism and its need to survive as a cipher for the regulatory reactions that guided the physiology of life in that harsh environment.

THE DISPLAY OF NATURE'S ECONOMY

After publishing his dissertation, Cowles joined the faculty in the Chicago Botany Department where he extended his studies of the dune complex with a new generation of students. He also taught classes about plant life on the dunes to public audiences at the Chicago Academy of Sciences. The academy had established the first public museum in the city in 1863, displaying its collection of natural history specimens from the Chicago region. After the original building burned in the fire of 1871, the museum

occupied several locations until 1893, when the directors hired the architects Reynolds Fisher and Norman Patton to design a new home for its collection in Lincoln Park (Figure 3.5).[27] In 1913, Cowles joined the Board of
Scientific Governors of the academy, an indication of the broadening influence of ecological thinking. The academy soon translated this dynamic
view of nature into a new form of display.

The arrangement of the museum in 1893 accommodated typical
nineteenth-century natural history exhibits on second and third floors.
The library was on the first floor while the basement housed the taxidermy
work, storage, and heating systems. Patton found most natural history
museums to be "simply storage warehouses for the safe-keeping of specimens"; his intention was to provide more effective display. He proposed
an interior organized in bays with freestanding columns at the end of each
library stack or display case. This structural system held up a vaulted ceiling, pierced by skylights, that brought natural light onto the locally gathered taxidermy specimens in glass vitrines. These were ordered from simplest to most complex on the second floor, while the cabinets on the third
floor were filled with various collections of smaller preserved specimens.[28]

Despite its many spatial virtues and thoughtful details, this sort of
display inadequately represented dynamic ecological interactions. Standing before a flattop case of specimens taken from Lake Michigan, the eco-
logically minded viewer might have asked: How do these organisms relate to their environment? How do they form their habitats? How can a
museum display make these relationships apparent? While speaking at
the Congress of Arts and Science convened during the St. Louis Universal
Exposition of 1904, the German plant ecologist Oscar Drude had anticipated that problems would result "when we attempt to change the accus-
tomed systematic arrangement of museums to one which shall represent
the ecological features of a given formation."[29] The old mode of display focused on the forms of specimens and their taxonomic arrangement, but
representing the "ecological features" of those specimens would require a
new arrangement to command a different mode of attention.

At the beginning of the new century, several American nature museums
had begun to transform their display formats.[30] Victoria Cain has shown that
a group of curators began mixing their pedagogical aims with new methods for attracting the attention of museum visitors, even appropriating the
language of mass marketing.[31] The most effective new form of display was
the habitat diorama, developed by Frank Chapman, the ornithologist and

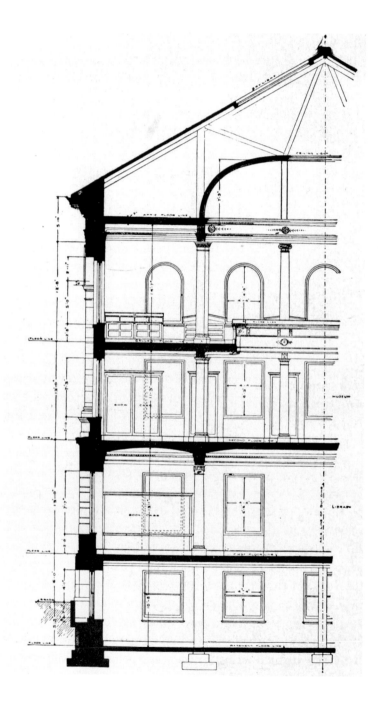

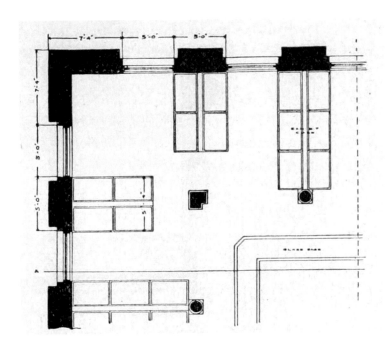

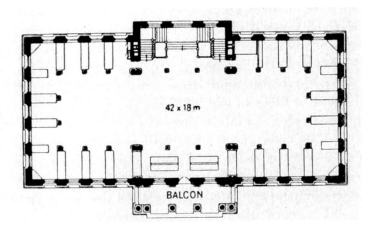

FIGURE 3.5. Plan, detailed plan of a corner of the museum, and section of the Chicago Academy of Sciences in Lincoln Park. Adolf Bernhard Meyer, *Studies of the Museums and Kindred Institutions of New York City, Albany, Buffalo, and Chicago: With Notes on Some European Institutions* (Washington, D.C.: U.S. Government Printing Office, 1905), 432–34.

curator of birds at the American Museum of Natural History in New York. A diorama could exhibit simultaneously the habits and the habitats of the specimen. In 1903, in an early example of this new format, Chapman arranged a display of Cobb's Island in Virginia in which birds preserved by taxidermy could be viewed in relation to one another and in the context of their environment.[32] The observer's view extended from the foreground of animal specimens and wax plants to the background, painted to imitate a horizon on the beach.[33] In its theatrical organization, the diorama even displayed a bird's wing movements as it descended toward its prey. The configuration of the specimens made the physical fact of flight visible and didactically demonstrated the bird's role in forming the character of the habitat.[34]

Shortly after Cowles joined the Board of Governors, the Chicago Academy of Sciences drafted a plan for dioramas like Chapman's for the main hall of the museum to represent the city's surrounding habitats, replacing the specimens held in glass vitrines. A view of these new displays allowed Chicagoans to imagine themselves immersed in the ecological interactions of the region. Even before there was a plan for the dioramas, the museum had already produced other dynamic displays. In 1912, Wallace W. Atwood, the geographer, geologist, and secretary of the academy, installed his patented Celestial Sphere under a skylight on the top floor—the first planetarium in the city. Those who entered the planetarium could observe the movement of Chicago's night sky over a full year as the fifteen-foot-diameter outer shell rotated around its axis.[35] Much like the panoramas of the nineteenth century but even more persuasive, Atwood's Sphere was enhanced by new mechanical equipment, to immerse the viewer in a scenic representation of stellar systems as they encircled the planet.[36]

Other specialists who were attentive to the dynamics of nature's economy promoted the use of habitat dioramas to display the panoramic changes of the Chicago region's ecology. The zoologist Charles C. Adams, also trained at the University of Chicago and briefly the director of the natural history museums at the universities of Cincinnati and Michigan, speculated that the new exhibits could correlate the processes affecting the region's physical conditions with the adaptations seen in the plant and animal life located there. He imagined that the "dried and pressed [plant] specimens which arouse so little interest" would soon be replaced by illustration of "plant societies and their ecological relations," a specific reference to Cowles's recently published research.[37]

In place of the few photographs that Cowles had published of the dunes, each describing a slice of time in the panoramic changes, the academy planned a continuous diorama that would re-create an immersive environment. Cowles's role in planning the exhibit remains unclear, but the influence of his ecological theory is plainly evident. Atwood, the acting director in 1916, announced a significant investment at the annual meeting, one focused on changing the methods of display used by the museum. On the second floor, he revealed a plan that would enclose most of the space with

> a continuous series of habitat groups, beginning at one side of the main stairway and encircling the entire museum floor . . . [to] represent the habitat groups encircling Chicago. So at the southeast of the building would appear those habitat groups associated with the south shore of Lake Michigan. A little to the west would come the Calumet Lake region, with its marshes and swamps and abundant bird life . . . [etc.,] each would appear in its proper place around the margin of the room . . . blended one into the other, a common background showing the landscape of this outlying district could be prepared.[38]

In blocking views through the windows with a continuous background image, the main display area of the museum would become totally internalized as a site for representing the Chicago region's ecology. As the diorama curved from one edge of the building to another, the relations of a particular habitat on display would correspond to the viewer's general orientation. The common background was intended to integrate the diverse taxidermy groups into a unified scene that, as we will see, transformed the use of photography from a piece of evidence used with scientifically objective criteria into an urban attraction.

Frank M. Woodruff, an ornithologist, photographer, trapper, taxidermist, as well as the curator for the academy, oversaw the construction of the "Chicago Environs Series." He had used enlargements from photographic negatives as early as 1910 for backdrops in various small "ecological installations" for the museum.[39] This technique would be extended in the new diorama series. While Cowles had used the term *panorama* figuratively in his writing, Woodruff produced a literally panoramic backdrop from enlarged photographs to display the processes of ecological interaction. A photography trade journal in 1919 described one of Woodruff's enlargements as the largest ever made. At ninety-six feet long and eleven feet high, one image was composed from multiple negatives that he had made on his field trips, each enlarged to eleven feet high by ten feet wide. The ten-foot width of one element of the enlargement was composed from three strips of photosensitive paper that were each approximately forty inches wide. The height of the image was determined by doubling the average height of a viewer, five and a half feet, to locate the horizon line at eye level. During the exposure of the eight- by ten-inch negative onto the ten- by eleven-foot pieces of paper, the latter was mounted on a printing board that had been built into a curve. The construction was set up around an enlarging camera to keep the entire image in focus. These large prints were then dismounted and developed in an immense tray as two men dragged the paper back and forth. One man wearing rubber boots climbed into the developer "armed with a swab mounted on a broomstick handle" (Figure 3.6).[40]

At its completion, 336 feet of enlarged photographs were integrated into the installation along the interior perimeter of the second floor of the museum. Woodruff described the geographic features pictured in the panoramic photograph in relation to each taxidermy group: "The first group . . . shows the Dune Region at the southern limit of the Calumet Region; the next one will be from where I left off at the Calumet River, continuing to the Calumet Lake, through the wooded swales and oak ridges, showing the transition stages from the prairie grass to the water plants, and then Calumet Lake with the nests and young of the canvas-back duck, redhead, and Canada goose, and the birds that nested in this region forty years ago." The whole diorama could be viewed continuously in either direction. Unlike the separate photographs that Cowles chose to illustrate specific transitions in the dune complex, each enlarged photograph was joined to the next, Woodruff explained, at a point "resembling the terminal of one scene and the beginning of the next one . . . perhaps a few leaves or a small tree could hide the joining." The photographs were integrated to hide their seams, he explained, like "wall paper on the wall."[41]

Woodruff's enlargements were referred to in museum journals as the "advent of a new art," a cheaper and more reliable technique for the mechanical manufacture of backdrops compared to "oil paintings costing thousands of dollars" such as those used in Chapman's dioramas in New York.[42] To color the massive prints, Woodruff replaced opaque paints with transparent colored oil tints that did not sacrifice the exactitude of detail, the correct exposure of light, or the rigor of the perspective offered by the camera lens. To add an image of a bird to the backdrop he would cut one out

FIGURE 3.6. Woodruff (in cap and suspenders, left), Atwood (in suit, right), and others developing the backdrop for the "Chicago Environs Series" [P-15b 1]. Chicago Academy of Sciences Institutional Archives. Chicago Academy of Sciences/Peggy Notebaert Nature Museum.

FIGURE 3.7. The "Dune Group" and the "Calumet River Group." Chicago Academy of Sciences/ Peggy Notebaert Nature Museum.

of a printed photograph and pin it to the panorama, a technique that enhanced the illusion of depth produced by the image. Depth was also added with painted shadows, projected from various objects in the scene; these were often extended from the panoramic image into the foreground or the reverse. The artificial shadows produced numerous overlaps between the photograph and the action figured by each taxidermy group. Woodruff's meticulous attention to detail is indicated by a letter he wrote to the board requesting funds for "a trained artist" to touch up some visual effects. He explained that in order to enhance the realism of artificial trees in the foreground, the skill of a painter would be uniquely qualified to add several greens that show "the varying shades of nature's colors."[43] Together, these techniques produced a unified realistic image of ecological dynamics at an architectural scale, held together by a single horizon line.

When aligned at the horizon, photographs of the "Calumet River Group," taken from two different vantage points, and four from the "Dune Group" reproduce the artifical visual continuity that would have been observed in the diorama at the museum (Figure 3.7). Although one image from the

Calumet River shows an osprey hunting its prey in the river and the other shows ducks in a marsh, the backdrop makes both events appear to be taking place simultaneously. Here is an important divergence between the ecologist's view of the region and its representation in the diorama. For Cowles, the dune complex was a landscape, never twice alike, in which the regulatory mechanisms of plants and animals indicated the physiological response to a dynamic physiography. By contrast, Woodruff's construction of static visual continuity between the organisms on display and their environmental context represented isolated instances of behavior in an impossible momentary harmony. These were not representations of specific regulatory responses to changes in the environmental conditions, but a collage of generic habits developed by each organism in its corresponding habitat.

The panorama transformed the photographs formerly used as facts requiring scientific explication into an immersive and spectacular spatial experience. One photograph of Miller Beach in the Indiana sand dunes was used as the frontispiece to Woodruff's *Birds of the Chicago Area* published by the academy in 1907. In 1916, Woodruff stitched together multiple images of the same location to form the backdrop for the museum (Figure 3.8).[44] Nestling one image into the next disrupted both the frame and the precise moment that it captured. The panoramic photograph represented an indefinite duration made up of fragments. Any viewer of the "Chicago Environs Series" was able to see the regional ecology through the curatorial composition of time, pictorial geography, and biological reenactment.

The representation was so complete and self-contained that the concept of an economy of nature could be apprehended even by a child's eye. Peter Mortenson, superintendent of the Chicago schools, remarked on the educational value of seeing "a representation of life in action" in the academy's diorama:

> The child who visits the museum catches the spirit of the Dune country and becomes familiar with all of its life in proper settings. Groups are built up in the fullest ecological sense. First there is the enlarged photograph as a background. This shows the habitat, the physiographic features, with the trees, plant life and water effects reproduced as nearly natural as is scientifically possible. . . . Mounted birds, animals and insects are shown against this background in a prepared foreground hunting food, feeding their young, and in every possible relationship which they maintain in actual life.[45]

The diorama represented the living environment as a translation of the ecologist's view: from the large geographic context in the rear to the object-scale of an organism in the front. These elements combined into an inhabitable yet autonomously regulated whole that, in its harmony, produced a psychological distance between the observer's everyday urban surroundings and the impenetrable unity of nature's economy, isolated from human interference. Unlike Cowles's individual images, the diorama also excluded traces of man's presence. The general public, including school children, would experience the difference between their city, shaped according to the needs of humans, and the diorama's closed world of nonhuman interactions. Constructing this representational unity in an urban building made the metaphor of a household of nature into a physical fact. Nature had been housed. The analogy of nature's economy to the regulated domestic interior, as the term *oikos* implied, was fulfilled by the viewer's experience of the totally integrated ecological interaction.

The Indiana dunes themselves, however, did not remain free of human

FIGURE 3.8. Compiled tree river panorama of Millers and Mineral Spring, Indiana, not yet enlarged for installation. Box 5, folder 8, Chicago Academy of Sciences Institutional Archives. Chicago Academy of Sciences/Peggy Notebaert Nature Museum.

influence. Beginning in 1906, the sand dunes had become a construction site for the world's largest steel plant, the Gary Works, named for Elbert H. Gary, J. P. Morgan's business partner, the president and chairman of the board of U.S. Steel (Figure 3.9). Through Morgan's uncompromising business tactics, U.S. Steel had become the first billion-dollar corporation, merging Andrew Carnegie's massive holdings with a network of local companies around the country. When the plant was built, the capitalization of U.S. Steel constituted 6.8 percent of the country's gross national product.[46] The corporation's effect on the dunes was more visibly powerful than its impact on the national economy. The Gary Works completely reconfigured the topography to suit the functions of the steel plant, laying railroad tracks in the sand and housing fifteen thousand workers in five hundred dwellings in the new town of Gary, Indiana. The apparent emptiness of the site, in the view of the leaders of this industrial conglomerate, was its main advantage. A writer for *Scientific American* captured the corporation's view of the dunes in his description of the location as "a dreary waste of drifted sand, entirely uninhabited and covered with a scanty growth of grass and scrub timer. . . . [On] a virgin site . . . the component parts of this, the greatest steel plant in existence, were therefore laid out with strict regard to the economical handling of enormous masses of raw material and finished product."[47]

As a reaction to the corporation's unregulated expansion into the dunes, the Prairie Club of Chicago initiated efforts to conserve the landscape from industrial interests with yearly festivals that raised awareness of the value of this ecology.[48] In late spring of 1917, the club produced two large pageants to support transforming the dunes into a national park. As many as forty thousand supporters gathered on Waverly Beach in Indiana to watch a dramatic historical narrative: reenactments of the region's development and interpretive dances inspired by the surrounding ecology. The pageant master also played the part of a Native American "Prophet," while nearly one thousand actors portrayed Indians, European explorers, soldiers, fur traders, and city planners. Some dancers were cast as waves, winds, nymphs, birds, or "tree hearts." The narrative, written by Thomas Wood Stevens, began with the explorer Father Jacques Marquette dying on the shores of Lake Michigan in 1675. It then revealed how "the Story of the West—the Progress of the Frontier—could not be written without the Indiana dunes."[49]

Cowles, a trustee of the Dunes Pageant Association, testified to support the proposal for a Sand Dunes National Park at a federal hearing, held

FIGURE 3.9. A view of the location of the Benzol Coke Plant of the Gary Works on Lake Michigan, surrounded by the dune complex. Photographs on October 6, 1916. Box 107, CRA-42-107-122, Calumet Regional Archives, Indiana University Northwest.

in 1917. He emphasized that the plant formations on the Indiana dunes were important to preserve because they represented a natural form of social mixing—"a common meeting ground of trees and wild flowers from all directions; and . . . as a picturesque battleground between plant life and the elements." Using metaphors of both congregation and war, as the historian Eugene Cittadino has shown, Cowles compared life on the dunes to the struggle for existence of the human populations in the adjacent metropolis.[50] The movements of sand that made the uncertainties of life on the dunes visible, he explained, were analogous to the human condition: "Our life is such a struggle. Nowhere perhaps in the entire world of plants does the struggle for life take on such dramatic and spectacular phases as in the dunes."[51] The spectacle and drama of environmental risk was reenacted daily in the dunes.

In contrast to the real uncertainty of life in nature and in the city, the habitat dioramas represented nature's economy as a static primordial image of ecological integration. This artificially constructed view of a suspended unity between organisms and their environment made the unregulated industrial interest of U.S. Steel appear all the more grotesque and alien to the reciprocity structuring this new view of a regulated nature. In the static diorama, the realism of the display produced a contemporary *tableau vivant* of the region's landscape in which succession, adaptation, and the struggle for existence were translated into visually accessible forms. The tranquility of the interior positioned the economy of nature as an image of harmonious relations; it offered a view of the region's original state of equilibrium that could be easily contrasted to the disturbing dominance of industrial interests. The reenactment of the dune complex's ecological history in the pageants and in the diorama became rhetorical foils against unregulated business. In the political battle to check corporate power, the dunes served as a natural symbol of a well-regulated economic system.

THE ECOLOGICAL LABORATORY

Despite the industrial transformations to Chicago's surrounding landscape, later ecological studies remained focused on the lives of organisms and their relations to the dunes. But in a new generation of ecologists who investigated the environment along the shores of Lake Michigan, the influence of industry was incorporated into their research as an undeniable force. While the academy presented an image of nature free of human interference, these young ecologists, trained in dunes, established laboratories to produce different representations of nature's economy. Translating what had appeared as ecological unity in the museum, their mechanical apparatus did not assume completeness; rather, they represented fragments of the dune complex, relying on the production of data to reconstruct the interconnected regulatory systems found in the field.

In 1911, one of Cowles's students from the University of Chicago, the zoologist Victor Ernest Shelford, made a field trip to the dunes to collect samples for his research on animal communities in the region around Lake Michigan. Like his teacher, Shelford took photographs, some of which included elements of urbanization near Gary (Figure 3.10). Behind the flattened land traversed by the tracks of the commuter rail running along the outskirts of town, the surrounding area revealed the sandy substrate beneath and beside the town. The photograph was labeled "succession with city growth." Borrowing Cowles's term to describe the dune complex, Shelford viewed the town of Gary as yet another part of the panoramic changes in the lake ecology. While Cowles had included dilapidated houses and people in images that illustrated his writings, Shelford's note on the photograph implied that human habitations were another form of animal community, much like the forms of shelter that he studied in his dissertation on the "Life-Histories and Larval Habits of Tiger Beetles" and their relation to the plant societies growing on the dunes.[52]

After receiving his degree in zoology, Shelford taught courses in animal ecology at the Hull Laboratories with his former thesis advisor, the physiologist Charles M. Child. The strong influence of physiology is immediately evident in Shelford's work, particularly in his determination to find direct cause-and-effect relationships to explain the changes in the habits of organisms in the dunes.[53] Unlike the botanical focus on large-scale forces and their consequent adaptations in dune vegetation, Shelford's research centered on animals' responses to environmental stimuli. He aimed to reproduce in the laboratory the natural relations between the organism and its environment in order to investigate how an animal's contribution to forming its immediate environment was an essential part of a regulatory system that worked to stabilize the conditions of its habitat.

The dedication to laboratory experimentation led Shelford to establish new methods of artificially simulating *in vitro* the physiological responses occurring *in vivo* that he called "social behaviors."[54] In his book *Animal Communities in Temperate America as Illustrated in the Chicago Region* (1913),

FIGURE 3.10. "Succession with city growth, Gary, Indiana." Photograph by Victor E. Shelford, 1911 [APF8-02349] University of Chicago Department of Botany Records Repository, Special Collections Research Center, University of Chicago Library. Also published in Victor E. Shelford, "Preserves of Natural Conditions," *Transactions of the Illinois State Academy of Science* 13 (1920).

he laid the groundwork for future experiments by studying animal communities in the Chicago region. He predicted that progress in this area would necessitate new forms of environmental control in the laboratory:

> The chief lesson which the author has drawn from his labors is that experimental study, conducted with due reference to the relations of the animals to natural environments, with conditions carefully controlled, and a single factor varied at a time, is one of the stepping-stones to future progress. . . . Though man is a land inhabitant, all the best work along these and many other lines has been done upon aquatic animals. The writer's course in the future will probably be . . . turned from the purely naturalistic method of study to a method made up of naturalistic observations and controlled experiments.[55]

Early studies of animal communities in water gave Shelford an immediate and predetermined combination of organisms and their milieu. This was an ideal model from which to start because changes made to the liquid medium surrounding the organism could be directly traced to its physiological functions.[56] Shelford soon sought to extend these methods of environmental simulation to other species in the Chicago region, including those living on the land.

Any attempt to identify an animal community, Shelford believed, required the observation of the responses of multiple organisms to the same stimulus.[57] But only by reducing the complexity inherent in the natural setting could Shelford measure the responses of one animal and relate them to the responses of others. Anticipating that the number of interdependencies of an animal community would be vast, he explained, made it necessary "to isolate particular animals and *construct* them into a society of real but limited relations."[58] While the construction of a habitat diorama made the ecological view of the organisms in its environment visible in an artificial re-creation of the natural landscape of the Chicago region, Shelford was aware that experimental apparatus would rely on the production of data—that was not immediately visual—to prove his hypothesis. He hoped that representing the interdependencies among the organisms that lived in the dunes by interpreting his experimental results could ground the knowledge of animal communities in the objectivity of experimental data.

Each subfield of ecology—botanical and zoological—therefore formed its own method of representing the relation of the organism to its environment. Cowles's naturalistic descriptions of plant adaptations and the surrounding flux of the dune complex were rendered in photographs; Shelford's analysis transcribed animal responses in the laboratory into data.[59] Rather than an organism's outward adaptations, it was its internal physiology that Shelford sought to understand as a system of regulatory responses to the stimuli in nature's economy. "Strictly speaking," he wrote, "the response is *the change or changes in the physical or chemical processes of the organism (or the part or parts concerned) which results from the disturbance.*"[60] The difference between Cowles and Shelford depended on the scale of their object of study in both space and time, and this difference was reflected in the methods they used to analyze and record change. While the botanist emphasized physiographic changes of a region, the zoologist focused on small physiological changes immediately around and within an organism. While the botanist recorded adaptations observed by the human eye and captured them with a camera, the zoologist experimented with methods for encoding animal responses in data that were not directly open to observation.[61] For Shelford, the organism's internalization of a stimulus and its translation into a response was the key to understanding the basic structure of life's regulatory machinery. His methods were not only designed to prove the existence of individual regulatory responses in an individual animal, however; instead he sought to prove the existence of collective responses as the regulatory behavior of animal communities. If he could demonstrate that common responses existed among organisms to stabilize a habitat, his research would prove that animal communities produced invisible economies that preserved the lives of multiple organisms at the same time.

In 1912 the embryologist Charles Zeleny, another graduate of the zoology program at the Hull Laboratories, returned to the University of Chicago to present his vision for a "Vivarium Building" on the Urbana campus of the University of Illinois. Two years later, Shelford, who probably attended Zeleny's presentation, joined the Illinois zoology faculty as well as the process of planning the new building. Contrasting a future Vivarium to the five-year-old Hull Laboratories, Zeleny hoped that the new facility would offer an unprecedented level of control over variables in the environmental conditions of biological experimentation. Until then, he explained, these experimental conditions had been largely overlooked: "The object of the facilities is to control temperature and light, both of which as antecedent conditions, so profoundly affect animal behavior, that critical experimenters would regard results obtained in an ordinary greenhouse as of very questionable value."[62] His specifications for the new laboratory were exacting. Zeleny insisted that any installation of experimental apparatus be protected from hot or cold water pipes; otherwise, resulting "irregularities in temperature make success of experiments impossible."[63] Even his earliest notes for the Vivarium included an entirely separate infrastructure for the laboratory machinery than those systems that serviced the building, including electricity, hot water, cold brine, compressed air, and sewer connections. His research into the environmental causes for what he called "compensatory regulation," the regeneration of organs in animals, depended on completely isolating the experimental organism from the surrounding architecture.[64] Unlike the order of nature's economy represented in enlarged colored photographs, laid out as a continuous diorama within an existing building, the Vivarium in Urbana required a hermetic mechanical enclosure that did not lend itself to public viewership. To this scientist's mind, it was only the apparatus, and not the building in which it was housed, that contributed to producing scientific results.

Zeleny made numerous sketches of the would-be Vivarium in 1911, some drawn with an architectural scale, others on gridded paper where each cell represented three feet (Figure 3.11). Basing his plans on the size

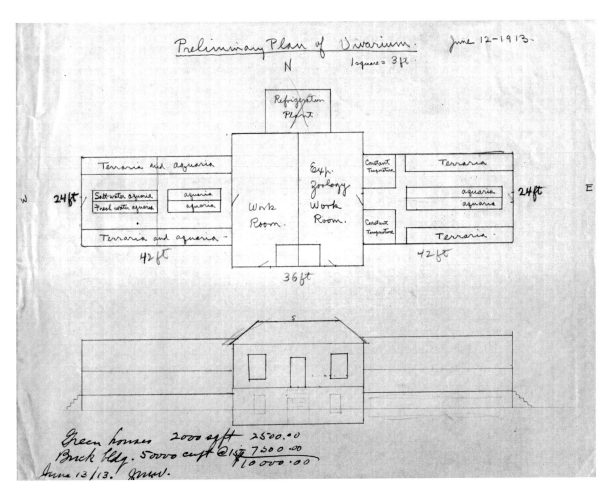

FIGURE 3.11. "Preliminary Plan of Vivarium, June 12, 1913." Charles Zeleny Papers, Record Series 15/24/22, Box 6, folder: Preliminary Plan of Vivarium. Courtesy of the University of Illinois at Urbana-Champaign Archives.

of the Illinois State entomologist's insectary, built on the Urbana campus in 1905, he drew a small square brick building, flanked at either side by rectangular glass houses containing terraria and aquaria—both salt and fresh water—for storing experimental specimens. In these drawings, he distinguished generic laboratories from "experimental rooms" housed in the central structure.[65] The latter would have a wall in common with "constant temperature rooms" located in the glass houses to the east. Detailed sketches of those rooms were labeled "40°F" and "90°F," with an additional note that anticipated the "range of temperature not to exceed ±1°." Zeleny's tireless efforts to sketch, annotate, detail, and specify his needs for laboratory space indicate that the conditions he required for his experiments made the building's distance from the apparatus it held essential to his research. Shelford became equally invested in the building's design as soon as he joined the Illinois faculty. Upon his arrival in 1914, he requested that a shed be added behind the square building that Zeleny had drawn to house what he called an "ecological laboratory."

Thus, plans for the apparatus and layout were nearly complete before the university even hired an architect. The architectural design of the Illinois Vivarium was finally given to the Illinois State architect, James B. Dibelka, and construction was completed at the end of 1915 (Figure 3.12).[66] With stripped-down beaux-arts elements on the exterior and modest furnishings in the domestically scaled interior, the building was designed to be easily modified with up-to-date laboratory equipment. This flexibility was a response to Shelford's request to the head of the zoology department to keep the Vivarium open to future changes. "Such buildings as this have not been standardized," he explained, "and the thing which is most certain to happen is that we shall have to modify interior details. For this reason the construction should be such as to permit of modification at the least possible expense."[67]

Despite their direct involvement in every aspect of the building's arrangement, neither Shelford nor Zeleny named the building "the Illinois Vivarium." This name came from the trustees' meetings, where the term *vivarium* gradually shifted from its conventional meaning—a small glass enclosure, a room, or structure in which animals could be stored—to a proper noun that referred to only this building, uniquely outfitted with the most technically advanced experimental equipment on the campus.[68] Shelford offered many criticisms of the layout as it was realized and concluded that for future laboratories, the "architectural style of the institution must not

FIGURE 3.12. "The Illinois Vivarium, 1918." Record Series 39/2/20, Box Vivarium-YMCA, folder: BUI Vivarium, 1916–17 Courtesy of the University of Illinois at Urbana-Champaign Archives.

be allowed to interfere with producing an adequate building."[69] But the building's inadequacy was not due to its style; rather, it was the result of the novelty of the scientists' apparatus. In fact, the building kept much of the organization from Zeleny's preparatory sketches: greenhouses flanked the main brick building and an additional laboratory to the north, as requested by Shelford, linked by an enclosed passageway (Figure 3.13). Although some shortcomings could be ascribed to poor planning and wartime shortages, most of the building's budget was dedicated to the purchase of the laboratory machinery. The fact that the building had no value to the scientists to represent their knowledge implied that it would necessarily be viewed as an obstacle to transformations in experimental equipment over the next years. Keeping this compromised infrastructure in working order required that Shelford and Zeleny develop a close collaboration with James M. White, the campus's supervising architect.[70]

Beyond overseeing the construction and maintenance of all the campus buildings, including the Vivarium, White was also a professor of architectural engineering and, since 1905, dean of the College of Engineering. As an undergraduate who had studied at that school of architecture, his early interests had focused on heating and ventilation.[71] Early in his career, he also published architectural guidelines for the design of modern farmhouses in which he extended lessons from domestic mechanical systems to rural architecture. The affinity between White's interest in ventilating farmhouses and Shelford's work at the Vivarium speaks to the range of contexts in which regulatory thinking took hold. If the systems in a farmhouse were to be tuned to animals, servants, and a family, White observed, their organization should service what he called "grouped dependencies."[72] White's recommendations were rigorous: in the technologically regulated interior, the behaviors of each adult human could be reduced to numerical requirements: about 1,800 cubic feet of air per adult per hour with approximately the same amount used for lighting. Thus, the designer of a ventilation system should calculate that each adult required 3,600 cubic feet of air per hour, or one cubic foot each second. Perhaps a similar calculation could be made for each animal in the farmhouse.[73]

Yet compared to the most technically advanced domestic interiors, the machines used for scientific research were significantly more sophisticated and powerful, capable of managing every environmental variable at far higher levels of precision.[74] Shelford's research relied so heavily on the reliable functioning of these systems that he dedicated his research

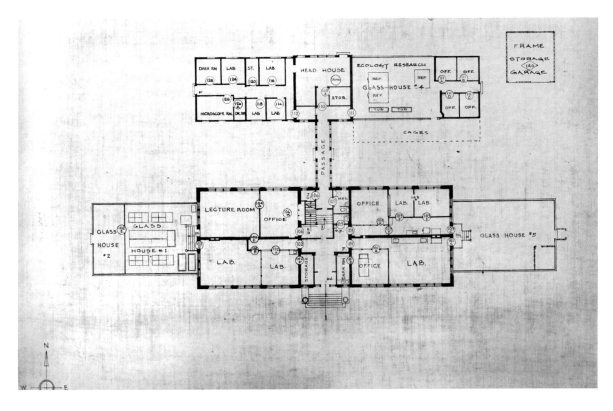

FIGURE 3.13. "Plan of the Illinois Vivarium as constructed." Charles Zeleny Papers, Record Series 37/3/809, Book 10. Courtesy of the University of Illinois at Urbana-Champaign Archives.

manual on animal ecology to Professor White thirteen years after moving into the Vivarium. White's "system of day-and-night centralized service to machinery," Shelford recalled, was the key to conducting his climate-simulation experiments by coordinating the action of each machine with the others so that they did not operate at cross-purposes.[75] In working closely with the architect, Shelford realized that controlling environmental dynamics required managing a range of interrelated variables; one change always caused others: "Temperature control involves heat sources, running water, refrigeration, circulating devices, and automatic control. Humidity control requires all that heat control does, and special equipment in addition. . . . Light control likewise involves temperature and humidity relations. Air movement influences evaporation and hence temperature and humidity."[76] White's control system far exceeded the capacity of any "traditional gardener," as Shelford observed, who formerly would have had to constantly "adjust ventilators and steam valves . . . for precise measurement and calibration."[77]

While the assembly and calibration of the laboratory was complex, Shelford's apparatus was not entirely unique. In fact, its replication was essential to producing verifiable results. By 1918 he could compare his measurements of animal reactions to those made by other scientists (Figure 3.14). These were all taken in seconds with a stopwatch, a common unit that bound together research from several different institutions.[78] Here was the essential difference between zoological and botanical ecology, between animal response and plant adaptation: unlike response, one could never accurately measure adaptation in the artificial environment of the laboratory because the exact amount of time elapsed during such a change could never be measured. Even in its apparent mechanical objectivity, the photographs used by Cowles only offered well-chosen instants of change that had been selected from an ongoing, dynamic, cyclical process. By contrast, physiological research on animal communities was organized around the technicality of measurements made according to discreet increments of time.[79]

The main difficulty in assembling the Vivarium apparatus was that the instruments of environmental control were not specifically designed for scientific purposes. Most of the scientists' machines were derived from various uses in industry. During the late stages of planning the building, for example, Zeleny wrote to White to consult "refrigerating and temperature devices which are installed in breweries" in advance of purchasing

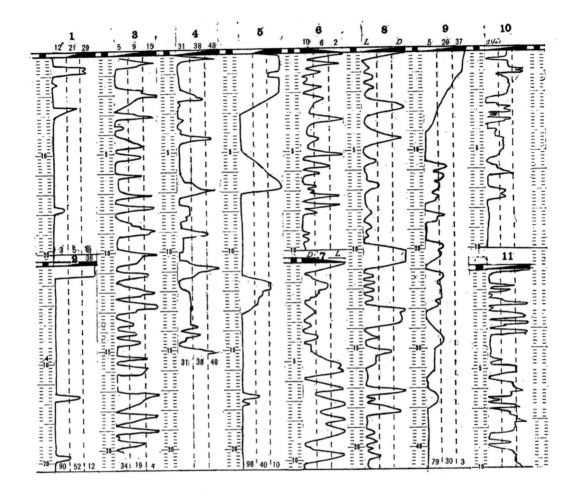

FIGURE 3.14. Graphs illustrating several stimuli and the reactions of several animal groups. Shelford's description is extensive: "Graph 1. A white-footed wood mouse in an evaporation gradient . . . (After Chenoweth.) Graph 2. A white-footed wood mouse in an air humidity gradient . . . (After Chenoweth.) Graph 3. A horned lizard in air humidity gradient . . . (After Weese.) Graph 4. A horned lizard in a substratum temperature gradient . . . (From Weese, unpublished.) Graph 5. A common toad in an air humidity gradient . . . . Graph 6. A small sunfish in an ammonia gradient in alkaline water. . . . Graph 7. A ground beetle in a light intensity gradient. Graph 8. The same individual ground beetle in an oblique cage intensity-direction gradient. Graph 9. An earthworm in an air, moisture gradient. . . . (From Heimburger, unpublished.) Graph 10. A single Paramecium in a temperature gradient in which the cool end was near the optimum. Graph 11. A single Paramecium in a temperature gradient which resulted in death at the end of 12 minutes." Victor E. Shelford, "A Comparison of the Responses of Animals in Gradients of Environmental Factors with Particular Reference to the Method of Reaction of Representatives of the Various Groups from Protozoa to Mammals," *Science*, n.s., 48.1235 (August 30, 1918): 227.

a cooling plant for experiments in the facility.[80] Further, the results of the research conducted in the Vivarium were often applied for practical concerns. For example, Shelford's research on the regulatory behavior of species in relation to seasonal changes, simulated by the machines, were framed to protect agricultural fields from the effects of such insects as cinch bugs and coddling moths. The industrial apparatus of the laboratory therefore bridged between the knowledge practices of ecologists and interests evolving from the market.[81]

With the assembly of this complex apparatus, the cost of scientific research grew to become an investment akin to those found in industry. And with the evolution of the scientists' research projects, the instruments became more tuned to generating experimental results. In 1927, for instance, Shelford replaced an outdated ammonia-driven cooling apparatus with a state-of-the-art air-conditioning machine (Figure 3.15). He contracted D. C. Lindsay of the Carrier Engineering Corporation to design a unit that could produce temperature conditions in forced air that were accurate to within a tenth of a degree Celsius.[82] In the captions attached to technical drawings he later published, Shelford described the space in which the specimens were held in isolated cages as a "room." The size of the mechanical instruments that controlled this room's interior conditions was equal to the volume of space it contained. Based on the scale, the cost, and the rapid rate of technological obsolescence, Shelford concluded that only experimental projects with funding of three years or more could be taken on with any hope of success. By his calculations, this was the amount of time that "interest, support, and enthusiasm" were at their highest. Ecological science in the laboratory gradually took on the characteristics of an enterprise, one that required investors, laborers, and management.[83]

As Shelford collected his research methods into a handbook for ecological experimentation, he also wrote a comprehensive naturalist's guide to the Americas using the descriptive methods that he had learned from Cowles and others at Chicago.[84] This late interest in field study illustrates his recognition of a limit to the explanatory value of the experimental data collected in a laboratory. Robert Kohler has interpreted Shelford's departure from the Vivarium as a result of the inadequacy of his experimental results. Indeed, on several occasions he publicly announced his doubts regarding the use of experimental facilities to answer questions that could be better addressed by field methods.[85] Yet he never fully withdrew from his commitment to connecting physiology and physiography in laboratory

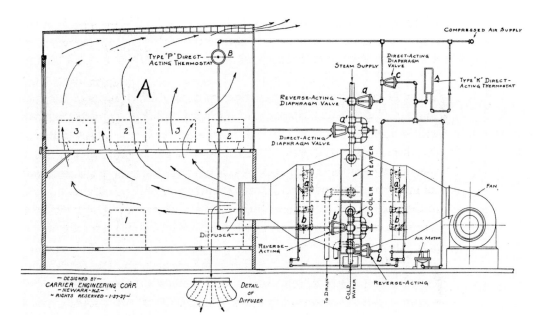

FIGURE 3.15. "A permanent Carrier-designed unit," designed in 1927 by the Carrier Engineering Corporation. Located in the glass house, room "A," the Johnson pneumatic thermostats at positions A and B automatically regulated the amount of steam and cold water used to counteract the fluctuations in temperature measured outside the room. Victor E. Shelford, *Laboratory and Field Ecology: The Responses of Animals as Indicators of Correct Working Methods* (Baltimore: Williams and Wilkins, 1929), 394.

simulations of environmental factors. Since Shelford's descriptive work did not disavow experiment, his position should be interpreted as a recognition of the complementarity of the two methods in producing ecological knowledge.[86] By shifting his object of study, or rather, broadening it, Shelford found that descriptive methods were essential in accounting for the influence of humans on ecological dynamics. We may recall the photograph of Gary in 1911 and the relation that he observed there between the dunes and the urban infrastructure that displaced them. Shelford acknowledged that man was also subject to the "physical environment" and hypothesized that humans, too, would eventually be tied into the "scope of modern scientific measurement."[87]

Two diagrams were drawn by Shelford to illustrate the differences in ecological dynamics caused by man's presence (Figure 3.16). The first diagram illustrated an "original biotic community of the deciduous forest of North America."[88] The circle at the center represented the food supply—nuts, fruit, blossoms, leaves, twigs, and bark—around which all the animals were organized. The arrows led from organisms that were sources of food to organisms that used them for food. Only a vague boundary organized the diagram around the center; the relations elaborated in the diagram related to a physical space only insofar as each animal would presumably be within the reach of the others as predator or prey. According to Shelford, this naturally occurring "biome," or plant-animal formation, could be compared "to an amoeboid organism, a unit of parts, growing, moving, and manifesting internal processes which may be likened to metabolism, locomotion, etc."[89] This metaphor of a microscopic organism's internal regulation helped explain the internal regulation of a macroscopic animal community as it moved through a forest and managed fluctuations in the food supply due to changes in the physical environment. Yet in the absence of human observation, these effects could never be measured. And after man was introduced into nature's economy, the diagram would need radical alteration. The habitat produced by humans fundamentally reorganized the form of the original forest community.[90]

The second diagram showed that man dominates the food network. What Shelford called a "ring of control" represented the technologies used by humans to limit the prevalence of dangerous predators. As in a farmhouse, domesticated animals such as cattle and hogs were inside the ring, located between man and the crops that replaced naturally growing foods.

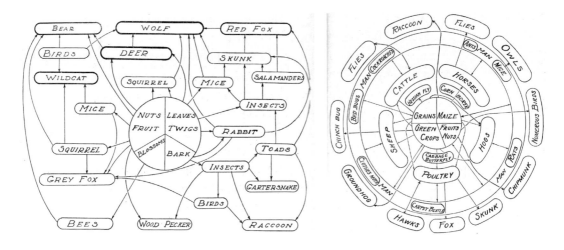

FIGURE 3.16. "The food network and general interrelations of the animals and plants of the original biotic community of the deciduous forest of North America." Right, "Showing the type of dominance which man exercises." Victor E. Shelford, "The Physical Environment," in *A Handbook of Social Psychology*, ed. Carl Murchison (Worcester: Clark University Press, 1935).

The animals within the ring also replaced the threatening wolves and bears that did not carry over from the first diagram. Yet new dangers emerged within the ring of control: crop pests and cockroaches replaced the insects of the original forest. Shelford compared primeval animal communities to a single-cellular organism, held together by internal associations, but man-dominated habitat added a regulatory barrier that clearly differentiated the center from the perimeter, producing functional hierarchies. The new system of relations, although more organized, was still dynamic, closer to the internal regulation of a complex organism than to one with a single cell. Arrows drawn over the ring of control showed how pests penetrated from the periphery to the center to consume food. Man's home, represented in the territory between the two concentric circles, was firmly located in one place, no longer mobile and flexible like that of the original biotic community represented by the first diagram. In an even more extreme way than a farmhouse, the Vivarium revealed Shelford's ring of control. Here science imposed an artificial order on the economy of nature by splitting it apart: extracting and housing specimens, regulating their surrounding conditions, and recording the data produced by a finely tuned apparatus. The experimental laboratory was perhaps the most complete instance of a man-dominated habitat.

In larger human communities, Shelford explained, control over the surroundings becomes more powerful; cities were merely an "intensification of man's dominance."[91] Citing the work of the sociologist Roderick D. McKenzie, Shelford saw human associations as an extension of other animal aggregations: they could be compared to ecological studies of bivalve mollusks, for example, that lived in communities called "*Spisula* cities." While Shelford viewed sociology as a subdiscipline of ecology, McKenzie, along with other members of the sociology department at the University of Chicago such as Ernest Burgess and Robert Park, exploited the overlap in these emerging fields. In their writings from the early 1920s, these social scientists borrowed the terms and metaphors of plant and animal ecology to set their theories of urban organization on rigorous ground.[92] Just as Shelford's illustration of a food network placed the food resources at its center, borrowing from other ecologists' diagrams, Burgess's well-known concentric diagram of a city placed the site of production in the central loop where the resources of the city were produced (Figure 3.17). Burgess even called the tendency of cities to grow outward from a central loop a process of "succession."[93] His theory sought to explain the growth of cities in general, and he applied his ideal model to Chicago to test its validity on an empirical case. If the organization of Chicago, or any other city, could be explained by analyzing its form and function as a system of interrelated forces, Burgess predicted that his research could establish a system of controls to avoid problems that he ascribed to a process called "disorganization." In both animal ecology and in the social sciences, an organism's internal modes of regulation became the preferred metaphor to explain the methods for managing aggregations of individuals. The diagram of physiological regulation was applied equally well to "nature's metropolis" as it was to nature's economy.[94]

Neither the ecological view of the city nor that of nature assumed a continuous state of internal stability. Rather, disruptions were an anticipated part of any existing configuration, and by this logic, the regulatory systems were tools developed by organisms or metropolitan centers to stabilize their environmental relations. With the intensification of man's dominance—the expansion of industry and urban growth—retaining order in the dune landscape required scientists to become politically active. Shelford's attitude toward these forces on the physical environment

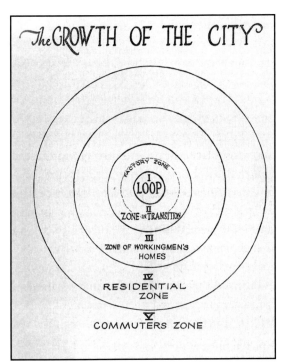
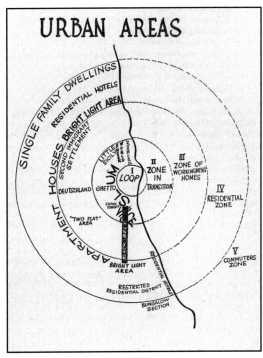

FIGURE 3.17. Left, the idealized diagram of a city; right, the same diagram applied to the areas of the city of Chicago. Burgess referred to the "black belt," a neighborhood in which many Southern blacks settled during the Great Migration, as a form of urban "disorganization." Ernest Burgess, "The Growth of the City: An Introduction to a Research Project," in *The City*, ed. Robert E. Park, Ernest W. Burgess, and Roderick D. McKenzie (Chicago: University of Chicago Press, 1925), 51, 55.

is evident from his efforts to preserve natural environments across the United States. In 1917, as the hearing to preserve the dunes in Indiana was being held, he established an advisory committee within the Ecological Society of America. Nearly thirty scientists in the committee, including Henry Cowles, offered advice to state and federal agencies for selecting sites for future preservation and recommended techniques for their management.[95]

Thus, Cowles and Shelford held a common interest in preserving the dunes and other ecological habitats. Despite employing different methods to represent ecological dynamics and their modes of regulation, the scientists' political position was coherent. Cowles viewed the dunes as an exemplary model for ecological study where the plants' collective capacity for regulating the dune landscape was immediately visible. Photographs describing this exchange in nature's economy pictured it at critical moments of flux. Translating this scheme into the three-dimensional diorama at the academy, set against a continuous photographic background, immersed the public viewer in a regulated world to which he did not belong. By contrast, Shelford's research offered a less dramatic and perhaps more technocratic image of ecological dynamics. The technicality of the laboratory apparatus did not produce a realistic image but presented man's dominance as intrinsic to the production of knowledge about ecological dynamics. What he represented was always the mediation of nature's regulatory systems through a network of mechanisms that resulted in tabulations of data. For Cowles, the dunes established a public image of regulation while for Shelford, the very act of preserving nature was one that would require even more investment, more management, and more systems of infrastructure for governmental regulation.

If we revisit the Gary Works, assembled by U.S. Steel on the dunes along the southern shore of Lake Michigan, we find the site of a company town, a center for human aggregation.[96] Spatial economic theory, based on the seminal work of Johann Heinrich von Thünen, would have explained the location of this community as an essential aspect in the confluence of raw materials, modes of transportation, machines, workers, and families that were gathered there for a common purpose: to maximize the factory's profitability. The dune complex, as Cowles, Shelford, and their fellow ecologists had observed, had been systematically reorganized according to the logic of industrial production rather than natural reproduction.[97] While the viewer of the diorama understood mechanical systems of production to be foreign to the natural systems of regulation that formed the dune complex, following Shelford might prompt a view of Gary as yet another ecological system, held together by its own internal regulatory action. Indeed, the urban sociologist, the animal ecologist, and the manager of the factory all viewed their objects of study as internal economies—what von Thünen called "isolated states"—that sustained unity by constantly adjusting their internal conditions to the dynamics of change that surrounded them.

CHAPTER 4

Imaging Brainwork

Organizing the factory according to the principles of regulation was central to studies conducted by such men of science as Andrew Ure in the 1830s.[1] As we have seen, these early attempts to systematically manage industry in Britain laid the intellectual groundwork for various practical changes in the conduct of American life around the late nineteenth century. The continued and expanded use of the term *regulation* indicates the broadening interest in tools for managing dynamic change, even changes occurring in the apparent harmony of nature. The protagonists in the preceding chapters participated in these expanded applications of regulatory thinking with comparisons they made among a variety of objects—household services, commodity markets, animal communities—and the long sought-after regularity of industrial production.

Yet the regulation of industry according to the forces of the market, which will be the topic of this chapter, was not only the result of physical transformations in machine assembly or the organization of a factory building. JoAnne Yates has shown the role of the instruments developed by managers for communicating their priorities, controlling processes of industrial production, and bringing oversight to the expanding domain of railroad operations.[2] The study of these instruments—including slide rules, bulletin boards, and instruction cards—as well as the diagrammatic images that managers drew of their "systems" for machine shops, helps situate managerial action among other forms of regulatory thinking that I described in earlier chapters. Just as the representations of ecology made the principles of natural regulation visually evident, for example, the tools used to govern modern production processes made industrial management into a legible form of knowledge.

For most of the twentieth century, historians of labor, technology, and business have discussed the impact of Frederick Winslow Taylor's doctrine of scientific management on politics, culture, and economics.[3] Architectural historians have also assessed the influence of Taylor's thinking, specifically its effect on modernist visual language such as that of Le Corbusier.[4] The present chapter adds to this work by concentrating on abstract notations of the labor process and the diagrams that described managerial operations as representations of regulation. With the invention of this representational mode, I aim to show how such an image of labor could be applied to any domain of production, and how it was especially effective in regulating production that did not have an immediate physical output. Architectural labor is one example of this, and it is the topic of the final chapter, where I describe the incorporation of these techniques in architects' offices. But to arrive at that point, this chapter must first show how regulatory thinking transformed the factory as an object of representation. An important distinction exists between regulation in mid- and late nineteenth-century factories: while Andrew Ure described regulation's automatic action as a "guiding intelligence" of the physical machinery, Taylor used the term "brainwork" to characterize his methods for regulating production through the collection of data, that is, through its rate and volume of output. Taylor's emphasis on brain*work* assumed management's direct engagement in the everyday inner workings of the factory, and Ure's notion of guiding intelligence remained a metaphor related to its capacity to organize the tasks of industrial production. Scientific managers' instruments, then, extended principles for regulating the mechanics of factory production into a new form of pragmatic reasoning—based in writing about, visually documenting, and rearranging factory operations—that tuned physically industrial output to fluctuations in the market.[5]

Industrial managers who followed Taylor sought out methods of representation that could account for all aspects of production—including management itself—in order to integrate them into a regulated whole. Such methods helped identify a pace for workflow and a sequence of production that minimized error and maximized profit. By fine-tuning the labor process with these methods, managers could sketch out a conceptual order that would structure any factory's organization. That managers used the word *harmony* to describe this goal is only one example of their belief that, at some point, an extensive system of industrial integration would become possible. They were committed to bringing factory labor ever closer toward an ideal form, shaped by their guidance, that they called "standard." By contrast, neither the regulation of temperature in private homes nor cold storage warehouses were viewed as means for producing an underlying order for structuring every aspect of daily life—these were primarily responses to a complex set of motivations that depended strongly on context. In the forms of representation used to regulate modern industrial labor, however, the managerial ambition to produce an image of order was unambiguously articulated.

Among the factors that required regulation in industrial production was the human body. Anson Rabinbach's rich historical study of French theories of fatigue, a concept used to describe the resistance of the body to work, aimed to "map out the lines of least resistance to the body's economy of force."[6] Human biology was a source for unpredictable stoppages, so the health of workers represented an important problem for industrial managers. "Occupational disease," as it was known, was a central concern in the systems they used to assert control over production.[7] Yet for those who followed Taylor's thinking, the body was only one of the many variables that needed to be integrated into the overall mechanical system. Thermostats were originally intended for factories, as we have seen, but industry was not the context in which that regulatory technology was best resolved; instead, the thermostatic interior was first established in the private house. Thus rather than focus on the body of the laborer, the discourse of scientific management viewed physical effort and the environment surrounding it as two elements within a vast system developed to control the operations related to production. Regulating the internal operations of a factory was primarily intended to synchronize the activities of labor with the economic and technological changes that occurred outside the plant.

To the process of industrial production, managers added representations of work executed in factories by both humans and machines. This addition was neither a natural part of the process nor was it necessary. Instead, it was a cunning addition that managers often claimed was continuous with the physical labor that it described. Claims to continuity helped naturalize the supervisory role of managers in the factory. Their efforts were what John Stuart Mill called "indirect labor" in his *Principles of Political Economy* of 1848, that is, a form of work that did not directly engage in the material manufacture of a commodity. For Mill, this was a supplement to direct labor, which included producing materials, maintaining tools, safety, worker training, and product distribution.[8]

The managers who followed Taylor, half a century after Mill, identified their work with the rest of the work in the factory, even if it was only indirectly related to the physical production of the industries they managed in machine shops and arsenals. This helped establish the idea that the engineering of machines, the ordering of work, and the surveillance of the shop were all indispensable to the operations of large-scale industry and required a unique expertise. But since a manager's labor was categorically different from that of a factory worker, their techniques—such as methods for data collection or mathematical analysis—were not identical to those of other workers, were not easily implemented, and therefore were not universally viewed as essential to the tasks of production. Writing about the role of engineers in the rise of corporate capitalism, David F. Noble observed: "Actually, these corporate engineers played a double role. As engineers in a capitalist system, they were professionally charged with the profit-maximizing advance of scientific technology. And as corporate functionaries, they assumed the responsibility for coordinating the human elements of the technological enterprise."[9] Putting these roles together, managers of machine-based factories, often trained as engineers, developed techniques to observe and represent labor that did not always expedite it, but regulated it to the demands of an owner or a group of investors. Their techniques therefore served purposes other than mere efficiency. By accelerating production on certain occasions and slowing it down at others, management conceptualized the factory as a time-based and mutable *form*.[10]

Against a fixed image of the interior, managers were like their ecologist counterparts in that they chose to measure the activities in the factory with formats that allowed them to perceive and record change. These formats helped identify errors related to mechanical movement or small deviations in the time of production. By observing action, they believed that they could constantly reorganize the production process through carefully calibrated interventions that restricted error to an acceptable range of deviation. Their interventions depended upon small instruments and everyday tools of the managerial apparatus that could be transported anywhere. Outside the context of the industrial machine shop, for example, the engineer Sanford E. Thompson worked with Taylor to formulate a mathematical description of the labor of a man and his wheelbarrow on a construction site using a stop watch. The result was a formula that integrated all the time-based tasks of loading a wheelbarrow, moving it, and then removing its contents.[11] Taylor insisted that the activities of brainwork be included in all descriptions of industrial labor processes, whatever their context. Isolating it, he argued, was only necessary to refine the methodologies for data collection and identify their use in planning production.

The importance of the term *scientific*, used by Taylor to describe his doctrine of management, was its indication that the system was based on methods of empirical observation. Insofar as the task of modern science has been to produce knowledge through the formulation, execution, and record of an experiment, a manager was most like a scientist in the way that the labor process was represented and analyzed. The factory was studied as if it was a natural phenomenon. In comparing a science such as ecology to industrial management, one sees the evident commonality in the tools developed by both fields: they were designed to produce representations of dynamic systems. The factory was an environment like any other that an ecologist might study, filled with living and nonliving things. Management represented it as a mechanical system with inputs and outputs in which the potential for error and lost profit was everywhere. It was the manager's job to locate error, control it, and thereby form the factory into a unity that could absorb technological change and sustain profitability in the face of economic fluctuations.

LOST WORK

Taylor's doctrine responded to an existing debate over "lost work" in the distribution of power through a factory building.[12] Lost work, or the energy absorbed by some form of mechanical resistance, was usually traced to the connections between a source of power and the machines on the factory floor. One of Taylor's fundamental contributions to the methods of industrial management was his extension of the search for lost work beyond the physics of power transmission. He looked at the relationships among machines, the men who operated them, and those who maintained them. By recording all the interruptions to the labor process, he was able to limit the amount of time and work that would be lost. The greater purpose of his intervention was to control production, not merely to increase the rate of output. Although the work process in the factory could become much faster if his methods were followed, Taylor's system also made it possible to slow down production as a response to errors and accidents.

Before Taylor published his notes on the lost work at the Midvale Steel Plant located in Nicetown near Philadelphia, the prevailing effort on the topic of lost work focused on models for creating an ideal tension in leather belts that connected the source of power to the machines.[13] There were two sets of belts: one that transferred power from a steam engine or other source to shafts hung from the ceiling, and another that connected the shafts to the machines below. The diameter of pulleys regulated the amount of power that the belts transferred from the shafts to the machines.

Andrew Ure published an early depiction of this system, set up for a cotton manufacturer in 1835 (Figure 4.1).[14] In this image, automated looms were aligned under the shafting mechanism with teams of women circulating between the rows of machines to correct errors, collect finished spools, and replace them with empty spools. The shafts were attached to beams that spanned from one column's top to the next. These determined the even placement of the machines on the floor. Cylindrical pulleys were attached to the shafts. Belts were hung from the pulleys to the machines, parallel to the columns. The resulting grid visually aligned the space to the mechanism. In unison, the system of shafts, pulleys, and belts moved all the machines with calibrated power, making it possible to execute nearly any form of production—from textiles to woodworking—at any speed.

Around 1880, the focus of many engineers who managed power distribution through this system was determining the coefficient of friction that most efficiently translated work between the belts and the pulleys to power the machines. If friction—defined as the ratio between the tension before and the tension after a belt rolls over a pulley—could be set as a constant, engineers believed that the tension in each belt could be fixed for an optimal transmission of power, an idealized solution to reduce lost work.[15]

Unlike these engineers, however, Taylor did not aim to fix the tension in the Midvale plant's belts according to an ideal coefficient of friction.[16] Instead, he argued that reducing the lost work would require constant supervision over the belts by paying close attention to the specificities of each machine. "Non-specialists," as he called them, who manned the belts were the primary obstacle to regulating the amount of lost work. He believed that supervision required a dedicated and well-informed employee. While errors could never be eliminated, supervision over the belts by someone with proper training was necessary to limit the effect of stretching, slipping, and, in the worst case, snapping. Every stretch in a belt produced a corresponding, although unpredictable, stretch in production time. If

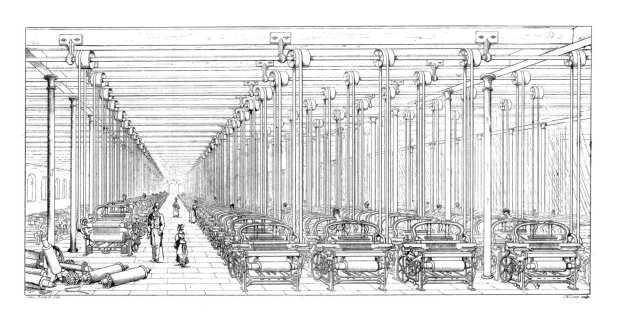

FIGURE 4.1. Power loom factory of Thomas Robinson Esq., Stockport. Andrew Ure, *The Philosophy of Manufactures* (London: C. Knight, 1835).

the tension, width, thickness, and speed of the belts could be limited to a range of acceptable values, the system could be tuned to produce a more predictable and continuous performance for each machine. Monitoring a factory's belting was essential for bringing this mechanical system under these predetermined norms.

Translating errors, delays, interruptions, and their attendant cost into data showed the potential problems that developed in belting. Taylor summarized these observations in a single table, but he did not organize the data that he collected into a standard method for belt maintenance.[17] His observations could not be immediately translated into a mathematical formula. The units of each datum only accounted for a limited number of variables and often did not reflect on any of the others. For example, the "average ratio that care and maintenance bears to first cost" was directly related but not measurable against the "average number of times each belt required tightening." As diagnostic tools, then, these measurements were useful in training an expert on the potential of error but were not yet formulated into a method for mathematically deriving predictive relationships of cause and effect. The table of data was simply a numerical representation of the error-ridden elements of the belting system, the costs associated with those errors, and a record of time lost to their repair.

If the potential for error in the factory's belting could be located and governed, Taylor believed, then it should also be possible for the interaction between each worker and each machine in the factory to be brought under more precise control. To achieve this, Taylor sought to develop a method that would allow him to predetermine time allotments for every step in the production process. Using the piece-rate system—the basis for paying laborers developed over a century of mechanized production—he analyzed the labor process into simple repeatable acts that were linked to a standard wage. Once each task was defined as a set of normative actions defined by Taylor, performed in a limited range of time, the knowledge of that task would no longer be the sole possession of any single worker in the factory.[18] In addition, instead of paying workers according to the total time they spent in the factory, Taylor proposed that they be paid a standard sum that had been assigned to each task. With a stopwatch for measuring the time required to perform each task, he collected data to establish the ranges by which to judge a worker's performance on a given task as faster or slower than normal. To give these observations functional power, faster work would be rewarded with higher wages, slower work with lower wages.[19] Taylor predicted that a broad implementation of this system would reveal enormous amounts of unused time: work that had been lost could now be made productive. Through equalization of labor tasks in both their value and allotted time, Taylor's updated piece-rate system would shift the way work was distributed in the factory from fixed positions in a hierarchy to a dynamic system in which every worker worked to a plan and was compensated on individual performance. This shift to measuring work and its compensation through normative units of time would not only potentially increase the total speed of production as desired but would also eliminate the threat of what was called "soldiering," working no more than was dictated by contract.

As the historian Daniel Nelson has shown, this form of task-based regulation was obviated by the power of the foreman.[20] Overseeing the production process as if it were a product of his imagination, a foreman usually resisted any challenge to his supervisory role. To erode a foreman's power, Taylor used the empirical data he collected about the production process to replace the foreman's rules of thumb with precisely defined instructions that fell into three general managerial categories: time-objects, speed-standards, and uniform policies.[21] Time-objects were encoded tasks made of simple actions, speed-standards were the norms assigned to those tasks, and uniform policies dictated the manner of pay. The complicated planning that resulted from this analytical division of work required a new administrative body. The forthright description of his system as a bureaucracy led Taylor to describe his reforms ironically as the introduction of "red tape" to the production process. To judge labor according to a predetermined set of normative criteria implied that the plant's regulation shifted from embodied "know-how" to the objectivity of data-based knowledge. In addition to representing the work process, the collection of numerical descriptions of the individual tasks allowed Taylor to integrate every possible contingency into his system of management. From errors in the production process to the "loss of men" due to economic downturns to accidents with injurious consequences, bureaucratic authority was formed around an objective translation of the owner's interest rather than the subjective considerations of a foreman.

In 1903, four years after moving from Midvale to the Bethlehem Steel Company and two years after his retirement, Taylor published the methods he used to replace the authority of the traditional foreman with the managerial agency of clerks. The essay, "Shop Management," described the disaggregation of the foreman's supervisory power into eight discrete functions, each assigned to a single clerk. Four circulated through the shop, and four were located in an office called a planning department. The clerks who supervised the workers and machines in the shop were a speed boss, a repair boss, an inspector, and a shop disciplinarian. As "executive managers," these men executed plans that had been outlined by the four clerks stationed inside the planning department, physically isolated within the site of production. Taylor explained that their isolation "merely concentrates the planning and much other brainwork in a few men especially fitted for their task and trained in their especial lines, instead of having it done, as heretofore, in most cases by high priced mechanics, well fitted to work at their trades, but poorly trained for work more or less clerical in its nature."[22] Replacing the approximations of overpaid mechanics whose skills were ill fitted for administrative tasks, the four clerical minds housed in the planning department were selected for their mental capacity to integrate a plan of an entire workday in the factory from the individual tasks that had been timed to a tenth of a second.[23]

Time allotments for individual tasks did not only apply to physical work; they also extended to the brainwork of the planning department. Taylor suggested that piece-rates could equally be used to organize and regularize the tasks of the clerks. Once clerical tasks would be governed by the same system that they were in charge of administering, the representation of their labor would be indistinguishable from the work directly involved in the production process.[24] What had once been described as a factory community, "a collective gathered for a common purpose," would become a matrix of tasks, including those executed by workers, machines, and managers, overlaid into a new unity.[25] The common purpose that motivated this unity could now be constantly redefined according to changes in market demand, technological developments, and owner involvement. The planning department took on what Taylor called "the functions of a clearing house" with up-to-date information on the activities of each worker at each machine at any given time in the shop as well as all the shifts in material costs and economic demand that occurred outside of the shop.[26] The bureaucratic authority of these clerks depended on forming an abstract map of all the tasks to be done, all those that had been fulfilled, and all the errors that had occurred and required attention. With this information, the planning department determined and constantly revised its plans, projecting a schedule of the near future and rarely repeating the activities according to a routine. Error was never excluded from Taylor's system; on the contrary, it was assumed in the system, a part of the labor process like any other.

The vast number of errors that lurked in the transmission of power through leather belts was Taylor's starting point in developing his managerial system. His acknowledgement, representation, and integration of error into the production process led to the extension of supervisory power over all the systems related to the factory's output. The clerical power in the planning department did not only coexist with but also derived from deviations in the physical labor of the factory. The relative independence given to the manager from the activities taking place on the shop floor gave him the distance he needed to produce an abstract representation of the labor process, in numerical form. This was much like the objective knowledge produced by a scientist about his subjects of study in a laboratory. The comparison of a manager to a scientist led Horace K. Hathaway, who had worked with Taylor at Bethlehem, to conclude that Taylor's system could be as powerful a tool for understanding machine shops as the scientific laboratory was for understanding nature. For Hathaway, the only difference between shop management and a laboratory apparatus was that the manager's observations took place directly in the shop, and their power was in their transportability. He claimed that without transporting the principles of management from one firm to the next, "they were of no more value than would be the principles of chemistry without a laboratory." The potential of the new system relied on measuring its effects in different factories. To apply the system, managerial instruments were designed to extend and refine Taylor's methods of data collection and analysis to a new set of standards that could be applied to a wide range of contexts and the mechanical operations that took place there.[27]

THE MATHEMATICS OF MANAGEMENT

Carl G. Barth, Taylor's main assistant at Bethlehem starting in 1899, developed compound slide rules to bring mathematical rigor to the processes of managing machinery in the shop. By their size and design, no larger than a foot in length, these instruments were essential to simplifying the clerical work of the planning department. Barth's training in mathematics, engineering, and mechanical drafting gave him the necessary background to recognize the potential value of slide rules to represent relationships

among various operations in the machine shop. Originally used for calculating complex arithmetical and trigonometric functions, slide rules in
Barth's hands could resolve complex multivariable calculations related to
machine maintenance and to maximizing their power and precision.[28] In
this regard, a predilection for visual thinking was crucial.[29]

Barth's attentiveness to graphic representation had led him to apply
analytical geometry to address a few unresolved problems in seventeenth-
century calculus.[30] In a short treatise that he never published, he described
his ambition to replace "the long-since discredited philosophy" of Gottfried
Leibniz with "a way of viewing the basic principles involved [in calcu-
lus] . . . in a graphic manner as an extension of analytical geometry."[31] The
insistence on transforming abstract mathematical problems into visual
representations was based on Barth's belief that calculation could be better understood when data were visualized in a curve or with the use of a
physical instrument. Similarly, slide rules shifted the process of calculation from the work of the mind to the intimate relationship between the
hand and the eye. With the simple manipulation of this physical instrument, a manager could quickly and accurately resolve all the variables to
determine the optimal power and speed of the machines used to build
metal tools.

To develop his first slide rule, Barth edited the data that Taylor had
collected in his experiments at Bethlehem with Maunsel White on cutting
so-called high-speed steel on a lathe.[32] Based on this preliminary analysis, he wrote an equation that related this data through three variables:
V, the cutting speed in feet per minute; F, the feed per revolution in inches;
and D, the depth of the cut in inches. After setting these three variables
onto the X, Y, and Z coordinates, he projected a doubly curved surface that
contained all the possible values from his equation, which approximated
Taylor and White's empirical data (Figure 4.2). He also plotted small circles
to show those original values deviated from his formula. This surface of
data became readily accessible in another visual form: a simple slide rule
in which two sets of givens could be fixed to determine the value of a third
variable (Figure 4.3).[33]

After a few years at Bethlehem, Barth returned to William Sellers and
Company of Philadelphia, where he had earlier worked as a draftsman.
This time, he worked in a more scientific capacity. He had three aims: to
repeat and refine Taylor's experiments in cutting steel, to improve the
exponential equation he had written based on the new data, and to make

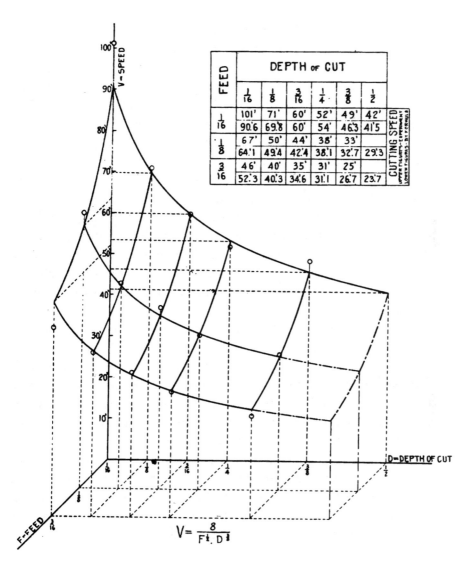

The table within the figure:

FEED	DEPTH OF CUT						CUTTING SPEED
	$\frac{1}{16}$	$\frac{1}{8}$	$\frac{3}{16}$	$\frac{1}{4}$	$\frac{3}{8}$	$\frac{1}{2}$	
$\frac{1}{16}$	101'	71'	60'	52'	49'	42'	UPPER FIGURES - EXPERIMENT
	90.6	69.8	60'	54'	46.3	41.5	
$\frac{1}{8}$	67'	50'	44'	38'	33'		
	64.1	49.4	42.4	38.1	32.7	29.3	
$\frac{3}{16}$	46'	40'	35'	31'	25'		LOWER FIGURES - BY FORMULA
	52.3	40.3	34.6	31.1	26.7	23.7	

$$V = \frac{8}{F^{\frac{1}{4}} \cdot D^{\frac{3}{8}}}$$

FIGURE 4.2. "Reproduction of original solid diagram showing relations between feed, depth of cut and speed." Carl G. Barth, "Supplement to Frederick W. Taylor's 'On the Art of Cutting Metals'—I," *Industrial Management: The Engineering Magazine* 58:3 (September 1919): 173.

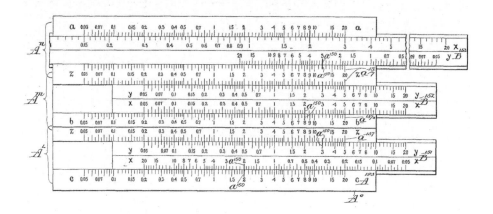

FIGURE 4.3. Patent drawing of Barth's slide rule for a lathe. The three sections, A^l A^m A^n, represent the three equations related to feed, depth of cut, and speed. Each slide, B^{151} B^{152} B^{153}, shows the solution to one variable in each of those equations. C. G. Barth, H. L. Gantt, and F. W. Taylor, Slide Rule, U.S. Patent 753,840 (issued March 8, 1904).

his slide rule more accurate to accommodate that data. He developed a new "empirical mathematical formula" that he believed would put metal cutting "on a strictly scientific basis."[34] In his view, holding together all the variables for determining the speed and feed of a lathe for cutting metal would exceed even the most adept mechanic's rules of thumb. Barth isolated twelve parameters in cutting metal on a lathe, not just the three as in his first slide rule, and he was able to represent eleven of them on a single new rule.[35] The instrument set each variable into relation with at least one other to find the points at which both were best satisfied. Once two were related, a third variable could be added, then a fourth, and so on. The slide rule, he explained, could identify a "speed-combination which [would] at the same time most nearly utilize all the pulling power of the lathe on the one hand, and the full cutting efficiency of the tools used on the other hand."[36]

Barth could also predict the approximate amount of time needed for a given operation on the lathe by using another set of "time slide rules" that he composed from disks that rotated around a pin. With this combination of instruments, he could set the piece-rates for all the tasks that would be needed to fabricate any metal part with a lathe. Wooden slides, pushed by his fingers through a "main frame," established relations between the

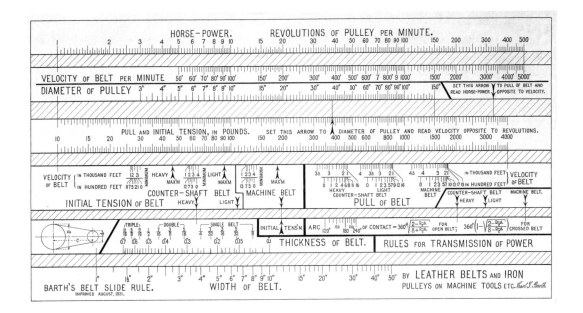

FIGURE 4.4. Carl G. Barth's Belt Slide Rule (Improved August, 1921). From Carl G. Barth Collection, Baker Library, Harvard Business School. The physical object, made of cherry wood, is located in Harvard's Collection of Historical Scientific Instruments. This representation is different from the one that was published in 1910, in which the instrument is shown in use as in the patent drawing in Figure 4.3. Here each strip is isolated above and below by a strip of hatch.

graduated ticks that were printed on either edge of paper strips that covered them. Not only would this slide rule make data available for a single machine, the same rule could be manipulated for use with other machines that were slightly different. A set of interchangeable slides could represent every lathe in the shop. If any machine needed to be altered according to shifts in the methods of production, the instrument that represented its function numerically could also be revised. With small alterations to his guiding equations, Barth continued to derive new sets of data that he translated into new sets of graduated ticks that were then printed onto new strips for slide rules used by the clerks who oversaw the machines in the shop: planers, gear cutters, boring machines, and others.

Beyond designing instruments to regulate machines, Barth also generalized Taylor's research on belts into another slide rule (Figure 4.4). This required systematizing and editing the data that had been collected at Midvale in Taylor's chart of belting errors. To relate each set of data to the next, Barth applied formulae that he derived from reading the ongoing work of engineers concerning the problem of power transmission. The process of translating Taylor's data mathematically into a set of ticks meant that he would need to derive new normative relations between the original empirical observations. The slide rule that resulted made it possible to calculate the material thickness of a belt as well as the diameter of a pulley by simply moving a set of slides through the frame. Horsepower could be just as quickly related to velocity as tension could be ascertained from measuring the diameter of a pulley.

The belt slide rule required a new kind of plot to visualize all the relations that Barth had calculated in a single diagram (Figure 4.5). Every vertical, horizontal, and diagonal line represented a unique relation among the variables. From the dimensions of the belt, its thickness and width, all the other variables could also be fixed: pull, horsepower, and speed in revolutions per minute. Just as he had done for the lathe, Barth translated the belting data three times: first into a set of equations, then into plots that made the data graphically visible in a diagram, and then finally onto the strips held together by a slide rule. By working on the belts in the factory, Barth's regulatory techniques expanded from their focus on individual machines to the infrastructure of transmission that connected the machines to the power source. Extending the mathematical regulation to a network of belts shows that a representational system based on data was flexible enough to incorporate the heterogeneous elements held in a factory building and establish the place of management at the head of a single internal system.

Collecting the variables of the production process in plots, diagrams, and slide rules translated the core elements of the production process— the machines below, the belting above, and the timing of manual tasks— into the neutral abstraction of numbers. Taylor's observations were collected to train a "specialist" on the methods for avoiding errors in belting, but a slide rule required only that a clerk learn how to use the instrument to start asserting managerial control over the entire system. Normalizing the tasks of brainwork with mathematics in this way established increasingly rigorous constraints on the tasks in the production process. With these constraints, new relationships could be formed by managers among machines, the men, and the planning department. Barth believed that this process had initiated the slow formulation of universal industrial standards that would guide industry into the future.

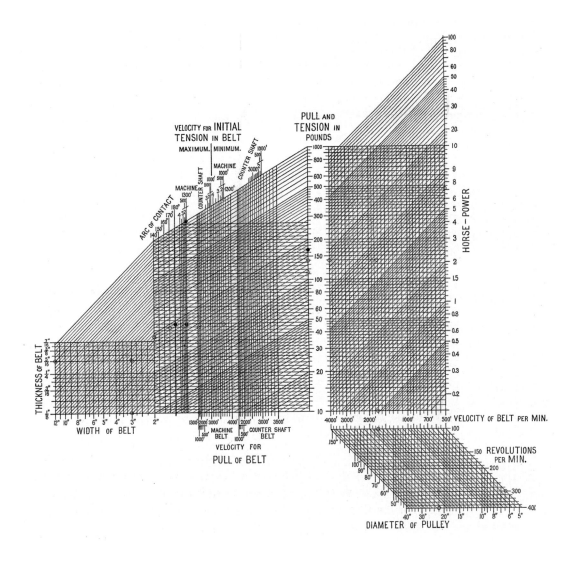

FIGURE 4.5. Carl G. Barth, "General Belting Diagram Incorporating the Author's Practice," *Transactions of the American Society of Mechanical Engineers* 31 (1910): plate 2.

The use of the term *standard* here requires clarification. Barth did not mean that standards were legal conventions that were set by an external agency. He viewed standards as a method for incremental development of an ideal that would be informed by the application of mathematical representations to the industrial labor process. The form of the machines, their individual parts, the methods of their use, even the instruments of their regulation would be under constant revision. Forming standards in the factory, he believed, would be the result of a collective effort by managers whose labor was the translation of real factories into abstract mathematical representations of industrial operations. In several publications, Barth illustrated his understanding of the process of standardization with a graph that showed steps rising under a curve that, over time, drew near to a horizontal asymptote (Figure 4.6). Each step along the curve represented a historical era of stability. With the passage of time, standards would accumulate force. Then, at some future moment, represented in the diagram as point 5, managerial standards would become so unified as to bring the curve to a plateau. If discrepancies in standards still existed after that, their differences would be so minor as to be negligible.[37]

With this progressive vision in mind, Barth imagined the possibility of bringing the machinery of every modern factory into what he called "musical harmony." The metaphor of music was central to his understanding of the unity that mathematical relations could bring to industrial production. Unlike Taylor's observational method of collecting data, the slide rule method translated actual machinery into an abstract numerical representation based on "empirical equations." Barth believed these would avoid the aggravation produced by managers "quarreling with men in the shop." The brainwork of management could be executed in isolation, or in Barth's words, "with God Almighty and a piece of paper and a pencil." Thus, with the aid of mathematical tools, a distance was established between the manager's representational work and the potential for real resistance at the site of production. While Taylor's tabulation of error operated at one level of abstraction from the reality of the factory, Barth's equations produced a greater distance that gave him the capacity to collect the work of machines, belts, and men into a set of interrelated equations. He spoke of a point at which "every machine tool in a machine shop is adjusted to certain musical chords, and they should be together, so that there is harmony. I do not mean that the physical noise is going to be less, but . . . there will be more or less music and everything running in harmony."[38] Barth

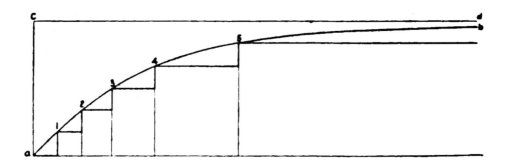

FIGURE 4.6. "Continuous vs. Step-by-Step Development." Carl G. Barth, "Standardization of Machine Tools." *Transactions of the American Society of Mechanical Engineers* 38 (1917): 896.

sought to produce something akin to music in regulating the differences among methods of industrial production; empirically derived equations set error-ridden machines into a unified system of order.

Barth later ventured to translate musical harmonies into a mathematical formula, also by means of a slide rule that related various scales and chords. Reversing the metaphorical relationship that he used to describe management through music, he subjected music to the same logic he used to organize the factory. To simplify the transposition of music from one key to another, Barth visualized the natural order of harmonic proportions with the tools he developed for machines and belting.[39] To Barth's mind, the process of industrial production resembled musical composition. In both music and the factory there was an explicit relationship of form to the passage of time. While the possibilities of producing new musical harmonies were infinite, their basis in mathematical proportions had already become a model of a universal system of composition. Barth's vision of harmonizing the mechanical elements in the factory sought to borrow music's universality to put industry on a similar ground. The standardization of modern industry, he believed, would be complete "when every drill press will be speeded just so, and every planer, every lathe, the world over, will be harmonized, just as musical pitches are the same all over the world."[40] By tuning all the organs of industry, the mathematics of management would guide them into a new form of modern order. In Barth's vision, management served as a global regulator, a universal brain that coordinated the rules of an intricate mechanical system to define and control differences into a stable industrial unity.

DIAGRAMS OF BRAINWORK

In 1905 James Mapes Dodge, the president of the Link-Belt Engineering Company, employed Barth at Taylor's suggestion.[41] Dodge invited Barth to apply his "Slide Rule System" to the company's shop in Philadelphia, where large-scale conveyors and hoists were being designed and fabricated. In the 1870s and 1880s Dodge had developed what he called "silent chain drives," an intricate assembly of pins and links used to move heavy industrial materials. The chains also took the place of leather belts for machinery located in the open, transferring power from a central source to cranes, for instance running through sheer trusses to load coal. The high-strength steel from which they were made helped them resist corrosion. Taylor and White had originally developed the steel alloy at Bethlehem in 1898. Beyond its stability in wet environments, it was also easier to cut in the shop and could carry heavier loads in the field.[42] Although Dodge used this experimental steel, he did not institute Taylor's system for organizing work in the shop until he decided to hire Barth. In handing over the management of the Link-Belt shop, Dodge expanded the distance between his executive power and the knowledge that guided the technology of the production process.

On his arrival, Barth observed that all the parts of the conveyor systems were drawn in a drafting room outside the machine shop. These drawings were then sent by elevator to a blueprint department above the shop to be reproduced and distributed to foremen who oversaw the conveyor's fabrication and assembly. The drawings did not indicate how the parts would be fabricated. All decisions about the process of making each part in the assembly were left to the foremen. Any task assigned to a worker was based on the foreman's understanding of the work to be done and his sense of the time required for its completion. Soon after arriving, Barth established a planning department on the floor with the machine shop to centralize the managerial tasks that were previously entrusted to the foremen. He believed that clerks needed to be close to the shop to receive up-to-date information on its activities.[43]

A chart published in 1909 by C. Willis Adams, the assistant superintendent of the Link-Belt operation, illustrated the planning department's effect on the production process (Figure 4.7).[44] Instead of allowing

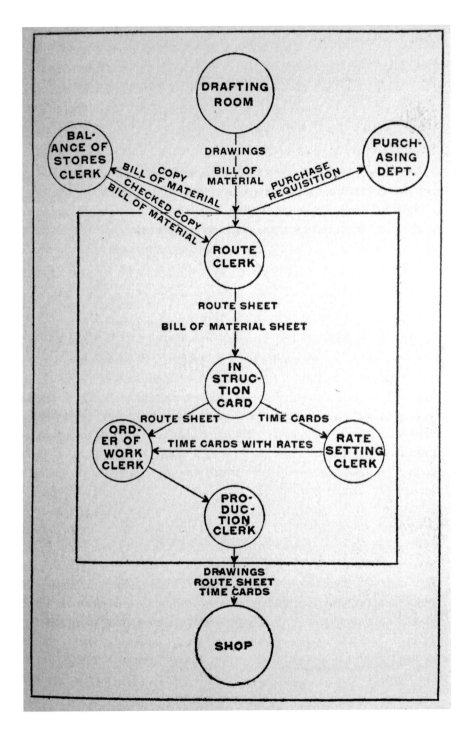

FIGURE 4.7. Chart showing how orders were handled through a planning department based on the operations of the Link-Belt Company factory in Philadelphia. C. Willis Adams, "How a Planning Department Works," in *How Scientific Management Is Applied* (Chicago: The System Company, 1911), 75.

drawings to be sent directly from the drafting room to the shop, managers mediated that process to displace the power of the foreman. Following Taylor's suggestion from "Shop Management," the clerks would plan the day's activities by breaking the total work down to individual tasks of roughly equal time allotments. At Link-Belt, the planning department was composed of clerks for routing, preparing instruction cards, setting piece-rates, and overseeing production; these jobs were assigned to each clerk based on his skills. Adams's chart translated their interrelations into a few circles connected by arrows inside rectangular boxes.

The chart conveyed neither the scale of the room occupied by the planning department nor its location in the factory. Instead, it diagrammatically connected the processes of brainwork with arrows that traced the flow of data held on documents as they moved from one clerk to the next. While the total labor of the factory was held in the larger rectangle that bound the diagram together, the smaller rectangle within it represented only the operations of the clerks in the planning department. After receiving drawings and bills of materials—listing the needed elements for each part's fabrication—from the drafting room, clerks would initiate operations to order and time the day's tasks in the shop. The routing clerk produced route sheets to schedule the development of each part from one machine to the next. An instruction card clerk analyzed the tasks at each machine into discrete movements and assigned the necessary tools. Piece-rates, set by the rate-setting clerk, were calculated and added to those instruction cards. The order-of-work clerk, using the information produced by his colleagues, determined the correct placement of each timed task onto each machine and its order of precedence. Finally, the translation of this clerical labor into physical labor was the job of the production clerk, who made sure that the product was finished and delivered on the date specified by the sales department.[45]

Unlike the image of an early nineteenth-century power loom factory, Adams's chart did not realistically illustrate the physical organization of the machine shop through the projection of linear perspective taken at eye level in the space. His drawing also escaped the notational systems found in architectural plans. The abstraction of equal-sized circles in the planning department represented the roughly equal-sized clerical tasks and their sequence. The space between the circles was determined arbitrarily, according to their placement in the rectangle. Without recourse to perspective or orthographic drawing conventions, the chart produced a non-spatial representation that operated as a virtual map by which brainwork could be visualized. Like the perceptual work of the brain, the diagrammatic arrangement of the circles revealed that the role of brainwork was to translate the day's activities in the shop through the fundamental perceptual categories of space and time. Work was positioned spatially in a map with "routes" and temporally with "rates." The instruction cards drawn in the planning department, in turn, articulated every step in an individual task from start to finish, mathematically organizing the order of each component in a task according to a decimal-based time allotment.[46] These were literally time maps that guided workers through each step in the process of fabricating a single part. The instruction cards brought together a series of planned tasks into timed routes that traversed the factory floor. Each part thereby passed from worker to worker, machine to machine, in a predetermined order, with a predetermined time allotment, and was finally added to the total assembly.

Barth spent over four years instituting this system at Link-Belt during which time he was also sending his techniques to other locations under the guidance of his assistants.[47] He trained H. K. Hathaway for several months before transferring him from Link-Belt to the Tabor Manufacturing Company, fabricators of molding machinery. When Hathaway arrived at the Tabor shop he found that it was poorly organized and losing money. His first improvements were to strengthen the machines and to construct new and better-organized tool rooms that held well-maintained sets of state-of-the-art tools. Then he added a planning department much like that established at Link-Belt. Using Barth's patented slide rules for regulating the machines and the belting in the Tabor shop, Hathaway soon stabilized the production process and eventually led the firm to produce sizable profits. The shop became one of the best-known examples of Taylor's system in action.[48]

In a photograph of the planning department at Tabor, taken around 1915, Hathaway numbered each clerk's desk (Figure 4.8). He explained: "The desks are numbered to indicate the route of the manufacturing order and the time cards accruing from it. Authority to issue an order is first received by the Production Clerk at Desk #1."[49] The image shows the production clerk standing with his back turned to the camera, off center, handing paperwork to his left, to the "Order Clerk" seated at desk #2 typing. The operations of the planning department traversed a circuit, a path that Hathaway called a "route" like those he described along the shop floor just

FIGURE 4.8. "A general view of the Planning Department at work in the Tabor Manufacturing Co., Tool Builders, Philadelphia." H. K. Hathaway, "On the Technique of Manufacturing." *Annals of the American Academy of Political and Social Science* 85 (September 1919).

beyond the wall. The shop was located on the other side of the window where the "recording clerk" stood who communicated the plans to clerks on the other side. Paperwork constantly moved around the room to anticipate the next step in the shop, and each unit of work was finalized when it arrived at "Desk #15," occupied by the "Costkeeper," seated farthest to the right in the photograph. The comparison of the planning department to the shop was an extension of his comparison of the whole operation of manufacture to that of a well-regulated machine. Hathaway wrote: "a complete system of management with all of the elements coordinated" would function "as in a well built machine."[50] Now Barth's metaphor of harmony could be applied to the bureaucracy of the planning department, as it, too, had become organized according to the same methods as the machinery in the shop. The unity of the clerks' mental labor was another machine made of increasingly regulated elements that needed to be tuned according to the force of time-based thinking. By the clerks' collective labor, the geometrical descriptions of parts drawn in the drafting room would be translated into processes made of small increments of time, accumulated into a route, along which the part would move as it traversed the factory floor.[51]

This bureaucratic work was made effective by another representational instrument, the bulletin board, visible in the rear of Hathaway's photograph of the Tabor planning department, manned by the "shop order of work clerk" and given the number 12. This was a tool for visual scheduling used by the clerks in the planning department as well as those clerks who circulated through the shop. All the tasks of a day had been timed and ordered into routes that were displayed in a code on two boards, one that hung on a wall facing the clerks who planned the day's work and the other facing the shop.[52] The bulletin board was an interface, a mode of communication, by which the planning department disseminated and constantly updated the plan being developed for a workday. Each column on the board represented the schedule for the work to be executed on one machine on that day. Work tickets were hung on hooks in the order that they would be performed, and upon their completion, they would be resubmitted to the planning department.

In large plants such as the Watertown Arsenal, where Barth began working in 1908, broad classifications of the production process distinguished different types of labor into distinct domains.[53] The variety of functions at the Arsenal required more clerks to work in the planning department than the fifteen that Hathaway enumerated in the photograph of the Tabor department or the four clerks depicted by Adams in his chart of the Link-Belt department. As Barth's bureaucratic machinery expanded, the bulletin board became more complex in its organization, conveying the massive amounts of information produced in the planning department as it flowed out to organize the activities on the shop floor.

Barth had several photographs made of the planning room at the Arsenal that pictured the clerks and their instruments (Figure 4.9 and Frontispiece). In one, the production clerk stands beside a piece of furniture that looks like a card catalog; this was the bulletin board devised by the Watertown clerks. The data-driven representation of production was contained into such physical assemblies, each of which was organized according to a system that could give order to the tasks in the shop. To hold all the work tickets produced by the department, the clerks employed a shelf of terraced boxes rather than rows of hooks for this bulletin board. Capital letters were painted on small panels that hung above the shelves to signify each department in the Arsenal: DB for the Blacksmith and Forge Department, DE for the Erecting Department, DM for the Machine Shop Department, etc. Each machine in its department was identified with one box in the racks. Instead of drawing a plan to indicate a machine's physical location, the clerks used this mnemonic system that combined letters and numbers to identify each machine. For example, C was used for gear cutters, D for drill presses, and a number ordered the machines from largest to smallest. The largest lathe would be designated L1 and the eighth largest boring mill was B8. To add a new task to a machine, a new work ticket would be written and labeled according to the assigned machine and its respective department. The same ticket would also include an estimated piece-rate, and the card would be placed at the back of the stack of other work tickets.

The board thus collected the plans for a working day in a coded system that assembled all the tasks to be performed on every machine in every department at the Arsenal in one place. Just as the chart of the Link-Belt planning department remained abstract and without reference to scale, the bulletin board offered no spatial description of the flow of work. The extraction of tasks from their physical location in the shop was necessary to ensure that the organization of the factory would follow a map of time rather than space. Using the bulletin board, the clerks could connect neatly one timed task to the next instead of resolving the impossible problem of visualizing the flow of tasks as an image of multiple overlapping movements that traversed the shop floor over the course of the day.[54]

FIGURE 4.9. The planning department in the Watertown Arsenal. The Production Clerk stands writing a note while a Gang Boss is captured in the window to the machine shop. Carl G. Barth Collection, Baker Library, Harvard Business School.

The horizontal surface of the shop, reconfigured by the logic of Barth's bulletin board, was made both vertical and abstract. As a card catalog, its forthright bureaucratic form allowed the distribution of tasks to be flexible and perpetually open to manipulation. Thus, the instrument could manage such contingencies as a fluctuation in a material's price or availability, an unexpected change in the design of the final assembly, the sudden initiation of a new job, and most usually, the constant accumulation of errors. To keep the bulletin board up-to-date required translating information gathered regarding the pace of work that took place in the shop into the finished work tickets that were extracted from each box. As Barth had originally noted, the proximity of management to the machines was essential for synchronizing the administration of production with the activities in the shop. The same photograph of the production clerk shows an exchange of information at the window between the planning department and the shop. The clerk hands new work tickets to a "gang boss" that will be added to the flow of work through the shop while the same window would, at other times, allow other gang bosses continuously to alert the clerks inside on the progress of the planned work for the day.[55] The separation ensured the abstraction of the plan from the actual physical work, but the window in the wall remained open to let information flow in both directions. New data allowed the planning department to reorganize the order of tasks, to add new tasks to the schedule, and to distribute them to the shop at the appropriate moment.

C. Willis Adams drew another chart in 1910 to describe the relationships among the planning department's so-called functional foremen and the gang bosses who circulated through the shop at Link-Belt (Figure 4.10). This drawing, like the diagram of the planning department's "interior," does not show actual spaces at the Link-Belt plant. Instead, smaller circles represent the various managerial operations in the plant. The smallest circles at the center of the chart represent the gang bosses, each of whom has been assigned to four of the five foremen. These were identified with slightly larger circles to the left of the gang bosses, drawn with double lines to mark them as extensions of the planning department, which was represented by the largest circle in the chart. The form of the notations produces a clear direction of movement: managerial power moves from left to right, from the concentrated power of the superintendent to the planning department to the foremen and finally to the gang bosses. The literal movement of the gang bosses in the shop, reduced to horizontal

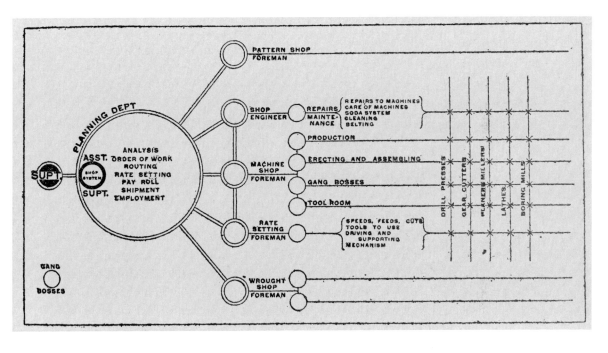

FIGURE 4.10. C. Willis Adams, "How a Planning Department Works," in *How Scientific Management Is Applied* (New York: The System Company, 1911), 79. A slightly altered version of this chart was published by Wilfred Lewis of the Tabor Manufacturing Company in his essay "Running Work by the New Rules." *Factory: The Magazine of Management* 7 (September 1911): 149.

lines, allows us to see the intersection of their encounter with the different types of machines in the shop. In fact, they intersected vertical lines, each labeled as a type of machine: drill presses, gear cutters, lathes, and boring mills. As horizontal lines of moving clerks intersected with the vertical lines of stationary machines, a conceptual image of managerial control was formed into a grid. The image produced of the power loom factory, from the 1830s, relied on gridded perspective lines that represented real beams, real shafts, real pulleys, and real leather belts. By contrast, the lines of Adams's diagram produced an abstract grid of managerial authority, notations that referred to no real object. The graphic simplicity of these notations visualized Barth's belief that management formed a harmonic order that guided and organized the processes of industrial labor.[56]

SABOTAGE: THE PRODUCTION OF THE NONPRODUCER

Despite the diagrams that represented a unified order of brainwork applied to industry, the adoption of Taylor's system in many factories was deeply contested. Hugh Aitken, in his seminal study of scientific management at the Watertown Arsenal, described a confrontation between Carl Barth and the head of the Arsenal, Colonel Charles B. Wheeler. The colonel opposed Barth's proposals for managing the production at the Arsenal because he felt that the shop could be more efficiently run without the addition of so many clerical workers that he called "nonproducers." Barth responded by contesting Wheeler's definition of the term *efficiency*. Rather than accept the view that efficient production was based on maximizing the amount of manual labor while minimizing the amount of management, he proposed an alternative ratio of total cost of the operation to a unit of output.[57] Barth's new ratio erased the distinction between physical work and brainwork to redefine efficiency as evaluating production as a function of minimized cost. Convinced of Barth's argument, Wheeler cautiously allowed him to proceed with his plans for integrating Taylor's system into the production process at the Arsenal in 1908. But over the next few years resistance heightened to the new system among the machinists, and in 1911 disagreements between workers and managers precipitated a strike.

Already in 1910, violent outbreaks of worker resistance in other factories had led to the establishment of a congressional Commission on Industrial Relations.[58] As a government industry run by the Ordnance Department, the Arsenal events proved to be particularly worrisome to both the union representatives and the politicians on the commission. Thus, central to the hearings, held in 1912, was the effect that the Taylor system was producing on the conditions of labor in the nation's machine shops. Taylor and his assistants, including Barth, were asked to participate in hearings to help identify the techniques that aroused the main opposition from the machinists.[59]

Representing the American Federation of Labor on the commission, James O'Connell returned to Wheeler's original concern over the high proportion of so-called nonproducers that had been added to the labor process at the Watertown Arsenal. When he posed the question to Barth, now a year after the strike, the issue no longer turned on the definition of efficiency. Instead, Barth immediately objected to O'Connell's devaluation of the clerical work of the planning department in relation to the physical work of the machine shop. He insisted that the brainwork of management had to be understood as work. "We haven't any non-producers," he protested; "I will not admit that for one second. We have direct and indirect workers. When I sit in my office, doing all kinds of things, I am working in [my own] way, and I am working like hell from morning to night too. . . . You want to forget this idea about producer and non-producer."[60] Beneath the obvious differences between direct and indirect labor, Barth believed, there was a more significant similarity: the relation of ownership to the managerial bureaucracy could not be financially distinguished from its relation to the direct labor in the shop. Managers and workers were both paid according to the tasks they performed based on normalized piece-rates. To Barth's mind, it would be essential to the future of industrial production that the indirect laborer—the manager—be recognized for his work in producing the order that governed the daily operations of the nation's industry. Despite the obvious hierarchy of power, it was crucial to the idea of a science of production that managers identify brainwork with physical labor.

Although Barth did not accept that the clerks in the planning department should be called nonproducers, the tools that were made available by brainwork were plainly applied by private industry to pursue the interests of investors who were fully removed from the production process. Thorstein Veblen wrote about the value of scientific management in the financial context of corporate industry in his book *The Engineers and the Price System* (1919). He explained that the relative scarcity of commodities and high cost of living in the United States after the First World War resulted from a "price system" that had been established at the end of the nineteenth century. The system relied on the managerial methods that controlled the rate and volume of production to maximize the profit margin for investors in industry. For Veblen, the price system was a form of sabotage. While he admitted that the term *sabotage* usually referred to the violent obstruction of production by workers—it was derived from "sabot," a wooden shoe that workers throw into machines—he believed that the same expression could be applied to the effect that the price system was exerting on the nation's productivity and general well-being. Raising prices when it was possible to charge more or lowering the cost of production by reducing the cost of labor, he explained, positioned the decisions of investors against the full productive capacity of industry. Quoting the definition of sabotage from the International Workers of the World as "the conscientious withdrawal of efficiency," Veblen explained that an arrangement by which managers acted on their interests of financial gain would always result in the manipulation of the factory against its maximum efficiency. A strike was simply an instance in which workers used a different set of tools to operate against full industrial capacity to achieve other purposes from those that motivated the price system. Both workers and investors participated in their own acts of sabotage.[61]

Yet a significant distinction between strategic acts of sabotage planned by workers and those executed on behalf of the captains of industry was that the price system that guided the latter had become, by 1919, an increasingly generalized financial imperative. Once the expansion of industrial production exceeded the expansion of demand, "the conscious withdrawal of efficiency" was the primary regulatory instrument for investors to defend against the possibility of overproduction that put their profit at risk. As Veblen explained: "The rate and volume of output have to be regulated with a view to what the traffic will bear—that is to say, what will yield the largest net return in terms of price to the business men who manage the country's industrial system."[62] The capacity to set the quantity of industrial output with the tools of managerial control had become a necessary aspect of the regulation of prices to guarantee stable profits. Barth's seemingly anodyne comparison of his standards for machines to musical harmony was clearly not an end in itself but part of a system that concentrated more control over the rate and volume of output in the hands of corporate investors. The best example of this was the consolidation of the steel industry that resulted in what Veblen characterized as "the stabilization of prices at a reasonably high level, such as would always assure reasonably large earning on the increased capitalization."[63]

Along with the concentration of authority over output in fewer hands, corporate finance was also gradually becoming interlocked through a unified system of credit. As American industries grew larger, they relied increasingly on a steady stream of investment. This was a central concern for the writers of the Federal Reserve Act of 1913. With this legislation, the financiers of the nation's industry sought to ensure that the banking system—which Veblen called a "syndicate of financial houses"—would be as methodically administered as well-managed factories.[64] The combination of centralized governance of industrial production on the one hand and credit on the other led Veblen to propose that the price system could still be corrected. Planning industrial production, he believed, should be left entirely in the hands of technologists like Barth, just as regulating the nation's credit should be managed by bureaucrats at the Federal Reserve Bank. Neither party, he observed, acted on its own selfish financial motives. They both sought to regularize output in relation to economic demand. Veblen's critique of financial greed among the captains of industry thereby doubled as an odd embrace of the bureaucratic order that promised to produce a universe of mechanical harmony. Veblen promoted the vision of a centrally managed industrial society that extended the power of regulation from the machines of production to the price and availability of commodities and finally to the system of finance and credit. Like Edward Bellamy's imagined socialist utopia, the inputs and outputs of modern production would be integrated into the expanded bureaucratic authority of brainwork.[65]

A drawing made by Barth around 1908 can be interpreted in light of Veblen's analysis (Figure 4.11). As the "First Comprehensive Diagram of a Taylor System Organization," it described the full extent of the managerial operation at the Smith and Furbush Machine Company in Philadelphia, makers of machines for textile manufacture. Like the diagram of shop management at Link-Belt, in which the clerical work of the planning department was related to the machines in the form of a grid, the right side of Barth's comprehensive diagram also showed a grid of managed machines. Yet, unlike the earlier diagrams, Barth included extensive information that described the functions of management beyond the shop, specifically as they related to dynamic shifts in the market. Overlapping lines connected departments that oversaw shipping, accounting, purchasing, and sales.

FIGURE 4.11. "First Comprehensive Diagram of a Taylor System Organization, about 1908. The Smith & Furbush Machine Co., as originally planned to meet its peculiar relation between the manager and the treasurer." There is a note at the bottom left, written by Carl Barth's son, J. Christian Barth, to explain that this is a photographic reproduction of the original drawing, drawn by his father on "manilla drafting paper." Carl G. Barth Collection, Baker Library, Harvard Business School.

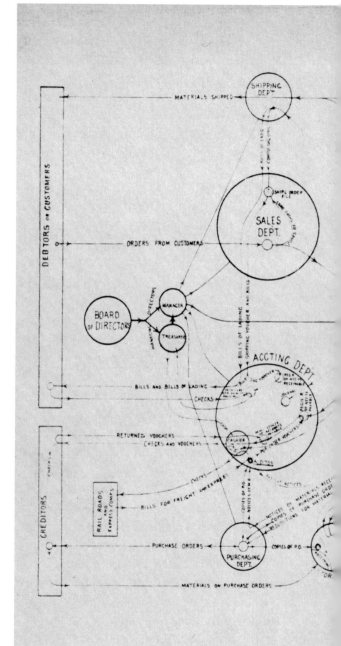

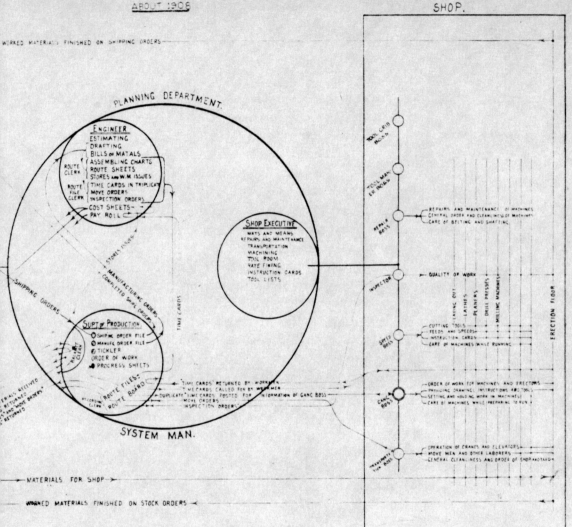

FIRST COMPREHENSIVE DIAGRAM OF A
TAYLOR SYSTEM ORGANIZATION
ABOUT 1906

THE SMITH & FURBUSH MACHINE CO., AS ORIGINALLY PLANNED
TO MEET ITS PECULIAR RELATION BETWEEN THE MANAGER AND THE TREASURER

Within each of these managerial nodes, Barth drew smaller circles that signified their discrete functions. From these circles, arrows traced the movement of paperwork from one set of clerks to another. As a whole, the diagram represented the transmission of decisions from a board of directors, a manager, and a treasurer to the rest of the company. The circular figures that represented these executive positions were located just to the right of boxes that framed creditors and debtors, that is, the two functions of capitalist investment and return. In the whirlwind of paperwork made visible by the diagram, Veblen's price system became the ground upon which these figures operated. As a message from the market moved from left to right, it was translated into a plan for setting the daily rate and volume of machine shop production. On the left, the diagram visualized the process by which a potential profit margin was calculated; on the right a corresponding quantity of output was produced to be sold at a set price. As management formed the infrastructure to transmit economic data from the market to the shop, it resolved what Barth called the "peculiar relation between the manager and the treasurer."

What is clear from Barth's diagram is that managers did not produce time-based representations of the factory to bring machine production into harmony with itself; they regulated production on behalf of a syndicate of investors and their representatives on a board of directors. Tabulations of data, instruments of mathematical calculation, and diagrammatic drawings produced a representation of the factory that could respond to the economic context and, under careful guidance, produce a profit even in an unstable market. Barth's metaphor of musical harmony idealized the role of management in the factory as a method for refining machinery and labor into a harmonious autonomous unity. Yet when he drew a more comprehensive diagram of management, the planning department visibly operated at the service of another system, regulating production to a financial context that was becoming, in Veblen's words, "a self-balanced whole, closed and unbreakable, self-insured against all risk and derangement."[66] Barth's notion of harmony was, ultimately, the harmony of one system nested inside another: industry was regulated as a function of finance. Managerial instruments were the tools that moved between these systems, between the factory and the market. The diagrams that made the regulation of industrial labor visible did not represent the atmosphere produced by toil, did not index moments of resistance, and did not portray the qualities of the space in a factory. Rather, these palpable attributes of modern industry were removed from the numerical partitioning of tasks into units of time, from the empirical formulas set onto slide rules, and from the flexible schedules organized in bulletin boards. The instruments of brainwork produced abstract representations of objects of modern industry as a system of dynamic relationships that could be regulated.

The production of the nonproducer was a particular kind of paperwork, one that contained an image and logic of flow and continuity but also the capacity to restrict the process of production. Translating this bureaucratic system into other domains of labor helped extend the techniques of regulation from industry to professions housed in offices, including the organization of large architectural practices.

CHAPTER 5

Regulation through Paperwork in Architectural Practice

In forming a modernist visual language, architects appropriated instruments of management used for industrial regulation such as diagrammatic drawings and mass-produced office furniture. Hyungmin Pai has written about the translation of managerial diagrams into representational methods for articulating so-called functional design in American architectural discourse around the 1920s and 1930s. Pai's history traces the turn toward diagrams to a shift in the profession during and after World War I, a time in which leaders of the American Institute of Architects were responding to the new organizational structure of real estate development and the building industry.[1] Yet even earlier, at the beginning of the twentieth century, an increasing number of technical, legal, and business motives had already entered architects' workplaces with the needs of clients, altering the forms of architectural labor. Pragmatic concerns—schedules, budgets, market conditions, and governmental regulations—brought the methodical intricacy of the American corporate business and the visible hand of management into the daily routines of large-scale practices.

With the expansion of their professional services, several firms employed methods used in production control to administer their offices. Some employed systems explicitly based on Taylor's methods for regulating industrial labor. These organizational systems describe a set of bureaucratic techniques that can be paired alongside the now-canonical images of modernism, such as photographs of factories and grain elevators.[2] In the years leading into the adaptation of these more articulate office management systems, some architects had already begun to reorient their office culture to meet the expectations of their corporate clients. Louis Sullivan recalled that Daniel Burnham was the first architect in Chicago to recognize and apply corporate values to his office's organization. Burnham's mental disposition, Sullivan believed, enabled him to produce a model of architectural practice congenial to the character of these integrated businesses—their "tendency toward bigness, organization, delegation and intense commercialism." As Thomas Hines's extensive study of this large Chicago office has shown, Burnham's ability to relate to executives who managed these complicated operations, combined with the methods he developed for office administration, brought his firm into alignment with the organizational structure of the corporate economy.[3]

Following Burnham, many of the larger modern architectural practices soon joined the general trend among clerical professions to employ managerial methods to organize their labor. These professions included sales, advertising, and accounting among other administrative services that would come to be called "white collar" work, largely based in offices. In this transformation of office dynamics, the processes of architectural production were redefined in professional journals in similar ways to those described in the journals of other professional societies such as the *Journal of Accountancy* or the *Journal of Marketing*. From these specialized discussions, it is clear that one result was that an architect's direct involvement in the execution of a design gave way to a more specialized task-based design process, for example, and the number of staff employed in non-design-related areas greatly increased. Given this reorientation, many statements that structured the incipient modernist discourse—the emphasis on function, efficiency, and the idealization of mechanical forms—can be situated in the context of a profession that increasingly performed a distinct type of paperwork; the clerical labor of regulation began to occupy a significant portion of an architectural office's daily activity.

Early twentieth-century architectural practices differed in their efforts to professionalize from those in the early nineteenth century. For architects of the earlier era, integrating architectural work into the prevailing economic order would have been a less immediate concern than simply getting paid for one's services. The few architectural professionals who worked in the United States at that time had been trained in Europe and viewed their labor through a model of practice formulated in fine arts academies. Given the absence of similar institutions in the American context, as Dell Upton and Mary Woods have shown, an antebellum generation of architects worked hard to secure the social status of architecture among other professions. Most architects' efforts were focused on assigning value to design as an intellectual commodity that they produced, so that it could be distinguished from the commodity of a physical building. Their techniques included assigning contractual power to drawings, producing publications such as pattern books and trade journals, initiating professional societies and schools, standardizing fees, and creating legal instruments such as licensure to establish their expertise.[4]

To organize a large architectural office like Burnham's required more than updating European gentlemanly practice with markers of modern professional status. Beyond distinguishing an architect's intellectual labor from the physical labor of a builder, the administration of large offices required certain kinds of business skills. In the opinion of Julius F. Harder of New York, a partner in the firm Israels and Harder, the traditional notion of an architect-as-artist represented a model of practice that would only produce continued poverty and social marginalization. Harder claimed that the very association of architecture with the fine arts had introduced a dangerous and misleading mystique regarding the labor that actually took place in architectural offices. Not only was this harmful to the social perception of the profession; it also devalued the labor of architects when it was compared to the more clearly defined tasks of businessmen and other professionals. Architects were not "befogged dreamers" he observed; "they are in reality fully as keen and of as large capacity in the business of money getting as any other constituency in American affairs."[5] To interface with a class of business clients, the twentieth-century architectural professional needed to extend his knowledge beyond the art of architecture and learn to conduct business with the administrative skills of a corporate executive.

Harder was also critical of architecture schools that patterned their pedagogy on European precedents. Prioritizing the study of historical architecture and the craft of drawing, he argued, was not appropriate for an economic context shaped by large business enterprises. Harder found schools to be at best "a limited imitation of real life," an isolated context in which true lessons of architectural practice could not be learned. Vaunting the value of experience, Harder recommended that future architects enter the profession as soon as possible to concentrate on the accumulation of practical knowledge rather than the theoretical knowledge offered in schools.[6] Many American architects who anticipated the growing influence of business held the same view: that corporations would soon change the character of professional training. Some students also shifted the focus of their studies toward more practical concerns. The thesis of Cyrus Foss Springall, for example, a student in the graduating class of 1912 at the Massachusetts Institute of Technology, was the design not of a building but of a system for the "business administration" of a hypothetical architectural office.[7] Generally, theses of students trained in the beaux-arts classical style included expertly rendered drawings of modern institutions such as libraries, banks, and train stations. Springall's predominantly written thesis, by contrast, included one diagrammatic plan of a generic architectural office interior (Figure 5.1). Certainly, when compared to the artful watercolors produced by his classmates, his modest drawing lacked aesthetic appeal, since it was nothing more than a straightforward subdivision of office space into functional rooms.

Yet the plan shows that Springall's approach to subdividing the space was an extension of his interest in reorganizing the labor of the modern architectural office. He labeled it in two different ways: either with a room's function—"Entrance Lobby," "Library," "Reception Room," "Drafting Room"—or with the name of a generic occupant: "Mr. Bolt," "Mr. Credit," and "Mr. Color," the partners of the hypothetical firm. Each name represented one of the three Vitruvian architectural virtues: firmness, commodity, and delight. In the plan, he placed business expert Mr. Credit close to the reception room to receive clients, hid technical Mr. Bolt in the smallest office in the space beyond an anteroom, and allocated artistic Mr. Color in a well-lit corner office buffered from the public areas by a busy clerical staff. Of the twenty employees in the firm, Springall projected that ten would be common draftsmen. One additional man, Mr. Color's assistant, would manage the drafting room, the filing clerk, and the "office boys." This was the supervising architect, the equivalent of a superintendent or factory foreman. Other expert positions included a designer, a detailer, an inspector, an engineer, and a specifications writer. Each man would answer to one or another partner, depending upon the latter's set of skills.[8]

The collective labor of an architectural office, Springall speculated, was like that of an industrial plant and could be managed with a similar system of instruments—requisition slips, time cards, cost books, etc.—that he derived from reading Frederick Winslow Taylor's *Principles*. "The principles of scientific management" wrote Springall, "[have] made little headway in the professions and particularly the architectural profession. Some objection to the introduction of systematic methods may be urged with the excuse that architecture is essentially a fine art and to handle it

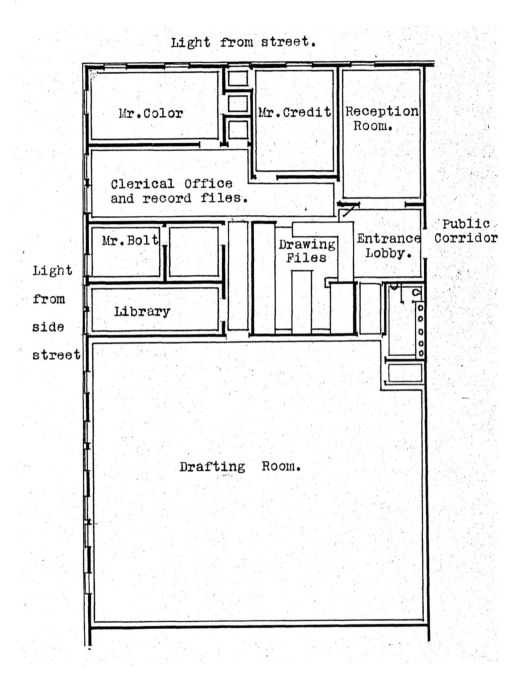

Light from street.

Mr.Color

Mr.Credit

Reception Room.

Clerical Office and record files.

Mr.Bolt

Drawing Files

Entrance Lobby.

Public Corridor

Light from side street

Library

C

Drafting Room.

FIGURE 5.1. "Suggested Arrangement for an Architectural Office." Cyrus Foss Springall. "The Business Organization of an Architectural Office" (BS thesis, Massachusetts Institute of Technology, Department of Architecture, 1912).

as a factory would be handled would lower the aesthetic viewpoint and the distaste for prosaic detail would handicap an artistic man and conflict with his best work."[9] Springall understood that the architect-cum-businessman, as sketched out by Harder, would produce a tension in professional practice between the aesthetic and monetary notions of value, but he saw no need to compromise one for the other. The architect, he pointed out, "is in the business of selling his technical skill and knowledge."[10] Compared to early American professionals, who simply sought to distance the status of an architect from that of a builder by assigning value to the labor of design, Springall realized that the value of this labor was not fixed. Instead, it would depend upon the capacity of an architect to sell his labor as a service in the corporate-led marketplace by making a commodity of his "skill and knowledge." Defining the product of an architectural office as a set of integrated services—from design to construction administration—was a critical starting point for scientifically managing the labor in a firm. The tasks of an architectural office were not related to the machines of industry but to the tools of mechanical drawing, structural and budgetary calculations, and paperwork. In the context of the architect's practice, Springall translated Taylor's planning department into a managerial zone that he labeled "clerical office."

Differences remained between planning the tasks of an architectural office and those of a factory. To translate techniques such as time study and routing to regulate architectural labor required defining the work of an office as a set of tasks. Each drawing by a draftsman would now be treated as analogous to a part of a complex industrial assembly. In this respect, Springall's attempt to convert the process of design into more specialized duties, supervised by Mr. Color's assistant, can be related to the general effort to reform offices in other clerical professions. Based on the experience of applying Taylor's principles at the Chicago Ferrotype Company between 1915 and 1916, for example, William H. Leffingwell formalized the process of administering office labor in his book *Scientific Office Management* (1917). His recommendations were as copious as they were concrete. Beyond translating the methods of brainwork that Taylor recommended for a planning department into the context of office labor, Leffingwell also wrote extensively about topics related to the physical appointment of interiors. He offered drawings that outlined an efficient distribution of aisles between desks, the location of drinking fountains, and the correct conditions of lighting. He even recommended methods for calculating the number of toilets needed based on the number of men and women who occupied a given office space. More completely than any of Taylor's disciples who managed factories, Leffingwell considered every aspect of the physical conditions that surrounded the employees in the office as critical for the performance of the tasks within the time they allotted to them.[11]

This focus on the physical space of an office can be found in other publications of this type. The frontispiece of *Office Management* (1918) by Lee Galloway, a professor of commerce and industry at New York University, was an image of the atrium of the Larkin Administration Building in Buffalo, opened in 1906.[12] Galloway's book was one of several that regarded the configuration of office work in that building as exemplary of a full integration of management systems into clerical work. The business press referred to it as "a model administration building" that represented "a magnificent monument to fidelity to a business ideal."[13] Without naming the architect, the publishers presented to an audience of office managers the organization of labor around an atrium, the various furnishings, and the ventilation system as significant improvements for moving work along desks as well as circulating air through office space. These aspects of the building, when considered as a system, exemplified a wide-ranging regulatory infrastructure that they hoped to reproduce. The massive mail-order company's bureaucratic needs, materialized in the design for desks and various other implements of office work, were held as paradigmatic.

Despite his direct involvement in designing the Larkin Building's physical infrastructure, and contrary to the trend of many professional practices, Frank Lloyd Wright claimed to have not appropriated managerial methods of organization to structure his architectural office. In his *Autobiography*, Wright emphasized that his refusal to engage in office administration was unusual. He wrote: "There was never organization in the sense that the usual architect's office knows organization. Nor any great need of it so long as I stood at the center of the effort. Where I am, there my office is: my office is me."[14] Rejecting managerial culture was important for Wright because it enabled him to equate the labor of the office with his singular authorial identity. This statement of total control was nothing less than a variation on the Sun King's declaration of absolute power—*L'état, c'est moi.* Using the organizational structure of "the usual architect's office" as a foil, Wright could define his authorship as both centered and unified.

But the issue of authorship was not a concern in the articles published on office organization by the architectural press.[15] These writers viewed the methods of managing an architectural office as offering a solution to the increasing difficulty of synchronizing the labor of a firm with the pace of urban development and client demands. In 1916, Daniel Paul Higgins, who managed John Russell Pope's large office in New York, wrote articles in the *Architectural Review* on "The 'Business' of Architecture." The quotation marks in the title reveal business's still uncommon and often unwelcome presence in architectural discourse. Higgins used Pope's office as a model to warn his readers that the organization of architectural production was becoming an increasingly significant part of the total labor of an office that could not be ignored. Like the Taylorists who viewed the work of a planning department as an essential investment in most forms of factory production, Higgins positioned office administration at the center of modern architectural work. For any office to succeed in the corporate economic context, Higgins wrote, it would necessarily be organized around the needs of a client who viewed design as a service like any other: "Business men are interested in employing only such architects as are equipped to represent their financial as well as their artistic interests."[16] Representing the client's artistic interest was clear enough to most trained architects, but representing the client's financial interests remained less obvious. Higgins meant that a properly managed architectural office would need to be equipped with tools that could organize the labor of a firm. These would make possible a high volume of work and a fast pace when a job demanded it. A slower pace could be followed when a client's funding was unstable or when the potential profit from a project required more time to develop.

To produce this flexibility, Higgins described tools to regulate the firm's output. For example, he explained the value of an accounting statement that would constantly update the relative profitability of jobs at various points in their completion. Based on this data, the supervising architect could modulate the amount of work dedicated to a job by shifting workers to the more profitable accounts. Further, to trace an overly expensive task to the work of a single employee, Higgins described a "draughting-room card record" that noted all the time spent by each worker on each drawing.[17] Both systems were premised on the extraction of data from the firm's daily operations, a model of control patterned on Taylor's studies of leather belts and timed tasks in machine shops during the 1880s and 1890s. Each drawing, each calculation, and each specification produced a corresponding record of the period of time spent on that task. These data were collected in a body of paperwork that the supervising architect used to manage the pace of architectural production. The management of the office required the constant production and arrangment of data.

Not all offices could be structured in the same way, Higgins acknowledged, but one configuration that he recommended was summarized in a single diagram (Figure 5.2). It was drawn according to the same graphic methods that factory managers used to visualize the operations of a planning department. At the top was an image of the architect seated with some paperwork stacked on his desk and a telephone beside his left hand. Among all the circles and lines of the diagram, his was the only empty circle as it uniquely connected "clients" to a "business department." The same circle also formed the vertex of a triangle that revealed his executive power over three other departments. Presumably, as the point of interface with clients, the architect would no longer have time to draw his own ideas. Therefore, with no instruments of design on his desk, he communicated his ideas into the telephone. At the other end of the line, the transmission of his voice would be received by someone in the "designing department" who would give form to his ideas in sketches and models. This group of designers was, in turn, overseen by the "supervising architect's department." His was a primarily managerial position that would employ the "draughting department," the large rectangle at the bottom of the diagram, to elaborate the designers' sketches. At the same time, the supervising architect maintained direct communication with the architect regarding the normative rates for various drawing tasks, the hiring and firing of draftsmen, and the arrangement of a schedule that maximized the profitability of various jobs. Positioned at the center of the diagram as well as the center of the firm's operation, the pace of the transmission of work from the designers to the draftsmen to the departments of "engineering" and "inspection" was entrusted to the supervising architect. These smaller departments, and smaller circles, were responsible for calculating dimensions of structural elements and specifying bills of material. Once the thoughts of the executive architect had been given form, structure, and cost, the final set of construction drawings and specifications could be sent to a contractor.

In this model of practice, the labor of an architectural office was identified neither with a collective, as it would have been in an atelier, nor with a singular author such as Wright, but distributed through an organization of subdivided tasks, one of which was to coordinate the flow of labor to meet

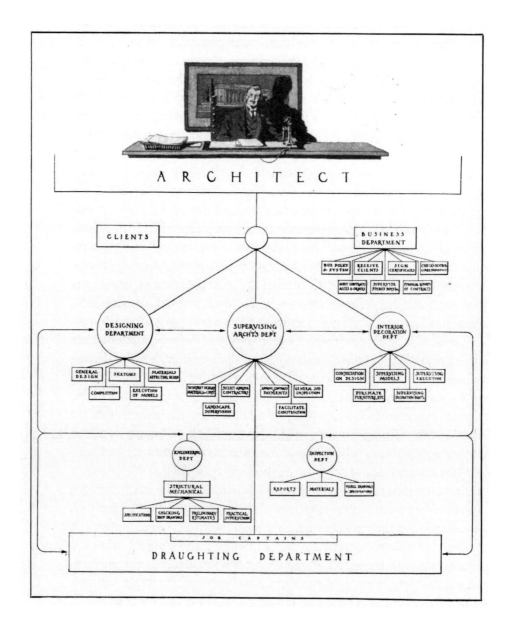

FIGURE 5.2. Daniel Paul Higgins, "Chart of a Complete Office Organization for the Architect." *Architectural Review* 6 (March 1918): 39.

the pace and volume of demand. The relationship of the architect pictured in Higgins's diagram to the rendering of a classical building that hung behind him was aptly represented by his looming shadow, projected from the lower left. When compared to the heightened attention given to architectural representation in Wright's practice, where drawings were often marked, in one way or another, by the architect's hand, the managerial system in the diagram distanced the architect from a direct claim to authorship. The production of drawings was one of the many tasks delegated to the various departments that also included calculating structures, superintending construction, and writing specifications. Higgins summarized the functions of office management in a single statement: "A 'business organization' is the machine by means of which all the other forces of architecture and building are made effective."[18] The mechanical metaphor—fundamental to regulatory thinking—did not represent the formal description of the modernist object of design; it characterized the administrative core of a modern architectural office. The brainwork of management kept the office up-to-date, allowing it to compete with other offices that were similarly expanding in scope and growing in scale. Perhaps most importantly, the management of an office ensured its wholeness from the tendency of large companies to fragment as teams of workers took on their tasks with greater expertise.

An exemplary application of managerial methods to a firm's production process, although by no means the only one of its kind, can be found in the large architectural office of Albert Kahn.[19] In his book, *Making the Modern*, Terry Smith provocatively compared the organization of Kahn's office to the operation of its most significant client, the Ford Motor Company. From the vantage point of cultural history, Smith could extend Higgins's mechanical metaphor from 1918 to equate both the office's products and its method to machines: "Like the Ford Company itself, the office became a machine for the production of even more refined, technically beautiful, economically efficient, and abstractly inhuman machines."[20] Two mechanical metaphors, in fact, compared two different classes of objects: places of work (offices and factories) and products of work (automobiles and buildings). Both equations, however, require significant qualification. First, the methods of management used in the automotive industry were different from those used in the architectural office. Ford's factory managers aimed to transfer tasks from men to machines to maximize the labor of the workers employed. By contrast, the manager of Kahn's office did not replace workers with machines, even if their skills could be made increasingly specialized. Second, in the formation of the assembly line at the Highland Park factory, for example, Ford's engineers organized the manufacture of an automobile in a sequence based on each task and its approximate duration. The production process could thus be continuously refined because the products that were being produced were nearly identical.[21] In architectural production, by contrast, each set of drawings, structural calculations, and specifications would differ by project, depending upon a building's location, function, budget, and client. The management of Kahn's office was more like a machine shop than a plant for car assembly in that it was organized around the fact that nothing designed by the staff was ever exactly the same, even if two buildings looked alike. Regarding Smith's equation of Kahn's buildings to Ford's Model T, another discrimination should be made. The business of architecture provided a service just as the earliest American professionals had defined it: an architectural office did not deliver a three-dimensional product, a commodity like an automobile or any other immediately useful object. Instead, it provided a set of drawings and instructions to a general contractor who organized the acquisition of materials and the industrialized construction systems on a site. Even if management made Kahn's office more profitable by specializing certain tasks and scheduling them according to the demands of its internal economy, income always depended on a contractual agreement for a service and not the purchase of a predefined product.

A closer look into Kahn's office makes the difference between architectural and industrial labor more explicit. Located in downtown Detroit, the office occupied the top floor of the Marquette Building, after it was remodeled from a power facility into a loft building in 1916. Unlike the office of Burnham and Root, located in the Rookery Building, which was designed by that firm, Kahn's office occupied this converted industrial building by adding the infrastructure that was needed for the firm's daily operation. "The offices were especially designed by Mr. Kahn," explained the author of a profile published in *Architectural Forum*, "with the idea of affording his organization every advantage and up-to-date facility for taking care of his business interests."[22] Rooms that housed individual departments—mechanical, structural, and design—were located at three corners of the plan (Figure 5.3). In between these were more rooms, including two large drafting rooms located at adjacent edges. The rooms divided the otherwise continuous space interrupted only by columns. Most of the divisions between the rooms were made of glass. Thus, from the designers' office at one corner of the building,

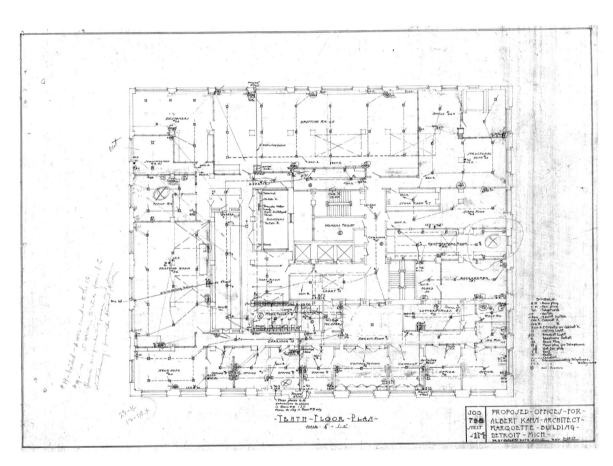

FIGURE 5.3. Proposed Offices for Albert Kahn, Architect, Tenth floor of the Marquette Building in Detroit, Job 798, Sheet 1M, March 23, 1917. The symbol key to the right includes "B.P., Basic plug," "F.P., Fan plug," "Tel., Telephone," "S, Switch," "3ps, 3 point switch," and "I.C., Intercommunicating telephones," and the dashed lines running throughout the plan indicate the location of conduit. This drawing, from the Bentley Historical Library, is an annotated version of the plan published in *Architectural Forum* 29:5 (November 1918). Courtesy of Albert Kahn Associates, Inc.

it would be possible to see the activities in each of the two drafting rooms through a series of glass walls. The specification typists, the superintendent's room, the bookkeeper, and even a corridor running alongside one of the drafting rooms were similarly separated by glass. Only the offices along the corridor that led out of the reception area had opaque walls. So despite the division of different sorts of tasks into separate rooms, an overall visual connection produced an apparent unity to the office.

While all these tasks had been collected in one architectural space, the work in the office remained highly differentiated and decentralized. No clear sequence of work could be traced from one room to the next. Instead, as in a machine shop organized by the Taylor system, the tasks and their order were constantly updated. The inevitable misalignment between the physical disposition of rooms and the routing of work made a telephone network essential. Its presence is visible in the plan from the numerous small annotations added to every wall: the note "Tel." often appears in corners or next to the columns beside a small arrowhead that points to the outlet; it is often supplemented by an additional note, "I.C.," for inter-communicating telephones, making up an internal network that could also be extended to positions marked "I.C.X." An image published in the *Architectural Forum* profile of Kahn's office shows a receiver located on a table below two plaster casts hanging on the wall (Figure 5.4). Thus information could be relayed through to a telephone operator, located between the reception room and the lobby, who coordinated the intercommunication system at a switchboard, connecting the caller to external lines. Higgins's image of a managerial network headed by an architect seated behind a telephone from 1918 was made concrete in the well-lit interior of the drafting room. Here, the value of electrified communication was visibly present in organizing the tasks of the architectural office.

The telephone network indicates the exigency of communicating among the firm's departments, an answer to the inevitable problem of workers moving constantly from one place to another to transfer tidbits of information as they emerged from the labor process.[23] But this was by no means the only technique used to control workflow or the rate and volume of output on the office at any given time. Control over labor required collecting and integrating vast quantities of data to oversee the status of the tasks in each day. The same profile of the Kahn office published a two-page montage of blank forms, including eighteen different pieces of paperwork (Figure 5.5). These were documents developed by the superintendent to transmit and archive

FIGURE 5.4. A view of the large drafting room in the office of Albert Kahn, Inc., in the Marquette Building. This room is labeled #25 in the plan above. Notice the telephone receiver at the lower right. From George C. Baldwin, "The Offices of Albert Kahn, Architect, Detroit, Michigan," *Architectural Forum* 29.5 (November 1918): 127.

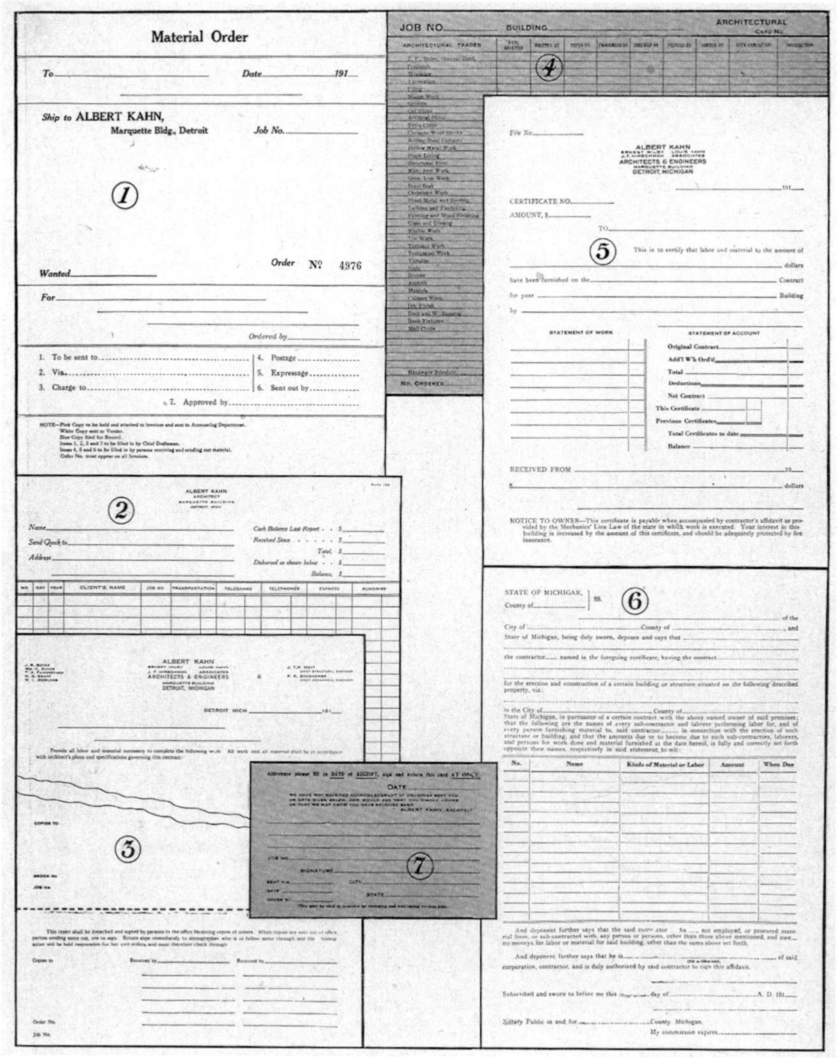

FIGURE 5.5. Reproduction of the forms used in Albert Kahn's offices. These included: "1, a material order form; 2, an expense account sheet; 3, a work order on contractors form; 4, a schedule of subcontracts; 5, certificate for payments; 6, the reverse side of the payment certificate; 7, 'follow-up' receipt card; 8, 'follow-up' return card; 9, superintendents' daily report; 10, superintendents' weekly report; 11, superintendents' report; 12, receipt card; 13, draftsman's time card; 14, office print record; 15, contractors' print record; 16, progress record of drawing; 17, office record of the commission; 18, graphic progress chart." George C. Baldwin, "The Offices of Albert Kahn, Architect, Detroit, Michigan," *Architectural Forum* 29:5 (November 1918): 128–29.

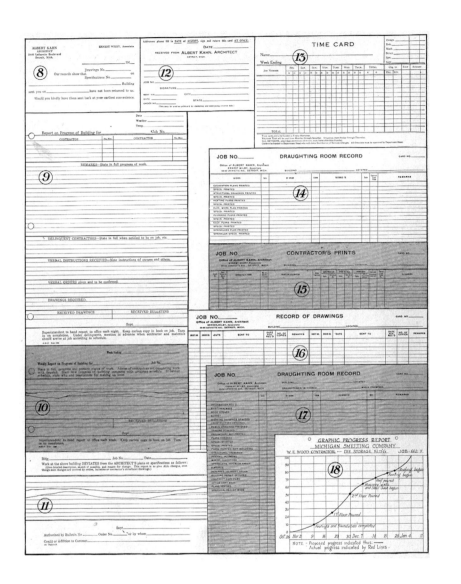

information on the routines in the office. The telephone circuitry that ran through the conduit at the ceiling was, then, another part of this intricate system of paperwork.

These mundane artifacts of professional practice—material orders, schedules, certificates of payment, time cards, etc.—were profiled because they represented the core elements of the office's organizational system.[24] While the telephone network tied the voices of designers to the ears of draftsmen and the glass walls visually tied separate departments together in the office, this collection of forms used in the practice produced an infrastructure of control that, like the management of timed tasks in the machine shop, tabulated the data related to the daily activities of architectural production through the medium of paper.

Compared to the managers of the Ford Company's factories who sought to arrange work along a linear path and centralize control, the heads of Kahn's office utilized the telephone network and the system of paperwork to govern their operations from a virtual center into one coherent whole. "Albert Kahn Incorporated" was a name that eventually came to represent not one man, but the wholeness of the office, covering over the ambiguity of this collection of services gathered under one architect's name.[25] The man, Albert Kahn, was no longer directly involved in the design of all these buildings, but as a corporate executive his name gave a symbol to the corporation and a sign of its stability. In place of the centralized power embodied in a single author, the order produced by these managerial instruments allowed the operation to continue its work in the absence of its namesake. This regulated and multifaceted body emerged from the medium of paperwork, the unifying force for the operations of the office.[26]

Reflecting on the influence of Kahn's office in 1939, the architect and industrial designer George Nelson observed that it had been "barely twenty years since the factory was 'discovered' to be architecture—architecture, moreover, that is quite as valid in its way as any of the antique monuments which ornament the pages of textbooks." In historicizing the turn toward the factory as a model for modern architectural form, Nelson noted that the status of this building type depended on the wide circulation of photographs of industrial architecture designed by Kahn's office. While these buildings had become internationally recognized emblems of the machine aesthetic, their centrality to modernist visual discourse was not Nelson's focus.[27] He insisted that his readers should also appreciate the functions of the well-managed office that lurked behind these images of functional buildings. "The outstanding fact about the organization of Albert Kahn, Inc.," he observed, "is its completeness."[28] For Nelson, the images of these factory buildings could not convey the remarkable unity of the large firm that designed them. In the text, he cataloged the enormous size and diversity of the operations at Kahn, Inc., a scope and scale of services that only continued to grow after its founder retired.

Perhaps Nelson was responding to promoters of the machine aesthetic who identified the formal unity of industrially manufactured objects with the functional forms of the factories, particularly those designed by the Kahn office.[29] In the exhibition of *Machine Art* at the Museum of Modern Art in 1934, organized by Philip Johnson and Alfred Barr, the items on display represented material proof of modernism's arrival in the forms produced by industry. Although they were forged in dusty machine shops around the nation, these visually simple objects were displayed in the museum as pure aesthetic creations, allowing their viewers to forget their place in the vast infrastructure that governed the engines of industry. As the art historian Jennifer Jane Marshall has shown, the Platonism of Barr's discourse around these objects, their apparent equivalence to one another, and the objective photographic images made for the catalog revealed an alliance in the modern movement between technical precision and metaphysical certainty.[30] In this case, the machine aesthetic conflated the ancient belief in ideal forms with the modern belief in the idealized completeness of well-managed industry. Just as musical metaphors were used to describe the effect of management on industry—bringing the mechanical systems of production into so-called harmony—both the machined objects in the museum and the photographs of factories designed by Kahn, Inc. substituted one form of order for another: in place of the primordial order of nature, they represented a new order of machines.[31] This idealized visual language of abstract form symbolized the power of managerial organization while hiding the practical processes based in the collection of data used to govern industrial production as well as the production of modern architecture.

When the architectural historian Henry-Russell Hitchcock described the architecture of Kahn, Inc. in 1947 as "the architecture of bureaucracy," he also conflated managerial order with formal abstraction. For Hitchcock, the images of the factories indicated "a certain rightness, straightforwardness, and cleanliness both actual and symbolic, which is the proper generalized expression of an efficient workplace."[32] Again, the claim that efficient work could be expressed in the form of architecture relied on a substitution of the complex infrastructure of regulation used to organize Kahn, Inc. with an image of factories that symbolized well-managed labor. This argument entered the same metaphysical trap as the *Machine Art* exhibition. The tools of management were a set of instruments for collection of data—some of which were made visible in graphs and diagrams—to stabilize the profitability of the office in response to a host of external fluctuations. We should not mistake images of factories with the systems of their management or the changes in the professional office. To find the image of regulation in architecture, return to the eighteen pieces of paperwork that mediated and organized the labor on the tenth floor of the Marquette Building. Recall, also, the circuitry and telephone networks that covered the office interior with conduit. These are not stable images of modern order when compared to a photograph of a factory or a machine-made part because, as a system, these instruments were always revised or replaced to respond to fluctuations in practice. Regulation did not offer an essential image of order and stability for modern architecture; it was the dynamic infrastructure that helped organize so many aspects of American life during the twentieth century.

Conclusion

In the Introduction, I used the example of Frank Lloyd Wright's Larkin Administration Building to point out the limitations of focusing on either the monumental forms or the advanced technical systems housed within this iconic building. It proved impossible to detect any hard lines separating the building's design from its role in organizing the company's operations, the machinery that treated its interior air, and the instruments that facilitated the workers' intercommunication. While some historians of modern architecture reduced this building's complexity by focusing on architectural form rather than technology (Vincent Scully) or by exposing the arrangement of machinery without considering the building's administrative function (Reyner Banham), my aim has been to account for the coexistence of such divergent aims—to account for the multifaceted aspects of regulation as a central feature of the encounter between architecture and modernism.

In keeping with the inclusive breadth necessitated by this approach, throughout the book I have taken care to focus attention on detailed descriptions of buildings, machines, and various techniques of representation that occupied crossing-points among architectural design, management, and environmental control. Assembling these interrelated but often misaligned procedures has required developing historical narratives from heterogeneous cultural references, each drawn from a range of sources. For example, regulatory metaphors from human physiology were fundamental to those who explained the usefulness of the thermostat's environmental sensitivity. And, in an apparent reversal, mechanical metaphors were essential for ecologists to explain an organism's physiological interaction with its environment. The capacity of an organism's physiology to explain a machine, or the reverse, indicates that regulation was neither a specifically technical issue nor uniquely fit as a scientific term; rather, it was an interpretive tool employed by different groups to different ends.

To describe the history of regulatory thinking, I have needed to make connections among various forms of evidence rather than prioritizing one type over another. Again, in the case of ecology, neither the representation of environmental interactions in an enlarged panoramic photograph nor the data recorded by the laboratory apparatus could exhaustively capture the activity of such dynamic systems. Only in the combination of museum display and empirical research could ecological concepts receive both a public image and internal discourse. Similarly, the instruments and paperwork developed by managers for machine shops could not fully explain the massive transformations in labor resulting from their supervision. But as these systems, developed for mass production, were appropriated for organizing office labor, including various architects' offices, they give clearer evidence of regulation's logic as it was applied to different forms of labor.

To capture the pervasiveness of regulation in such instances, among others, I have followed the advice of the French economist Michel Aglietta, who studied capitalist regulation in the United States after the Civil War: regulation's history, he explained, is constituted from acts of "social creation." Aglietta sought to write a concrete theory of regulation, one set against the abstractions endemic to equilibrium theory. His position was based on the definitive role of time, not as a variable within a plastic system of political economy, but as a historical force that produces qualitative change.[1] In place of the rhythm of crisis and equilibrium that often punctuates economic models of change, for Aglietta, regulation's history focuses on the methods by which social institutions change and are reproduced. This means that shifts in those institutions are neither self-evident nor derived from first principles. There are no universal precepts that explain their transformation or how they take on various forms. In lieu of the focus provided by an overarching explanatory system, a definitive event, or the inevitability of a root cause in this history, I have developed narratives that trace temporary alignments among scientific theories, legal codes, representational tools, and technical instruments. In the cases I have collected, and in many others that I did not, these alignments helped develop unique opportunities for agents who aimed to manage the dynamics of the economy and the environment.

Such narrative involutions are essential to this history and run against well-known stories of setting standards, technical refinement, or increased efficiency. These have been the dominant modes for explaining architectural modernism's engagement with machine-based production.[2] But such historiographical tropes are inadequate to the complex role of regulation in so many domains of life in this period. For instance, while thermostats first served industrial interests, they were not uniquely suited to that context. Thermostats gained their value from the diversity of their application. This was especially true in households, where they played a definitive role in the discourse on modern housework. Thus in both contexts, home and factory, the instrument participated in the task of management, but to different ends. Or in another case, merchants sought to regulate the market in perishable commodities by mechanically refrigerating them, but only with a range of legal codes could their value be guaranteed. To put these examples in more general terms: for those who sought to assert control over their material surroundings, their intentions could be better developed in their transformation through auxiliary fields. Similarly, plenums, thermophones, bulletin boards, slide rules, and drafting room card records exemplify a set of objects that simultaneously occupied the technical and bureaucratic territory of regulatory thinking. Clerical instruments and methods of data collection were intricately tied to managing the marginal errors and deviations in the mundane operations of technologies. While systems of tabulation may appear to be supplementary to machinery, we have seen that they were in fact central to shifting fundamental cultural concepts. For example, the assembly of ecologists' laboratory apparatus helped redefine *nature* through automated measurements, while the statistical data recorded by managerial instruments brought a new technicality to the rather abstract meaning of *labor*.

At many times, in the chapters above, I have felt that the term *modernism* was inadequate to the historical complexity that I sought to describe. I have often been tempted to replace that word with a seemingly broader term: *modernization.* In American history, modernization aligns with an intellectual movement from the 1960s and 1970s, in which historians sought social scientific explanations for the transformation of the society from its structure around the colonial period to the industrial nation that it became after the Civil War.[3] Robert H. Wiebe's now-canonical book, *The Search for Order,* traced this process into the final decades of the nineteenth century to reveal a reorganization of society according to the "regulative, hierarchical needs of urban-industrial life."[4] "The Middle Class," "the Trust and Wall Street," and "the Political Machine" were all terms that Wiebe selected as examples of what he called "a national habit" of expression that aligned with this new system of governance.[5] These concepts were central to his persuasive and enduring description of a shift in people's routines as bureaucratic and administrative bodies entered into many domains of American life.

Other histories of the period explained the processes of modernization through the interplay of sociological categories: economic informality versus corporate hierarchy, a demographic shift from rural to urban settlement, or the transfer of community-based civil society to large-scale political institutions. These pairings provide bridges between the unfamiliar past and the present. In this way, social relations appear gradually to conform to a modern ideal of rationality.[6] Yet the history of regulation that I have described shows that many transformations in social institutions after the Civil War cannot be explained along such linear paths. Any realistic description of the pragmatic, ephemeral, and often unacknowledged alliances among diverse agents in this period would resist terminological abstractions or oppositions used by historians of the modernization process. Assemblages of machines, buildings, images, data, and clerical paperwork gave provisional meaning to a set of unsettled concepts that still characterize a now-familiar modern lexicon: comfort, freshness, environment, and efficiency, to name a few. Yet the meaning given to those terms never settled into an axiomatic definition. "Modernism," as I use it, relies on expanding the types of objects that serve as examples to explain the cultural value given to such commonly used expressions.

Because the history of modern architecture in the United States, like everywhere else, includes more than great masterworks, historians need to develop methods that help assess the roles that mundane buildings, their technical features, and their functions have played in giving shape to modern life. To examine regulation as an interpretive tool used by various agents, including architects, their clients, and a host of others, has been my attempt to give narrative force to the visual forms of some less-than-striking buildings, to the ways these buildings helped organize the things they contained and the methods by which they integrated a relentlessly changing set of technological amenities. Expanding the architectural history of modernism beyond its alignment with other fields of cultural production—literature, plastic arts, and performance arts—can ward off the whiggish teleology of modernization. At the same time, such cultural alignments among the arts should not serve as the self-evident proof of modernism's existence. This book's ambition is to explore the contradic-tory impulses on which the history of modernism rests. There can be as many books written about the misalignments found among architectural work and the divergent motives of industry and science as those that have already been written about their complementarity.

In collecting a few episodes in the history of regulation, I have sought to position architecture in a diverse field of archival material to begin to unpack images of modern American life that have become so familiar and firmly implanted in cultural history that they barely require explanation. I hope to have offered some distance from the apparent inevitability of the modern habits that we see in these images: images of hygienic homes, fresh food, wildlife preserves, mechanized production, and so on. Perhaps this study will suggest the usefulness of retrieving some distance from our amenities of environmental control, communication, and real-time service. If, for no other purpose, this might begin to reveal how none of these systems was assumed to be part of an inescapable future. I hope to have contributed some rudimentary methods for undermining the relent-less myth of automatic processes that change our buildings, cities, and the lives we live within them. The historical analysis of regulation as a social creation reveals that modern techniques for governance are an essential, if unacknowledged, part in modernism's history.

Acknowledgments

Much of my thinking for this project was shaped by my dissertation committee in the History, Theory, and Criticism section of the Department of Architecture at the Massachusetts Institute of Technology: Mark Jarzombek, Arindam Dutta, and Edward Eigen.

I am deeply grateful to Reinhold Martin for his guidance and support at all stages of the project's development. I am honored to have been involved in a project with the Temple Hoyne Buell Center for the Study of American Architecture at Columbia University under his directorship. Reinhold's editorial presence in this project was generously buttressed by Pieter Martin, whom I thank for his patience and sage advice in crafting the book with the staff and board of the University of Minnesota Press.

The book would never have become a book without the meticulous editorial interventions of Carol Krinsky. Helping shape the manuscript would have been enough, *dayenu*, but John Krinsky's inspired comments could not have happened without her. John was more involved than he ever could have known, from the start.

Sylvia Lavin read the manuscript at a critical juncture. But more important, she represents a model scholar, one from whom I have learned so much. The dynamics of our little group at UCLA could only be complete with the friendship of Dana Cuff, Diane Favro, Cristobal Amunategui, and Margo Handwerker. Jason Payne has been a dear friend and an invaluable colleague. I have learned so much from the students in my seminars over nearly a decade. I am particularly thankful to Megan Meulemans and Brigid Boyle for their help with images and permissions.

The project was supported by several UCLA Senate Faculty Research Grants, the NSF Science and Society Dissertation Improvement Grant, and a Graduate Research Fellowship from the Canadian Center for Architecture. The Hyzen Travel Grant, Henry Luce Foundation Grant, and Royal Fund were awarded toward dissertation research and writing while I was a student in the Department of Architecture at MIT. Anne Deveau was central to every aspect of life in HTC.

Some of my greatest friendships began in the kennel: Zeynep Celik Alexander, Tijana Vujosevic, Lucia Allais, Lauren Kroiz, Florian Urban, Janna Israel, Fabiola Lopez-Duran, Ijlal Muzaffar, Pamela Karimi, and Patrick Haughey. That group was then supplemented with a wonderful set of collaborators in Aggregate: Danny Abramson, John Harwood, Timothy Hyde, Jonathan Massey, Meredith TenHoor, and John May.

Archival research would not have been possible without the help of numerous archivists, including Dawn Roberts and Steve Sullivan at the Notebaert Nature Museum; William Maher at the University of Illinois, Urbana-Champaign; and Melissa Murphy at the Baker Library at the Harvard Business School.

I have been fortunate to receive feedback on many parts of this project from presentations in conferences, seminars, and workshops at Oberlin College, the Society of Architectural Historians, Machine Project, Cornell University, the UCLA History of Science Colloquium, Princeton School of Architecture, University of Massachusetts Dartmouth, Temple Hoyne Buell Center for the Study of American Architecture at Columbia University, the Radcliffe Institute for Advanced Study at Harvard University, Los Angeles Forum for Architecture and Urban Design, and the Van Alen Institute.

My scholarly identity has been shaped by a group of friends who now exist in various parts of the educational complex: Richard Cho, Alex Kentisis, Bharath Nath, Mira Henry, and Gautham Rao. More recently, my conversations on architecture took root with Lisa Tilney, Matt Seidel, Adam Ruedig, Lauren Kogod, and Andrew Atwood. A few late but very welcome additions to my thinking came from Ra'anan Boustan, David Ruy, and Chris Kelty. To all these people I owe so much, but none is responsible for the shortcomings of this book.

Finally, and most important, I always feel endless support from my family: Miriam, Rami, and Keren Osman, Maya and Adam Osman-Krinsky. The Neimarks (and Geffens) produced the love of my life, Anna Neimark: they all know the wild intelligence and warmth she possesses and has transmitted to Sasha and Jacob. I am forever indebted to their tolerance for my absences on so many weekends. I dedicate this book to my father, from whom I learned about the immediate value of regulation to his life, a value that he transmitted to me and others in so many lessons I cannot possibly enumerate them.

Notes

INTRODUCTION

1. Alfred D. Chandler Jr., *The Visible Hand: The Managerial Revolution in American Business* (Cambridge, Mass.: Belknap Press of Harvard University Press, 1971). Chandler began the history of these enterprises by tracing the means of cooperation that were established among large-scale railroad companies from 1850 to 1900. The sequel to his first book is also enormously useful, especially the U.S. section: *Scale and Scope: The Dynamics of Industrial Capitalism* (Cambridge, Mass.: Belknap Press of Harvard University Press, 1990), 47–234.

2. The term *modernizing*, as used by Chandler, was also commonly found in the writings of historians grouped by Louis Galambos in what he called an "organizational synthesis," in his "The Emerging Organizational Synthesis in Modern American History," *Business History Review* 44:3 (Autumn 1970): 279–90. Chandler's students contributed heavily to this literature; see Jerry Israel, ed., *Building the Organizational Society: Essays on Associational Activities in Modern America* (New York: Free Press, 1972).

3. Martin J. Sklar, *The United States as a Developing Country: Studies in U.S. History in the Progressive Era and the 1920s* (Cambridge: Cambridge University Press, 1992). See also Martin J. Sklar, *The Corporate Reconstruction of American Capitalism, 1890–1916: The Market, the Law, and Politics* (Cambridge: Cambridge University Press, 1988). The shift away from classical political economic thinking was the topic of Harold U. Faulkner's *The Decline of Laissez Faire, 1897–1917* (New York: Rinehart, 1951). For an excellent history of the intellectual transformations in political economic thought in this period, see Daniel Rogers, "Twilight of Laissez-Faire," in *Atlantic Crossings: Social Politics in a Progressive Age* (Cambridge, Mass.: Belknap Press, 1998), 76–111.

4. For a classic account of the political and economic processes involved in American modernization at the end of the nineteenth century, see Robert H. Wiebe's *The Search for Order, 1877–1920* (New York: Hill and Wang, 1967). A wide-ranging treatment of the problems of control in this period can be found in James R. Beniger, *The Control Revolution: Technological and Economic Origins of the Information Society* (Cambridge, Mass: Harvard University Press, 1986).

5. Frank Lloyd Wright, "The Art and Craft of the Machine," *Journal of the Western Society of Engineers* 6 (1901): 359.

6. The most thorough treatment of Wright's lecture is Joseph Siry, "Frank Lloyd Wright's

'The Art and Craft of the Machine': Text and Context," in *The Education of the Architect: Historiography, Urbanism, and the Growth of Architectural Knowledge*, ed. Martha Pollack (Cambridge, Mass.: MIT Press, 1997), 3–36.

7. Frank Lloyd Wright, *An Autobiography* (New York: Duel, Sloan and Pearce, 1943), 150–51. The earliest critical reception of the building was Russell Sturgis's "The Larkin Building in Buffalo," *Architectural Record* 23 (April 1908): 310–21. For an extended analysis of the environmental system and nearly every other aspect of the Larkin Building, see Jack Quinan, *Frank Lloyd Wright's Larkin Building: Myth and Fact* (Chicago: University of Chicago Press, 2006).

8. Vincent Scully, "Frank Lloyd Wright and Twentieth Century Style," originally in *Problems of the Nineteenth and Twentieth Centuries* (Princeton, N.J.: Princeton University Press, 1963); republished in *Modern Architecture and Other Essays* (Princeton, N.J.: Princeton University Press, 2003), 110.

9. Reyner Banham, *The Architecture of the Well-Tempered Environment* (Chicago: University of Chicago Press, 1969), 27.

10. Banham cited only a few books that preceded his, most prominently James Marston Fitch, *American Building: The Environmental Forces that Shape It* (1947; repr. New York: Schocken Books, 1975). Later pertinent writing included his own revised edition of *The Architecture of the Well-Tempered Environment* (Chicago: University of Chicago Press, 1984). An important challenge to some of Banham's claims was the historically nuanced essay by Robert Bruegmann, "Central Heating and Forced Ventilation: Origins and Effects on Architectural Design," *Journal of the Society of Architectural Historians* 37:3 (October 1978): 143–60. More episodic treatment of this material can be found in Luis Fernández-Galiano, *Fire and Memory: On Architecture and Energy*, trans. Gina Cariño (Cambridge, Mass.: MIT Press, 2000) and in Sven-Olov Wallenstein, *Biopolitics and the Emergence of Modern Architecture* (New York: Princeton Architectural Press, 2009). See also my "Banham's Historical Ecology," in *Neo-avant-garde and Postmodern Postwar Architecture in Britain and Beyond*, ed. Mark Crinson and Claire Zimmerman (New Haven: Yale University Press, 2010), 231–50. For another interpretation of Banham's environmental preoccupations, see Amy Kulper, "Ecology without the Oikos: Banham, Dallegret and the Morphological Context of Environmental Architecture," *Field: A Free Journal for Architecture* 4:1 (December 2010): 67–86.

11. Banham, *The Architecture of the Well-Tempered Environment*, 27–28. Alan Colquhoun, reviewing Banham's first book from 1960, *Theory and Design in the First Machine Age* (New York: Praeger, 1960), saw it as too dogmatically accepting of the idea that modern architecture was a branch of technics, leaving no room for explaining the productive misinterpretations of technology that underlay the machine aesthetic. See Alan Colquhoun, "The Modern Movement in Architecture," *British Journal of Aesthetics* 2:1 (1962): 59–65.

12. George Twitmyer, "A Model Administration Building," *Business Man's Magazine* 19 (April 1907): 43.

13. For an excellent history of risk in nineteenth-century American society, see Jonathan Levy, *Freaks of Fortune: Risk and the Rise of American Capitalism* (Cambridge, Mass.: Harvard University Press, 2012).

14. Two recent reevaluations of Banham's polemical position in his essay "1960: Stock-taking," *Architectural Review* 127 (February 1960), are Anthony Vidler, "Taking Stock: Architecture 2013," and Felicity D. Scott, "I want to argue that contemporary scholarship be cast as a sort of ongoing counter-memory to familiar historical narratives," *Log* 28 (Summer 2013): 12–20, 79–86. On Banham's place in environmental debates, see Daniel Barber, "The World Solar Energy Project, ca. 1954," *Grey Room* 51 (Spring 2013): 65–67.

15. Among Latour's attempts to define what he has called a collective, as opposed to society, is his *Reassembling the Social: An Introduction to Actor-Network-Theory* (Oxford: Oxford University Press, 2005). He writes: "the question of the social emerges when the ties in which one is entangled begin to unravel; . . . the social as normally construed is bound together with already accepted participants called 'social actors' who are members of a 'society'; when the movement toward collection is resumed, it traces the social as associations through many non-social entities which might become participants later; if pursued systematically, this tracking may end up in a shared definition of a common world, what I have called a collective, it may fail to be reassembled; and, lastly, sociology is best defined as the discipline where participants explicitly engage in the reassembling of the collective." Ibid., 247.

16. Among his examples are doors, door-closing mechanisms, texts, speed bumps, and keys. See Bruno Latour, "Where Are the Missing Masses? The Sociology of a Few Mundane Artifacts," in *Shaping Technology/Building Society: Studies in Sociotechnical Change,* ed. Wiebe E. Bijker and John Law (Cambridge, Mass.: MIT Press, 1992), 225–58.

17. Bruno Latour, "A Cautious Prometheus? A Few Steps Toward a Philosophy of Design (with Special Attention to Peter Sloterdijk)," keynote lecture, "Networks of Design" meeting, Design History Society, Falmouth, Cornwall, September 3, 2008, published in *In Medias Res: Peter Sloterdijk's Spherological Poetics of Being,* ed. Willem Schinkel and Liesbeth Noordegraaf-Eelens (Amsterdam: Amsterdam University Press, 2011), 157. His assertion relies on the work of the philosopher Peter Sloterdijk, who has proposed that using technical objects as metaphors to replace the abstraction of philosophical concepts such as "Being" reveals the material substrate that has been organized by what he calls "design." The first two volumes of a trilogy on "spheres" by Peter Sloterdijk are translated by Wieland Hoban as *Spheres,* vol. 1: *Bubbles, Microspherology*; vol. 2: *Globes, Macrospherology* (Los Angeles: Semiotext(e), 2011–14). See also the treatment of "immune systems" in Peter Sloterdijk, *The World Interior of Capital,* trans. Wieland Hoban (Cambridge: Polity Press, 2013).

18. This preference for empirical and practical issues can be traced to Latour's reading of American pragmatism, a philosophical movement contemporaneous with the development of regulatory systems. Pragmatists rejected the use of reductive abstractions to explain human action. For the intersection of Latour's thinking with this philosophical tradition, see his "What Is Given in Experience?," *boundary 2* 32:1 (2005): 223–37. This essay is a review of Isabelle Stengers, *Thinking with Whitehead: A Free and Wild Creation of Concepts,* trans. Michael Chase (Cambridge, Mass.: Harvard University Press, 2011).

19. The biological theory associated with the German term *Umwelt* is that environment cannot be understood outside of the ways in which it is shaped by an organism. Georges Canguilhem and Maurice Merleau-Ponty took up the theory of Jakob von Uexküll to

ground the relation of organism and environment, the former for his history of vitalism in biology and the latter for his project of expanding the terrain of phenomenology. See Jakob von Uexküll, *Theoretical Biology* [1920], trans. D. L. Mackinnon (New York: Harcourt, Brace, 1926). For a recent translation of von Uexküll's later writing, see *A Foray into the Worlds of Animals and Humans*, trans. Joseph D. O'Neill (Minneapolis: University of Minnesota Press, 2010). See also Giorgio Agamben, "Umwelt," in *The Open: Man and Animal*, trans. Kevin Attell (Stanford, Calif.: Stanford University Press, 2004). A nuanced history of a revision of mechanistic milieu with a vitalist notion of *Umwelt* is found in Georges Canguilhem, "The Living and Its Milieu," *Grey Room* 3 (Spring 2001): 7–31.

1. THE THERMOSTATIC INTERIOR AND HOUSEHOLD MANAGEMENT

1. The coincidence of Shelley's novel with experiments like those of Dr. Ure have led to many historical speculations on the relationship between science fiction, popular culture, and the electrical explanation of life. See, for example, Iwan Rhys Morus, *Frankenstein's Children: Electricity, Exhibition, and Experiment in Early-Nineteenth-Century London* (Princeton, N.J.: Princeton University Press, 1998).

   As the story goes, on June 16, 1816, Lord Byron, Percy Shelley, Mary Shelley, and Byron's doctor John Polidori met and discussed the relationship of electricity to the phenomenon of life. Mary Shelley described the event as the origin of her thinking about *Frankenstein* in her preface (London: Henry Colburn and Richard Bentley, 1831): "They talked of the experiments of Dr. [Erasmus] Darwin, I speak not of what the Doctor really did, or said that he did, but, as more to my purpose, of what was then spoken of as having been done by him, who preserved a piece of vermicelli in a glass case, till by some extraordinary means it began to move with voluntary motion. Not thus, after all, would life be given. Perhaps a corpse would be re-animated; galvanism had given token of such things: perhaps the component parts of a creature might be manufactured, brought together, and imbued with vital warmth." See also *The Diary of Dr. John William Polidori: 1816, Relating to Byron, Shelley, etc.*, ed. William Michael Rossetti (London: Elkin Mathews, 1911), 96–135.

2. "Full, nay, laborious breathing, instantly commenced. The chest heaved, and fell; the belly was protruded, and again collapsed, with the relaxing and retiring diaphragm. This process was continued, without interruption, as long as I continued the electric discharges. In the judgment of many scientific gentlemen who witnessed the scene, this respiratory experiment was perhaps the most striking ever made with a philosophical apparatus." Andrew Ure, "An Account of Some Experiments Made on the Body of a Criminal Immediately after Execution, with Physiological and Practical Observations," *Journal of Science and the Arts* 6 (1819): 290. See also the riveting description by Peter MacKenzie, "The Case of Matthew Clydesdale the Murderer—Extraordinary Scene in the College of Glasgow," in *Old Reminiscences of Glasgow and the West of Scotland*, vol. 2 (Glasgow: James P. Forrester, 1890), 49.

3. John (Giovanni) Aldini, *An Account of the Late Improvements in Galvanism, with a Series of Curious and Interesting Experiments Performed before the Commissioners of the French National Institute, and Repeated Lately in the Anatomical Theatres of London, to Which Is*

Added an Appendix Containing Experiments on the Body of a Malefactor Executed at Newgate, and Dissertations on Animal Electricity, 1793 and 1794 (London: Cuthell and Martin and J. Murray, 1803). Animal electricity was discovered by his uncle Luigi Galvani; see *Commentary on the Effects of Electricity on Muscular Motion*, trans. Margaret Glover Foley (Norwalk: Burndy Library, 1953).

4. Georges Canguilhem, "Machine and Organism" [1947], trans. Mark Cohen and Randall Cherry, in *Incorporations*, ed. Jonathan Crary and Sanford Kwinter (New York: Zone Books, 1992), 44–69. See also Edward George Tandy Liddell, *The Discovery of Reflexes* (Oxford: Clarendon Press, 1960); Georges Canguilhem, *La formation du concept de réflexe aux XVIIe et XVIIIe siècles* (Paris: Vrin, 1977). On the tie between neurophysiology and the reflex, see *On Animal Electricity: Being an Abstract of the Discoveries of Emil du Bois-Reymond* (London: John Churchill, 1852).

5. An excellent summary of the difference between the reflex concept and the Cartesian theory of mechanical movement can be found in the partial translation of Canguilhem's *Le formation du concept de réflexe* in *A Vital Rationalist: Selected Writings from Georges Canguilhem*, ed. François Delaporte, trans. Arthur Goldhammer (New York: Zone Books, 1994), 182–85.

6. W. V. Farrar, "Andrew Ure, FRS, and the Philosophy of Manufactures," *Notes and Records of the Royal Society* 27 (February 1973): 299–324.

7. "These two descriptions [by Ure] are far from being identical. In one, the combined collective worker appears as the dominant subject, and the mechanical automaton as the object; in the other, the automaton itself is the subject, and the workers are merely conscious organs." Karl Marx, *Capital*, vol. 1 [1867], trans. Ben Fowkes (London: Harmondsworth, 1976), 544. Marx also addresses the automatic workshop in *The Poverty of Philosophy* (Moscow: Foreign Languages Publishing House, n.d.), 140–43. For more on the relationship of Ure's automatic factory system and the calculating engines designed by Charles Babbage, see Simon Schaffer, "Babbage's Intelligence: Calculating Engines and the Factory System," *Critical Inquiry* 21:1 (Autumn 1994): 203–27.

8. Andrew Ure, *The Philosophy of Manufactures: Or, an Exposition of the Scientific, Moral, and Commercial Economy of the Factory System of Great Britain* (London: C. Knight, 1835), 367. This passage was famously quoted by Friedrich Engels, *The Condition of the Working-class in England in 1844* (London: Swan Sonnenschein, 1892), 223. See also Andrew Zimmerman, "The Ideology of the Machine and the Spirit of the Factory: Remarx on Babbage and Ure," *Cultural Critique* 37 (Autumn 1997): 12; Mohinder Kumar, "Karl Marx, Andrew Ure and the Question of Managerial Control," *Social Scientist* 12:9 (September 1984): 63–69.

9. For more on the metaphysical implications of "mechanical intelligence," see Jessica Riskin, "The Defecating Duck, or, the Ambiguous Origins of Artificial Life," *Critical Inquiry* 29:4 (Summer 2003): 599–633. See also Simon Schaffer, "Enlightened Automata," in *The Sciences in Enlightened Europe*, ed. William Clark, Jan Golinski, and Simon Schaffer (Chicago: University of Chicago Press, 1999), 126–68.

10. The patent was granted on October 20, 1830. For an abstract of his paper, see Andrew Ure, "On the Thermostat or Heat Governor, a Self-Acting Physical Apparatus for Regulating Temperature," *Abstracts of the Papers Printed in the Philosophical Transactions of the Royal Society of London* 3 (1830–37): 67. The bimetallic strip was not Ure's invention, but

John Harrison's, and was originally used in navigation. The H3 timepiece, as Harrison called it, was published in *A Description Concerning Such Mechanism as Will Afford a Nice, or True, Mensuration of Time* (London, 1775). See A. J. R. Ramsey, "The Thermostat or Heat Governor, an Outline of Its History," *Transactions of the Newcomen Society* 25 (1945): 53–72. Credit for inventing the first thermostat is often given to Cornelius Drebbel (1572–1632), a Dutch alchemist who also used his furnaces to regulate the temperature of transmutation; see F. W. Gibbs, "The Furnaces and Thermometers of Cornelis Drebbel," *Annals of Science* 6:1 (1948): 36. See also Otto Mayr, *The Origins of Feedback Control* (Cambridge, Mass.: MIT Press, 1975).

11. Andrew Ure, *A Dictionary of Arts, Manufactures and Mines* (London: Longman, Brown, Green, and Longmans, 1853), 843–45.

12. Ure, *The Philosophy of Manufactures*, 25–26.

13. Robertson Buchanan, *A Treatise on the Economy of Fuel and Management of Heat* (Glasgow: Hedderwick, 1815). For a few clearly illustrated examples of the steam heat system devised by Boulton and Watt, see Jennifer Tann, *The Development of the Factory* (London: Cornmarket Press, 1970), 111–19.

14. William Newton, *London Journal of Arts and Sciences* 8 (1832): 307–17. The descriptions follow the following titles: "To Andrew Ure, of Burton Crescent, in the county of Middlesex, doctor of medicine, for his having invented an apparatus for regulating temperature in vaporization, distillation, and other processes.—[Sealed 20th October, 1830.]" and "To Andrew Ure, of Finsbury Circus, in the county of Middlesex, M.D. for his having invented an improved apparatus for distilling.—[Sealed 31st March, 1831.]"

15. Ure, *The Philosophy of Manufactures*, 27.

16. Canguilhem, "Machine and Organism."

17. Andrew Ure, "An Experimental Inquiry into the Modes of Warming and Ventilating Apartments," read before the Royal Society on June 16, 1836, *Architectural Magazine* 4 (April 1837): 161.

18. Robert Stuart Meikleham, *The Theory and Practice of Warming and Ventilating Public Buildings, Dwelling-houses, and Conservatories: Including a General View of the Changes Produced in Atmospheric Air, by Respiration, Combustion, and Putrefaction, with the Means of Obviating Its Deleterious Agency; and a Description of All the Known Varieties of Stoves, Grates, and Furnaces; with an Examination of Their Comparative Advantages for Economising Fuel and Preventing Smoke* (London: Thomas and George Underwood, 1825). See also, in Meikleham's pseudonym, Walter Bernan, *On the History and Art of Warming and Ventilating* (London: George Bell, 1822). For nonindustrial applications, see Jean Baptiste Marie Frédéric, marquis de Chabannes, *On Conducting Air by Forced Ventilation, and Regulating the Temperature in Dwellings: With a Description of the Application of the Principles as Established in Covent Garden Theatre and Lloyd's Subscription Rooms, and a Short Account of Different Patent Apparatus for Warming and Cooling Air and Liquids* (London, 1818). See also Thomas Tredgold, *Principles of Warming and Ventilating Public Buildings* (London, 1824).

19. Jayne Elizabeth Lewis, *Air's Appearance: Literary Atmosphere in British Fiction, 1660–1794* (Chicago: University of Chicago Press, 2012). For Boyle's early experiments on air, see Steven Shapin and Simon Schaffer, *Leviathan and the Air Pump: Hobbes, Boyle, and the Experimental Life* (Princeton, N.J.: Princeton University Press, 1985).

20. A few key works in the secondary literature of nineteenth-century ventilation include Robert Bruegmann, "Architecture of the Hospital: 1770–1870, Design and Technology" (PhD diss., University of Pennsylvania, 1976). Robin Evans's analysis of Jeremy Bentham's ventilation system for the Panopticon is in *The Fabrication of Virtue: English Prison Architecture, 1750–1840* (Cambridge: Cambridge University Press, 1982). Michel Foucault, Blandine Barret Kriegel, Anne Thalamy, François Beguin, and Bruno Fortier, *Les machines à guerir (aux origines de l'hôpital moderne)* (Brussels: Pierre Mardaga, 1979). For an excellent analysis of a twentieth-century case of hospital ventilation, see Annemarie Adams, *Medicine by Design: The Architect and the Modern Hospital, 1893–1943* (Minneapolis: University of Minnesota Press, 2008). See also Sven-Olov Wallenstein, *Biopolitics and the Emergence of Modern Architecture* (New York: Princeton Architectural Press, 2009).

21. Robert Bruegmann, "Central Heating and Forced Ventilation: Origins and Effects on Architectural Design," *Journal of the Society of Architectural Historians* 37:3 (October 1978): 143–60. See also Neville S. Billington, "A Historical Review of the Art of Heating and Ventilating," *Architectural Science Review* 2:3 (1959): 118–30; Benjamin Walbert III, "Infancy of Central Heating in the United States: 1803–45," *Association for Preservation Technology Bulletin* 3:4 (1971): 76–87; Eugene S. Ferguson, "An Historical Sketch of Central Heating: 1800–1860," in *Building Early America: Contributions to the History of a Great Industry*, ed. Charles E. Peterson (Radnor: Chilton Book Company, 1976), 165–85.

22. By the middle of the century, a theory of ventilating mines had been formalized. See J. J. Atkinson, "On the Theory of the Ventilation of Mines," *Transactions of the North of England Institute of Mining Engineers*, December 1854, 73–222, 321–40. For an example of writing that dealt with the conditions of health related to the industrial workplace, see Charles Turner Thackrah, *The Effects of Arts, Trades, and Professions: And of Civic States and Habits of Living, on Health and Longevity: with Suggestions for the Removal of Many of the Agents which Produce Disease, and Shorten the Duration of Life* (London: Longman, Rees, Orme, Brown, and Green, 1831).

23. Ure, "An Experimental Inquiry," 174–76.

24. Ibid., 161.

25. For a history of the concept of animal economy, see Bernard Balan, "Premières recherches sur l'origine et la formation du concept d'économie animale," *Revue d'histoire des sciences* 28 (1975): 289–326.

26. Ure, "An Experimental Inquiry," 164–66.

27. With N. L. Sadi Carnot's 1824 *Reflections on the Motive Power of Heat and on Machines Fitted to Develop that Power*, trans. Robert H. Thurston (New York: John Wiley and Sons, 1890), scientific theories of thermodynamics were developing around the same moment as the studies on ventilation. For the formulation of the term "thermo-dynamics," see William T. Kelvin, "An Account of Carnot's Theory of the Motive Power of Heat with Numerical Results Deduced from Regnault's Experiments on Steam," *Transactions of the Royal Society of Edinburgh* 16 (January 2, 1849): 113–64. For a beautiful essay on the effect of thermodynamic thinking, see Michel Serres, "Turner Translates Carnot," in *Hermes: Literature, Science, Philosophy* (Baltimore: Johns Hopkins University Press, 1982), 54–62.

28. Charles Sylvester, *The Philosophy of Domestic Economy: As Exemplified in the Mode of*

Warming, Ventilating, Washing, Drying, & Cooking, and in Various Arrangements Contributing to the Comfort and Convenience of Domestic Life, Adopted in the Derbyshire General Infirmary (London: Barnett, 1819); William Strutt, *The Philosophy of Domestic Economy* (Nottingham: H. Barnett, 1819). For more on Strutt, see M. C. Egerton, "William Strutt and the Application of Convection to the Heating of Buildings," *Annals of Science* 24:1 (1968): 73–87. On the hospital, see V. M. Leveaux, *A History of the Derbyshire General Infirmary, 1810–1894* (Cromford: Scarthin Books, 1999); Paul Elliott, "The Derbyshire General Infirmary and the Derby Philosophers: The Application of Industrial Architecture and Technology to Medical Institutions in Early-Nineteenth-Century England," *Medical History* 46:1 (January 2002): 65–69.

29. Ure made additional careful studies of the ventilation of the Long Room at the Custom House, although the conditions there remained notoriously difficult to fix. See "Experiments at the Custom House with Boyle's System of Ventilation," *Sanitary Record* 2 (February 15, 1881): 318. In the same article the author mentions that Michael Faraday also investigated the conditions of the Long Room in the middle of the century.

30. David Boswell Reid, *Rudiments of Chemistry; With Illustrations of the Chemical Phenomena of Daily Life* (Edinburgh: William and Robert Chambers, 1836), 45–54.

31. Charles James Richardson, *A Popular Treatise on the Warming and Ventilation of Buildings* (London: John Weale, 1839). See also Cecil D. Elliott, *Technics and Architecture: The Development of Materials and Systems for Buildings* (Cambridge, Mass.: MIT Press, 1992), 285–86.

32. David Boswell Reid, *Brief Outlines Illustrative of the Alterations in the House of Commons, in Reference to the Acoustic and Ventilating Arrangements* (Edinburgh: Neill and Company, 1837).

33. For the exchange between Barry and Reid, see Moritz Gleich, "Architect and Service Architect: The Quarrel between Charles Barry and David Boswell Reid," *Interdisciplinary Science Reviews* 37:4 (December 2012): 332–44. Also see Peter Collins, *Changing Ideals in Modern Architecture, 1750–1950* (London: Faber and Faber, 1965), 237–38.

34. David Boswell Reid, *Illustrations of the Theory and Practice of Ventilation, with Remarks on Warming, Exclusive Lighting, and the Communication of Sound* (London: Longman, Brown, Green, and Longmans, 1844), 70.

35. "Reid's Air Brewery," *Punch, or the London Charivari* 10 (1846): 168.

36. William MacKenzie, "On the Mechanical Ventilation and Warming of St. George's Hall, Liverpool," *Proceedings of the Institution of Mechanical Engineers* 14 (June 1863): 194–208.

37. Montgomery C. Meigs, "General M. C. Meigs on the Heating and Ventilating of the U.S. Senate Chamber," *Sanitary Engineer* 9 (1884): 431. See also William C. Dickinson, Dean A. Herrin, and Donald R. Kennon, eds., *Montgomery C. Meigs and the Building of the Nation's Capital* (Athens: Ohio University Press, 2001).

38. David Boswell Reid, *Ventilation in American Dwellings: With a Series of Diagrams, Presenting Examples in Different Classes of Habitations* (New York: Wiley and Halsted, 1858), viii.

39. Ibid., 5. Dr. Elisha Harris, the physician-in-chief of the New York Quarantine Hospitals, wrote the introduction to Reid's *Ventilation in American Dwellings*. His "Outline of the Progress of Improvement in Ventilation" was specifically concerned with their value for sanitation. In Wisconsin, Reid spoke to the State Agricultural Society on public health, where he asked: "How many are the death-bed scenes where a little knowledge

of the pulse, of respiration, of the influence of a vertical or a horizontal position, of heat and cold, and of dry and moist air, would have averted a fatal termination! Is there a house that should not have its Florence Nightingale?" "The Practical Development of the Resources of Science, in Relation to Agriculture and the Health and Habitations of the People," September 27, 1860.

40. Reid, *Ventilation in American Dwellings*, 5.

41. Catharine E. Beecher, "How to Redeem Woman's Profession from Dishonor," *Harper's New Monthly Magazine* 31:186 (November 1865): 710–16.

42. Beecher was developing her political position in her *Treatise on Domestic Economy, for Use of Young Ladies at Home and at School* (Boston: Marsh, Capen, Lyon, and Webb, 1841). On the relationship between Beecher's feminism and her home designs, see Dolores Hayden, *The Grand Domestic Revolution: A History of Feminist Designs for American Homes, Neighborhoods, and Cities* (Cambridge, Mass.: MIT Press, 1981), 55–63. Hayden's analysis builds on the work of Kathryn Kish Sklar, *Catherine Beecher: A Study in American Domesticity* (New Haven: Yale University Press, 1973).

43. The Marxist literature on domestic labor begins with Marx's own discussion of reproduction in *Capital*, extended in Friedrich Engels, *The Origin of the Family, Private Property and the State* [1884], trans. Tristram Hunt (New York: Penguin Books, 2010). Selected works that further investigate these subjects include Wally Seccombe, "The Housewife and Her Labor under Capitalism," *New Left Review* I/83 (January–February 1974): 3–24; Joan W. Scott and Louise A. Tilly, "Women's Work and the Family in Nineteenth-Century Europe," *Comparative Studies in Society and History* 17:1 (January 1975): 36–64; Eli Zaretsky, *Capitalism, the Family & Personal Life* (New York: Harper and Row, 1976); Mary O'Brien, "The Dialectics of Reproduction," *Women's Studies International Quarterly* 1:3 (1978): 233–39; Bonnie Fox, ed., *Hidden in the Household: Women's Domestic Labour under Capitalism* (Toronto: Women's Press, Fernwood Books, 1980).

44. See Lewis W. Leeds, *Lectures on Ventilation: Being a Course Delivered in the Franklin Institute* (New York: John Wiley and Sons, 1868). For Beecher's reaction to Reid's work on the Houses of Parliament, see Catharine Beecher and Harriet Beecher Stowe, *The American Woman's Home: Or, Principles of Domestic Science; Being a Guide to the Formation and Maintenance of Economical, Healthful, Beautiful, and Christian Homes* (New York: J. B. Ford, 1869), 419–32. For the relationship between the Sanitary Commission and the work of women's organizations during the Civil War, see Lori D. Ginzburg, *Women and the Work of Benevolence: Morality, Politics, and Class in the 19th-Century United States* (New Haven: Yale University Press, 1990), 133–73.

45. Beecher, *Treatise on Domestic Economy*, 268.

46. Reyner Banham, *The Architecture of the Well-Tempered Environment* (Chicago: University of Chicago Press, 1969), 96. Banham notes that James Marston Fitch, in *Architecture and the Esthetics of Plenty* (New York: Columbia University Press, 1961), used Le Corbusier's *machine à habiter* to describe Beecher's house.

47. Beecher and Stowe, *The American Woman's Home*, 426. For a treatment of Beecher's plumbing system, see Maureen Ogle, *All the Modern Conveniences: American Household Plumbing, 1840–1890* (Baltimore: Johns Hopkins University Press, 1996), 18–19, 31.

48. Thomas P. Hughes, *Networks of Power: Electrification in Western Society, 1880–1930*

(Baltimore: Johns Hopkins University Press, 1983). See also David E. Nye, *Electrifying America: Social Meanings of a New Technology, 1880–1940* (Cambridge, Mass.: MIT Press, 1990), esp. chap. 6, "A Clean, Well-Lighted Hearth."

49. Arthur E. Kennelly, "Electricity in the Household," *Scribner's Magazine* 7 (January 1890): 115.

50. "The Automatic Electric Heat Regulator. Manufactured by the Perfect Hatcher Company, Elmira, NY (F. Rosebrook, Inventor)," in *International Electrical Exhibition, 1884: Reports of the Examiners of Sections V, VI & VIII* (Philadelphia: Franklin Institute, 1885), 78–81. Frank Rosebrook's patent is Electric Regulator and Alarm for Incubators, U.S. Patent 271,991 (issued February 6, 1883). "Hatching by Electricity," *Electrical World*, August 2, 1884, 35. For a description of the device directed at architects and builders, see "A Sensitive Automatic Heat Regulator," *Manufacturer and Builder* 18:1 (January 1886): 19.

51. Butz was brought to court for a patent infringement of Julien M. Bradford's "improvement in electrical heat and vapor governors for spinning and weaving rooms," U.S. Patent 222,234 (issued December 2, 1879). See "The Butz Thermo-Electric Regulator Company v. The Jacobs Electric Company," in *Decisions of the Commissioner of Patents* (Washington, D.C.: Government Printing Office, 1888), 515. For a history of patents related to temperature control, see Barry Donaldson and Bernard Nagengast, *Heat and Cold: Mastering the Great Indoors. A Selective History of Heating, Ventilation, Refrigeration and Air Conditioning from the Ancients to the 1930s* (Atlanta: ASHRAE, 1994), 197–204.

52. It is hard to find proof that Butz ever used this term "damper flapper," but it has become part of the origin myth of the Honeywell Corporation. See http://honeywell.com /About/Pages/our-history.aspx.

53. The Butz Thermo-Electric Regulator Company was sold to the Consolidated Temperature Controlling Company in 1888 and eventually merged with several other companies. In 1926 the company became known as the Minneapolis-Honeywell Regulator Company, now Honeywell, Inc.

54. "Automatic Heat Regulation by Electric Means," *Manufacturer and Builder* 20:11 (November 1888): 259.

55. William Penn Powers patented a "vapor disk," a nonelectric thermostat that regulated the heat produced by the furnace. Thermostat, U.S. Patent 424,617 (issued April 1, 1890). This pneumatic system was the basis of the Powers system. The use of condensed air may be related to the company's innovative methods of using a plenum chamber to treat the air, bring it to a controlled temperature, and move it throughout the domestic interior. Powers Regulator Company, *The Powers Systems of Automatic Temperature Control* (Chicago: Powers Regulator Co., 1901), 17.

56. Most of the regulatory instruments discussed in this chapter were not available to the vast majority of American families. For example, only a third of the nation's homes were wired for electrical regulation around 1920. For the expansion of electrical utilities, see Hughes, *Networks of Power*.

57. Ruth Schwartz Cowan, "The 'Industrial Revolution' in the Home: Household Technology and Social Change in the 20th Century," *Technology and Culture* 17:1 (January 1976): 1–23. Reworked in her *More Work for Mother: The Ironies of Household Technology from the*

Open Hearth to the Microwave (New York: Basic Books, 1985). See also David P. Handlin, "Good Housekeeping," and "The Heart of the Home," two chapters in *The American Home: Architecture and Society, 1815–1915* (Boston: Little, Brown, 1979), 386–486; Glenna Matthews, *"Just a Housewife": The Rise and Fall of Domesticity in America* (New York: Oxford University Press, 1987), esp. chap. 6.

58. The term *management* had, since its early use, been associated with the household econ-omy. Only in the 1850s did the industrial meaning of the term, relating it more directly to labor and technology, come into use. One example is Charles Pierce, *The Household Manager: Being a Practical Treatise upon the Various Duties in Large or Small Establishments, from the Drawing-room to the Kitchen* (London: G. Routledge, 1857).

59. Daniel T. Rodgers, *The Work Ethic in Industrial America, 1850–1920* (Chicago: University of Chicago Press, 1974), 182–209.

60. The influence of social Darwinism on Edward Bellamy and Lester Ward was signifi-cant, and Gilman was an avid reader of both. See Charlotte Perkins Gilman, *Women and Economics: A Study of the Economic Relation between Men and Women as a Factor in Social Evolution* (1898; repr., New York: Harper and Row, 1966). See also Hayden, *The Grand Domestic Revolution*, 183–205.

61. Edward Bellamy, "A Vital Domestic Problem, Household Service Reform," *Good House-keeping* 10:4 (December 21, 1889): 74–77. For more on Bellamy's influence on feminist thought, see Mari Jo Buhle, *Women and American Socialism, 1870–1920* (Urbana: University of Illinois Press, 1983), 49–103. Bellamy was not an entirely liberal thinker. As Arthur Lipow has shown, the utopia he espoused erased many of the individual liberties as-sociated with democratic society. See his *Authoritarian Socialism in America: Edward Bellamy and the Nationalist Movement* (Berkeley: University of California Press, 1982).

62. Charlotte Perkins Gilman, "What Diantha Did," *The Forerunner* 1 (1909–10): 14. For Gilman's views on housekeeping in industrialized society, see her "The Waste of Private Housekeeping," *Annals of the American Academy of Political and Social Science* 48 (July 1913): 91–95.

63. J. H. Kinealy, "Temperature Regulation," *Transactions of the American Society of Heating and Ventilating* 9 (1904): 65.

64. [Mary] Pattison, "Scientific Management in Home-Making," *Annals of the American Academy of Political and Social Science* 48 (July 1913): 96. The vast literature on the appli-cation of Taylor's methods to household labor includes Martha B. Bruere and Robert W. Bruere, "The Elimination of Waste in the Household," *Journal of Home Economics* 2 (June 1910): 292–97; J. B. Guernsey, "Scientific Management in the Home," *Outlook* 100 (April 13, 1912): 821–25; Francis E. Leupp, "Scientific Management in the Family," *Outlook* 98 (August 12, 1911): 832–37; Frank B. Gilbreth, "Scientific Management in the Household," *Journal of Home Economics* 4 (December 1912): 438–47; and M. Atkinson, "The Application of Scientific Methods to Housekeeping," *Living Age* 259 (October 24, 1908): 227–33. For the relationship between Taylor's doctrine and the domestic setting, see Martha Banta, *Taylored Lives: Narrative Productions in the Age of Taylor, Veblen, and Ford* (Chicago: University of Chicago Press, 1993).

65. Margaret E. Dodd, *Chemistry of the Household* (Chicago: American School of Home Economics, 1907), 14.

66. Theodore Hough and William T. Sedgwick, *The Human Mechanism: Its Physiology and Hygiene and the Sanitation of Its Surroundings* (Boston: Ginn and Company, 1906), 201.

67. The late eighteenth-century discourse on comfort was related to a "culturally progressive rather than physically natural" view of the home. John E. Crowley, *The Invention of Comfort: Sensibilities and Design in Early Modern Britain and Early America* (Baltimore: Johns Hopkins University Press, 2003), 292. For an excellent history of American advertising, see Roland Marchand, *Advertising the American Dream: Making Way for Modernity, 1920–1940* (Berkeley: University of California Press, 1986).

68. Adrian Forty, "Hygiene and Cleanliness," in *Objects of Desire: Design and Culture, 1750* (London: Thames and Hudson, 1992), 156–81.

69. Alfred G. King, *Progressive Furnace Heating: A Practical Manual of Designing, Estimating and Installing Modern Systems for Heating and Ventilating Buildings with Warm Air* (New York: Sheet Metal Publication Company, 1914), 156.

70. Banham's analysis of the reciprocal relationship between Wright's domestic architecture and environmental control is in *The Architecture of the Well-Tempered Environment*, 104–21. For a short historical account of the relationship between architects of the period and reformers, see Gwendolyn Wright, "The Progressive Housewife and the Bungalow," in *Building the Dream: A Social History of Housing in America* (Cambridge, Mass.: MIT Press, 1981), 158–76. For the later development of the picture window, only possible after the automated control of the interior environment, see Sandy Isenstadt, "'The View It Frames': A History of the Picture Window," in *The Modern American House: Spaciousness and Middle Class Identity* (Cambridge: Cambridge University Press, 2006), 179–214.

71. Mary Pattison, "Domestic Engineering: The Housekeeping Experiment Station at Colonia, New Jersey," *Scientific American* 106 (April 13, 1912): 330–31; "Experiment Station to Solve Housekeeper's Problems," *New York Times*, March 26, 1911; "Making the Home Efficient," *New York Times*, July 25, 1915. For Pattison's biography, see William Nelson, *Nelson's Biographical Cyclopedia of New Jersey*, vol. 2 (New York: Eastern Historical Publishing Company, 1913), 745–50.

72. Christine Frederick, *The New Housekeeping: Efficiency Studies in Home Management* (Garden City: Doubleday, Page, 1913), originally published in *Ladies' Home Journal* 29 (September–December 1912).

73. Mary Pattison, *Principles of Domestic Engineering: Or, the What, Why and How of a Home; an Attempt to Evolve a Solution of the Domestic "Labor and Capital" Problem, to Standardize and Professionalize Housework, to Re-organize the Home upon "Scientific Management" Principles, and to Point Out the Importance of the Public and Personal Element Therein, as Well as the Practical* (New York: Trow Press, 1915), 30.

74. Christine Frederick, *Household Engineering: Scientific Management in the Home* (Chicago: American School of Home Economics, 1921), 96. Later she published a book on advertising, *Selling Mrs. Consumer* (New York: Business Bourse, 1929). Janice Williams Rutherford, *Selling Mrs. Consumer: Christine Frederick and the Rise of Household Efficiency* (Athens: University of Georgia Press, 2003).

75. The literature on the mechanization of the kitchen is large. Its architectural history begins with Sigfried Giedion, *Mechanization Takes Command* (Oxford: Oxford University

Press, 1948; reprint, Minneapolis: University of Minnesota Press, 2013). A recent synopsis is in Juliet Kinchin and Aidan O'Connor, *Counter Space: Design and the Modern Kitchen* (New York: MoMA Publications, 2011).

76. Frederick was also not the first to apply this visual language to housework. See Hyungmin Pai, *The Portfolio and the Diagram:* Architecture, Discourse, and Modernity in America (Cambridge, Mass.: MIT Press, 2002), 176–97. For the relationship between Frederick's diagrams and Bruno Taut's in *Die Neue Wohnung,* see Nicholas Bullock, "'First the Kitchen—Then the Façade,'" *Journal of Design History* 1 (1988): 177–92. On the contribution of Frank Gilbreth's wife, Lillian Gilbreth, to movement analysis in the kitchen, see Laurel D. Graham, "Domesticating Efficiency: Lillian Gilbreth's Scientific Management of Homemakers, 1924–1930," *Signs* 24:3 (Spring 1999): 633–75. See also the diagrams for motion in Frank B. Gilbreth, *Bricklaying System* (London: M. C. Clark Publishing, 1909). The mechanistic representation of bodily movement is contextualized in a broad intellectual history of fatigue by Anson Rabinbach, "Time and Motion: Etienne-Jules Marey and the Mechanics of the Body," in *The Human Motor: Energy, Fatigue, and the Origins of Modernity* (New York: Basic Books, 1990), 84–119.

77. For an excellent critique of the virtues ascribed to labor in the political economic thought of Thorstein Veblen's *Theory of the Leisure Class* (New York: Macmillan, 1899), see Theodor W. Adorno, "Veblen's Attack on Culture," in *Prisms,* trans. Samuel Weber (Cambridge, Mass.: MIT Press, 1967), 75–94. Like Gilman, Veblen viewed the isolation of women in the home as an indication of the bankruptcy of the capitalist profit motive. Veblen's view was first published as "The Barbarian Status of Women," *American Journal of Sociology* 4:4 (January 1899): 503–14.

78. Barber-Coleman Company, *An Electrical System of Temperature Control* (Rockford: Barber-Coleman Company, 1931).

2. COLD STORAGE AND THE SPECULATIVE MARKET OF PRESERVED ASSETS

1. Edward Bellamy, *Looking Backward* (Boston: Houghton Mifflin, 1889), 30–31.

2. Arthur Lipow has written that Bellamyism, and the Nationalist movement that grew out from it, was a precursor to at least two political movements: totalitarian collectivist ideologies and bureaucratic statist or "corporate" liberalism. *Authoritarian Socialism in America: Edward Bellamy and the Nationalist Movement* (Berkeley: University of California Press, 1982), 2. For the novel's position in the context of American reactions to technology, see John F. Kasson, *Civilizing the Machine: Technology and Republican Values in America, 1776–1900* (New York: Penguin Books, 1984), 191–202.

3. In the novel, Bellamy projected another profound change in his view of the utopian future: the manner in which humans interacted with their surroundings. Instead of individual responses to the weather, such as the use of an umbrella in rain or a ventilating fan in heat, the government would guide a collective mechanical system that responded to rainfall and extremes in temperature. Publicly owned renewable natural resources were responsible for producing the electricity that warmed and cooled the entire population to any degree that it desired. For more on this, see William B. Meyer, "Edward Bellamy and the Weather of Utopia," *Geographical Review* 94:1 (January 2004): 43–54.

4. "Editor's Study," *Harper's New Monthly Magazine* 95:569 (October 1897): 798.

5. For a history of the transition from harvested ice to mechanical refrigeration, see Richard Osborn Cummings, *The American Ice Harvests: A Historical Study in Technology, 1800–1918* (Berkeley: University of California Press, 1949); Jonathan Rees, *Refrigeration Nation: A History of Ice, Appliances, and Enterprise in America* (Baltimore: Johns Hopkins University Press, 2013).

6. Mary Yeager Kujovich, "The Refrigerator Car and the Growth of the American Dressed Beef Industry," *Business History Review* 44:4 (Winter 1970): 460–82. Kujovich wrote her dissertation on the meatpacking industry under Alfred Chandler, "The Dynamics of Oligopoly in the Meat Packing Industry: A Historical Analysis, 1875–1912" (PhD diss., Johns Hopkins University, 1973). It was published as *Competition and Regulation: The Development of Oligopoly in the Meat Packing Industry* (Greenwich, Conn.: JAI Press, 1981). Chandler referred to Kujovich's early research; see Chandler, *The Visible Hand: The Managerial Revolution in American Business* (Cambridge, Mass.: Belknap Press of Harvard University Press, 1977), 299–302, 391–402.

7. The technology depended on the capacity to mechanically compress liquid ammonia and combine it with water. This low temperature mixture separates as temperature rises and the ammonia expands into vapor. Machines were built to circulate the cool liquid mixture through coils that withdrew heat from the air inside the rail car. At the same time, as the mixture warmed in the coils, the ammonia would expand into vapor to be recompressed and saturated back into water so that it could reproduce the refrigeration effect in another cycle. See Oscar Edward Anderson Jr., *Refrigeration in America* (Princeton, N.J.: Princeton University Press, 1953). See also Mikael Hård, *Machines Are Frozen Spirit: The Scientification of Refrigeration and Brewing in the 19th Century—A Weberian Interpretation* (Boulder, Colo.: Westview Press, 1994).

8. All through the 1880s Chase advertised his patented refrigerators for grocers called the "Cold Blast Roll Top"; see *The Grocers' Criterion* 18:33 (August 17, 1891): 16. He also designed the apparatus for a few cold storage buildings designed by William Gibbons Preston, the architect of the Quincy Market Cold Storage Company. For example, Preston's drawings for a small storage house in Elizabeth, New Jersey, notes the use of "A. J. Chase's System of Refrigeration," W. G. Preston Collection, Boston Public Library, vol. 24, 1–16.

9. For the controversies that surrounded the "bucket shops" that traded and speculated on futures, see Jonathan Ira Levy, "Contemplating Delivery: Futures Trading and the Problem of Commodity Exchange in the United States, 1875–1905," *American Historical Review* 111:2 (April 2006): 307–35.

10. See, for example, Jonathan Lurie, *The Chicago Board of Trade, 1859–1905: The Dynamics of Self-Regulation* (Champaign: University of Illinois Press, 1979).

11. The literature on the history of business cycles in the United States is vast, especially those dealing with the relationship to monetary policy. Maybe the most cited text is Milton Friedman and Anna Schwartz, *A Monetary History of the United States, 1867–1960* (Princeton, N.J.: Princeton University Press, 1971).

12. The institute was founded in 1868 as the Zymotechnic Institute. John Ewald Siebel, *Compend of Mechanical Refrigeration: A Comprehensive Digest of Applied Energetics and Thermodynamics for the Practical Use of Ice Manufacturers, Cold Storage Men, Contractors,*

Engineers, Brewers, Packers, and Others Interested in the Application of Refrigeration (Chicago: H. S. Rich and Company, 1899).

13. Mary E. Pennington published extensively on the quality of food as head of the Household Refrigeration Bureau. On Pennington's role in governmental regulation of food, see Lisa Mae Robinson, "Regulating What We Eat: Mary Engle Pennington and the Food Research Laboratory," *Agricultural History* 64:2 (Spring 1990): 143–53. See also Madison Cooper, *Eggs in Cold Storage: Theory and Practice in Preserving Eggs by Refrigeration, Data, Experiments, Hints on Construction, Etc., from Practical Experience, with Illustration* (Chicago: H. S. Rich and Company, 1899). F. Wm. Rane, Herbert H. Lamson, and Fred W. Morse, *The Cold Storage of Apples* (Durham: New Hampshire College of Agriculture and the Mechanic Arts, 1902).

14. Jean-Baptiste Say's "Law of Markets" and various restatements of it assumed an essential equation between supply and demand. See, for example, John Stuart Mill, *Essays on Some Unsettled Questions of Political Economy* (London: John W. Parker, 1844), 69.

15. Karl Marx, *Theories of Surplus Value*, trans. Emile Burns (Moscow: Progress Publishers, 1968), 493.

16. "If, for example, purchase and sale—or the metamorphosis of commodities—represent the unity of two processes, or rather the movement of one process through two opposite phases, and thus essentially the unity of two phases, the movement is essentially just as much the separation of these two phases and their becoming independent of each other. Since, however, they belong together, the independence of the two correlated aspects can only *show itself* forcibly, as a destructive process. It is just the crisis in which they assert their unity, the unity of the different aspects." Ibid., 500.

17. Ibid., 509. Later Marxists argued against what became known as the "inevitability doctrine" such as the Ukrainian economist Mikhail Ivanovich Tugan-Baranovskiï (1865–1919) in his *Theoretische Grundlagen des Marxismus* (Leipzig: Duncker and Humblot, 1905). The "crises debates" remained alive for many decades, and Marx's theory became the backbone of several theories of imperialism such as that of Rosa Luxemburg (1871–1919) in *The Accumulation of Capital*, trans. Agnes Schwarzschild (New Haven: Yale University Press, 1951) and of course that of Vladimir Ilyich Lenin (1870–1924), *Imperialism, the Highest Stage of Capitalism: A Popular Outline* (New York: International Publishers, 1970).

18. William Cronon, "Pricing the Future," in *Nature's Metropolis: Chicago and the Great West* (New York: W. W. Norton, 1992), 97–147. On grain silos, see Guy A. Lee "History of the Chicago Grain Elevator Industry" (PhD thesis, Harvard University, 1938). Also see his short article, "The Historical Significance of the Chicago Grain Elevator System," *Agricultural History* 11:1 (January 1937): 16–32.

19. Marx, *Theories of Surplus Value*. The American edition of Karl Rodbertus's *Theory of Crises* was published under the title *Overproduction and Crises*, trans. Julia Franklin (New York: C. Scribner's Sons, 1898). In the preface to the new edition of Francis Wayland's *Elements of Political Economy* (New York: Sheldon and Company, 1886), Aaron L. Chapin condensed the "second division on Consumption" to make "room for a new chapter in connection with it on Overproduction." See also Frederic Grimm, *Notes on Civilization, Over-production, Competition, Protection, Silver Question, Chinese, etc.: Giving a Cause for the*

Present Dull Times (San Francisco, 1886); Uriel H. Crocker, *Over-production and Commercial Distress* (Boston: Clarke and Carruth, 1887).

20. Martin J. Sklar, *The Corporate Reconstruction of American Capitalism, 1890–1916: The Market, the Law, and Politics* (Cambridge: Cambridge University Press, 1988), 43–85. See also his earlier article written with Carl P. Parrini, "New Thinking about the Market, 1896–1904: Some American Economists on Investment and the Theory of Surplus Capital," *Journal of Economic History* 43:3 (September 1983): 559–78.

21. Charles A. Conant, *A History of Modern Banks of Issue, with an Account of the Economic Crises of the Present Century* (New York: G. P. Putnam's Sons, 1896), 453.

22. Charles A. Conant, "Crises and Their Management," *Yale Review* 9 (February 1901): 375. This statement resonates with the biological theories developing at the time that, in turn, deployed economic metaphors to explain biological systems of regulation. See, for example, Frederic Edward Clements, "Nature of the Problem of the Cycle," *Geographical Review, Special Supplement: Report of a Conference on Cycles* 13:4 (October 1923): 657–59.

23. "The tendency to over-production resulting from unrestricted competition has been corrected to some extent during the past decade by the consolidation of industry and the restriction of production. The volume of production and the process of distribution have thus been brought under a higher degree of organization than before." Conant, "Crises and Their Management," 379.

24. "Chicago Produce Exchange," *Chicago Daily Tribune*, April 20, 1874, 5.

25. When Andreas wrote his history of Chicago in 1886, perishables were still considered "minor" commodities: "In May [of 1874] the Produce Exchange was organized. Its membership is composed of dealers in minor agricultural products, such as butter, eggs, poultry, etc. Co-operation and concert of action in dealing in this class of products, thus inaugurated, has resulted in the continued and successful operation of this Exchange." Alfred Theodore Andreas, *History of Chicago*, vol. 3 (Chicago: A. T. Andreas, 1886), 302.

26. Ibid., 123–52. See also Produce Exchange of the City of Chicago, *Constitution and By-laws of the Produce Exchange of the City of Chicago: Rules for Handling and Grading Butter, Cheese, Eggs, Fruits, Vegetables, &c: List of Members, &c.* (Chicago: The Exchange, 1884), 20–37. In the year of this publication the Exchange claimed 493 members including commission merchants, grocers, insurers, exporters, and even a few cold storage companies.

27. Samuel Macauley Jackson, *The Laws of Trade, as Adopted by the Board of Trade, the Union Stock Yards and Transit Company, the Lumberman's Exchange and the Produce Exchange of the City of Chicago Together with Some Practical Hints in Shipping &c.* (Chicago: Pitkin and Cruvek, 1878), 120.

28. The rules regulating the butter trade included "Rule 3: On spot sales the goods shall be ready for immediate delivery." While there were also rules set for the "future delivery" of butter, they were only carried over from one call to the next leaving no time for speculation as "to arrive" contracts had in the Board of Trade. Ibid., 20.

29. See Edward S. Davis, "Chicago: The World's Greatest Produce Market," *Fort Dearborn Magazine* 1 (January 1920): 14–15, 31; Chicago Mercantile Exchange, *Chicago Mercantile Exchange: The Great Central Market for Butter and Eggs, Its Methods of Operation and Position*

in the Industry (Chicago: Chicago Mercantile Exchange, 1923); Chicago Mercantile Exchange, *Getting Butter and Eggs to Market; a Detailed Account of How These Products Are Handled, and of the Channels through which They Pass, on Their Way from the Producer to the Ultimate Consumer* (Chicago: Chicago Mercantile Exchange, 1924); Lloyd S. Tenny, "Chicago Mercantile Exchange," *Annals of the American Academy of Political and Social Science* 155 (May 1931): 133–35. David Greising and Laurie Morse have written a brief account of the origins of the Chicago Mercantile Exchange in their chapter "Scrappy Survivor: The Early Years of the Merc," in *Brokers, Bagmen, and Moles: Fraud and Corruption in the Chicago Futures Markets* (New York: John Wiley and Sons, 1991), 73–74; so too has Charles R. Geisst, *Wheels of Fortune: The History of Speculation from Scandal to Respectability* (New York: John Wiley and Sons, 2003), 82–83. Finally, see Roy Ashmen, *A Brief Institutional History of Price Determination for Wholesale Butter; Chicago Produce Exchange, 1874–1894 and Chicago Butter and Egg Board, 1894–1919* (College Park, Md., 1973).

30. "Artificial Cold on Tap," *Chicago Daily Tribune*, November 1, 1888, 7. Fuller established a subsidiary to his New York company: the Illinois Refrigerating Construction Company. See also "Railway Industries," *Railway World*, November 10, 1888, 1062.

31. "Biggest in the World," *Chicago Daily Tribune*, November 14, 1890, 6.

32. Ibid.

33. Ibid. See also "The Great Cold-Storage Plant," *Chicago Daily Tribune*, July 7, 1891, 4.

34. For more on the complexity of the program, see Joseph Siry, *The Chicago Auditorium Building: Adler and Sullivan's Architecture and the City* (Chicago: University of Chicago Press, 2002).

35. Frank M. Lester, *Handbook of Chicago Stocks and Bonds* (Chicago: Jameson and Morse, 1891), 65.

36. Carl Condit, *The Rise of the Skyscraper* (Chicago: University of Chicago Press, 1952), 180. The same is stated in Carl Condit, *The Chicago School of Architecture* (Chicago: University of Chicago Press, 1964), 135. This is particularly strange given Condit's emphasis on technological novelty in this book as well as in his other writings. Another similar commentary comes from Hugh Morrison: "It is in reality architecture reduced to the most elemental terms of volumes and plane surfaces, and suggests, a generation ahead of its time, '*Die neue Sachlichkeit*' of modern German architecture." *Louis Sullivan: Prophet of Modern Architecture* (New York: W. W. Norton, 1935), 126.

37. Louis Sullivan, "The Tall Office Building Artistically Considered," in *Kindergarten Chats and Other Writings* (New York: Dover Books, 1979), 203; originally published in *Lippincott's* 57 (March 1896): 403–9. On the relationship between the steel grid and architectural modernism, see Colin Rowe, "The Chicago Frame: Chicago's Place in the Modern Movement," *Architectural Review* 120 (November 1956): 285–89. See also Carl W. Condit, "Sullivan's Skyscrapers as the Expression of Nineteenth Century Technology," *Technology and Culture* 1:1 (Winter 1959): 78–93. More recently, see Joanna Merwood-Salisbury, *Chicago 1890: The Skyscraper and the Modern City* (Chicago: University of Chicago Press, 2009).

38. For a treatment of the organic metaphor in American architecture, Sullivan and Frank Lloyd Wright in particular, see Donald Drew Egbert, "The Idea of Organic Expression and American Architecture," in *Evolutionary Thought in America*, ed. Stow Persons (New

Haven: Yale University Press, 1950), esp. 352–53. On the German case, which undoubtedly also influenced Sullivan, see Mitchell Schwarzer, "Ontology and Representation in Karl Bötticher's Theory of Tectonics," *Journal of the Society of Architectural Historians* 52:3 (September 1993): 267–80.

39. Louis Sullivan, *The Autobiography of an Idea* (New York: American Institute of Architects, 1924), 246. Lewis Mumford wrote that "Sullivan saw that the business of the architect was to organize the forces of modern society, discipline them for human ends, express them in the plastic-utilitarian form of a building." *Brown Decades: A Study of the Arts in America, 1865–1895* (1931; repr. New York: Dover Publications, 1971), 74.

40. Thomas Leslie, "Dankmar Adler's Response to Louis Sullivan's 'The Tall Office Building Artistically Considered': Architecture and the 'Four Causes,'" *Journal of Architectural Education* 64 (September 2010): 83–93. See also Mario Manieri Elia, *Louis Henry Sullivan* (New York: Princeton Architectural Press, 1995), 121–25.

41. Dankmar Adler, "Function and Environment," in *Roots of Contemporary American Architecture*, ed. Lewis Mumford (New York: Grove Press, 1972), 244; originally published with the title "The Influence of Steel Construction and Plate Glass upon Style," in *Proceedings of the Thirtieth Annual Convention of American Institute of Architects*, ed. Alfred Stone (Providence: E. A. Johnson, 1896), 58–64.

42. "Produce Cold Storage Fails," *Chicago Daily Tribune*, October 2, 1895, 8.

43. Quoted in Richard Nickel and Aaron Siskind, *The Complete Architecture of Adler & Sullivan* (Chicago: Richard Nickel Committee, 2010), 374.

44. "Want the Storage Houses Combined," *Chicago Daily Tribune*, March 16, 1894, 12.

45. Jean Ames Follett-Thompson, "The Business of Architecture: William Gibbons Preston and Architectural Professionalism in Boston during the Second Half of the Nineteenth Century" (PhD diss., Boston University, 1986), vi.

46. "Quincy Market Cold Storage Warehouse, Boston, Mass.," *American Architect and Building News* 12 (August 26, 1882): 98.

47. Ibid.

48. "Boston's Cold Corner," *Ice and Refrigeration* 9:6 (December 1895): 374, 384.

49. See Siebel, *Compend of Mechanical Refrigeration*, 192–95.

50. W. G. Preston Collection, Boston Public Library, vol. 22.

51. "Boston's Biggest Ice Chest," *Boston Daily Globe*, January 17, 1915, 45.

52. "Boston's Cold Corner," 394. For more on the tunnel construction and insulation of the pipeline, see Madison Cooper, *Practical Cold Storage* (Chicago: Nickerson and Collins, 1905), 105.

53. "The Thermophone Installation of the Quincy Market Cold Storage Co.," *Ice and Refrigeration* 12:1 (January 1897): 34.

54. Ibid. For more on the thermophone, see Michael Osman, "Listening to the Cooler," *Cabinet* 47 (January 2013): 85–87. See also Henry E. Warren and George C. Whipple, "The Thermophone, a New Instrument for Determining Temperatures," *Technology Quarterly* 8:2 (July 1895): 152. The patent is G. G. Whipple and H. E. Warren, Electrical Thermometer, U.S. Patent 540,008 (issued May 28, 1895). See also Louis M. Schmidt, *Principles and Practice of Artificial Ice-Making and Refrigeration* (Philadelphia: Philadelphia Book Co., 1908), 398–400.

55. See the statement of Charles H. Utley, the president of the Quincy Market Cold Storage and Warehouse Co., Senate Committee on Manufactures, *Foods Held in Cold Storage*, 61st Cong. 3rd sess., 1911, 140.

56. Davis revised a book written by the general superintendent of Swift and Co., F. W. Wilder, in 1905; see *The Modern Packing House: Complete Treatise on the Design, Construction, Equipment and Operation of Meat Packing Houses, According to Present American Practice, Including Methods of Converting By-products into Commercial Articles* (Chicago: Nickerson and Collins, 1921).

57. Hans Peter Henschien, *Packing House and Cold Storage Construction: A General Reference Work on the Planning, Construction and Equipment of Modern American Meat Packing Plants, with Special Reference to the Requirements of the United States Government, and a Complete Treatise on the Design of Cold Storage Plants, Including Refrigeration, Insulation and Cost Data* (Chicago: Nickerson and Collins, 1915), 3.

58. For more biographical information, see "H.P. Henschien Dead; Famed as Architect," *Chicago Daily Tribune*, February 13, 1959, A13. "H. P. Henschien established his independent practice in October 1914, and worked on his own until April 1916, when he joined forces with Robert J. McLaren. After McLaren's retirement in February 1929, the firm operated under the name 'H. P. Henschien, Architect,' until August 1937, when longtime associates W. H. Everds and Robert Crombie were made full partners. The firm then became known as 'Henschien, Everds and Crombie, Architects and Engineers.'" John F. Lauber and Jeffrey A. Hess, "The Rath Packing Company," Historic American Engineering Record No. IA-4I (February 1993): 21.

59. Upton Sinclair, *The Jungle* (New York: Doubleday, Page, 1906).

60. "A Double Hold-Up," *Puck*, October 6, 1910, 8–9.

61. Frederic C. Howe, *The High Cost of Living* (New York: C. Scribner's Sons, 1917), 53. His solution was the public ownership of all the cold storage plants in the nation as it was in Germany, Denmark, and Australia.

62. Herman Hirschauer, *The Dark Side of the Beef Trust: A Treatise Concerning the "Canner" Cow, the Cold Storage Fowl, the Diseased Meats, the Dopes and Preservatives* (Jamestown, N.Y.: Theodore Z. Root, 1905), 92–93.

63. For more on the pure-food issue, see Oscar E. Anderson Jr., "The Pure-Food Issue: A Republican Dilemma, 1906–1912," *American Historical Review* 61:3 (April 1956), 550–73. See also Harvey W. Wiley, *Foods and Their Adulteration Origin, Manufacture, and Composition of Food Products: Description of Common Adulterations, Food Standards, and National Food Laws and Regulations* (Philadelphia: P. Blakiston's Son, 1907).

64. Dr. Harvey Wiley, "Our Opportunities in an Unbounded Field," *Good Housekeeping* 54:5 (May 1912): 593a–o. See also "Dr. Wiley's Debut as Editor," *New York Times*, April 26, 1912. On Wiley, see Clayton Anderson Coppin and Jack C. High, *The Politics of Purity: Harvey Washington Wiley and the Origins of Federal Food Policy* (Ann Arbor: University of Michigan Press, 1999).

65. President of the Quincy Cold Storage and Warehouse Company, Charles H. Utley, testified: "There has not been, so far as my knowledge goes, sufficient evidence to show that the operation of the cold-storage business has been in any way responsible for or instrumental in advancing prices, or to show that the health of the public has been

unfavorably affected to warrant the enactment of such a bill as you have under consideration. Such feeling as has been aroused is largely due to a misapprehension and
lack of a full knowledge of the actual facts. If any measure should be desirable, the only
measure likely to accomplish results desired would be to establish government inspection." Senate Committee on Manufactures, *Foods Held in Cold Storage*, 61st Cong. 3rd
sess., 1911, 129.

66. Walter E. Clark, *The Cost of Living* (Chicago: A. C. McClurg, 1915); Eric Rauchway, "The
    High Cost of Living in the Progressives' Economy," *Journal of American History* 88:3
    (December 2001): 898–924. For more on food prices, see David I. Macleod, "Food Prices,
    Politics, and Policy in the Progressive Era," *Journal of the Gilded Age and Progressive Era*
    8:3 (2009): 365–406.

67. This was the general consensus of the investigations of cold storage prices. A federal
    investigation was initiated in 1912, led by George K. Holmes, chief of the Division of
    Production and Distribution in the Department of Agriculture. See his "Prevention of
    Waste and Seasonal Price Fluctuations through Refrigeration," *Annals of the American
    Academy of Political and Social Science* 50 (November 1913): 48–56. Also George K.
    Holmes "Cold-Storage Business Features: Reports of Warehouses," in *U.S. Department
    of Agriculture, Bureau of Statistics—Bulletin* 93 (Washington, D.C.: Government Printing
    Office, 1913). See also George K. Holmes, "Cold Storage and Prices," in *U.S. Department
    of Agriculture, Bureau of Statistics—Bulletin* 101 (Washington, D.C.: Government Printing
    Office, 1913).

68. Quoted by the commission from F. W. Taussig, *Principles of Economics*, vol. 1 (New York:
    MacMillan, 1911), 159–60. See House No. 1733, the Commonwealth of Massachusetts,
    *Report of the Commission to Investigate the Subject of the Cold Storage of Food and of Food
    Products Kept in Cold Storage* (Boston: Wright and Potter Printing, 1912), 93. See also F. W.
    Taussig, "Is Market Price Determinate?," *Quarterly Journal of Economics* 35:3 (May 1921):
    397–98. For more on Taussig, see Kyle Bruce, "Frank W. Taussig's Institutionalism,"
    Journal of Economic Issues 39:1 (March 2005): 205–20.

69. State Public Utilities Commission, State of Illinois, *Annual Report of the State Public
    Utilities Commission of the State of Illinois*, vol. 1: *Orders and Decisions* (Springfield: Illinois
    State Journal Co., 1915), 194–95. The "order to file a schedule of rates" made by the State
    Public Utilities Commission was upheld by the court despite the appeal made by the
    company; see *State Public Utilities Commission v. Monarch Refrigerating Company*, 267 Ill.
    528 (1915). The definition of cold storage as a public utility was settled differently in a
    number of contexts. In 1915, the Washington Supreme Court found that a cold storage
    warehouse could be a public utility: *State ex rel. Hill v. Bridges*, 151 P. 490, 492 (Wash.
    1915). But a Texas court found otherwise, in a different legal context: *Gulf States Utilities
    Co. v. State*, 46 S.W.2d 1018 (Tex. Civ. App. 1932). And under a 1919 North Dakota statute,
    cold storage companies were public utilities: *State ex rel. Herbrandson v. Vesperman*, 204
    N.W. 202 (N.D. 1925).

70. For the legal statutes of each state up until 1903, see Barry Mohun, *A Compilation of
    Warehouse Laws and Decisions: Containing the Statutes of Each of the States and Territories
    Pertaining to Warehousemen: Together with a Digest of the Decisions of the State and Federal
    Courts, in All Cases Affecting Warehousemen* (New York: Banks Law Publishing, 1904). See

also National Conference of Commissioners on Uniform State Laws, *Draft of an Act to Make Uniform the Law of Warehouse Receipts* (Cincinnati: Gibson and Perin, 1906). For legal reviews of the issue, see Francis Bacon James, "Practical Suggestions on Codifying the Law of Warehouse Receipts," *Michigan Law Review* 3:4 (February 1905): 282–89; and Barry Mohun, "The Effect of the Uniform Warehouse Receipts Act," *Columbia Law Review* 13:3 (March 1913): 202–12.

71. *Proceedings of the Nineteenth Annual Meeting of the American Warehousemen's Association* (Washington, D.C.: American Warehousemen's Association, 1909–10).

72. John H. Frederick, *Public Warehousing, Its Organization, Economic Services, and Legal Aspects* (New York: Ronald Press, 1940), 144.

73. This is Section 3 of the bill, as quoted by Chester Morrill, Assistant to the Solicitor, Department of Agriculture in House Committee on Agriculture, *Cold Storage Legislation*, 66th Cong. 1st sess., 1919, 6.

74. Ibid., 826.

75. Susanne Freidberg's sustained discussion of the concept of freshness and its place in American modernity is in *Fresh: A Perishable History* (Cambridge, Mass.: Belknap Press of Harvard University Press, 2009).

76. *Cold Storage Legislation*, 42. The issue of "freshness" in the hearings is discussed through-out; for a few exchanges, see ibid., 125, 181, 384.

77. Bruno Latour, "A Cautious Prometheus? A Few Steps Toward a Philosophy of Design (with Special Attention to Peter Sloterdijk)," in *In Medias Res: Peter Sloterdijk's Spherological Poetics of Being*, ed. Willem Schinkel and Liesbeth Noordegraaf-Eelens (Amsterdam: Amsterdam University Press, 2011), 157.

3. REPRESENTING REGULATION IN NATURE'S ECONOMY

1. This phrase comes from Carl Linnaeus's *Oeconomia naturae* [1749], trans. Isaac Biberg, in *Miscellaneous Tracts Relating to Natural History, Husbandry, and Physick*, ed. Benjamin Stillingfleet (New York: Arno Press, 1977), 37–130. Robert Clinton Stauffer quotes: "how is it possible that so vast a World of Animals should be supported, such a great variety equally and well supplied with proper Food, in every Place fit for Habitation, without any especial Supertendency and Management, equal to, at least, that of the most prudent Steward and Householder?" "Ecology in the Long Manuscript Version of Darwin's *Origin of Species* and Linnaeus' *Oeconomy of Nature*," *Proceedings of the American Philosophical Society* 104:2 (April 19, 1960): 239. See also Stauffer, "Haekel, Darwin, and Ecology," *Quarterly Review of Biology* 32:2 (June 1957): 138–44; Gertrud Himmelfarb, "The Specter of Malthus," in *Victorian Minds: A Study of Intellectuals in Crisis and Ideologies* (Chicago: Ivan R. Dee, 1995), 82–110. For more recent scholarship in this vein, see Trevor Pearce, "'A Great Complication of Circumstances': Darwin and the Economy of Nature," *Journal of the History of Biology* 43:3 (Fall 2010): 493–528. On Linnaeus's use of the phrase, see Lisbet Koerner, *Linnaeus: Nature and Nation* (Cambridge, Mass.: Harvard University Press, 1999).

2. The environmental historian Donald Worster has pointed to the various related mean-ings that are held together in the term *ecology: Nature's Economy: A History of Ecological Ideas* (Cambridge: Cambridge University Press, 1994). For more histories of ecology,

see Sharon Kingsland, *The Evolution of Ecology* (Baltimore: Johns Hopkins University Press, 2005) and Robert P. McIntosh, *The Background of Ecology: Concept and Theory* (Cambridge: Cambridge University Press, 1985). For an ongoing project on the history of ecological thought starting with the Greeks, see F. N. Egerton, "A History of the Ecological Sciences," *Bulletin of the Ecological Society of America* 82–94 (2001–13), online: http://esapubs.org/bulletin/current/history_links_list.htm.

3. Charles Darwin, *On the Origin of Species* (London: John Murray, 1860), 62. The origins of this concept are traced by Trevor Pearce, "From 'Circumstances' to 'Environment': Herbert Spencer and the Origins of the Idea of Organism–Environment Interaction," *Studies in History and Philosophy of Biological and Biomedical Sciences* 41:3 (2010): 241–52.

4. The midcentury shift in French natural history, examined by Edward Eigen, from the descriptive methods used in the museum to *in vivo* experiments made in field laboratories played out differently in American ecological science at the beginning of the new century. See Edward Eigen, "The Place of Distribution: Episodes in the Architecture of Place," in *Architecture and the Sciences: Exchanging Metaphors,* ed. Antoine Picon and Alessandra Ponte (New York: Princeton Architectural Press, 2003), 52–79.

5. Ernst Haeckel, *Generelle Morphologie der Organismen: Allgemeinen Anatomie der Organismen* (Berlin: Georg Reimer, 1866). For a discussion of the formalization of the term *ecology* in the American academy, see *Proceedings of the Madison Botanical Congress: Madison Wisconsin August 23 and 24* (Madison: Tracy, Gibbs, 1894), 35–38. The topic is introduced by A. S. Hitchcock, a professor of botany at Kansas Agricultural College: "It concerns itself with the adaptive processes of the plant, and with what the Darwinian school has brought forwards and made popular. What we want is a term for this latter part of the science. Shall we use ecology which the committee recommends, or some other term? If ecology is used the recommendation of the committee is that it shall be spelled with an initial E, instead of Œ." Ibid., 36.

6. Claude Bernard, *Lectures on the Phenomena of Life Common to Animals and Plants,* trans. Hebbel E. Hoff, Roger Guillemin, and Lucienne Guillemin (Springfield: Charles C. Thomas, 1974). See also Eugene Debs Robin, ed., *Claude Bernard and the Internal Environment: A Memorial Symposium* (New York: M. Dekker, 1979). Georges Canguilhem, *A Vital Rationalist: Selected Writings from Georges Canguilhem,* ed. François Delaporte, trans. Arthur Goldhammer (New York: Zone Books, 1994), 261–84. See also his preface to Claude Bernard, *Leçons sur les phénomènes de la vie communs aux animaux et aux végétaux* (Paris: Librarie Philosophique J. Vrin, 1966), 7–14. Annie Petit, "Claude Bernard and the History of Science," *Isis* 78:2 (June 1987): 201–19.

7. For example, William Davis, a Harvard physiographer, studied the factors determining the cyclical changes in flood plains of rivers as they were affected by tides, temperature, and topography. William M. Davis, "The Geographical Cycle," *Geographical Journal* 14 (November 1899): 481–504. Maybe the most famous work of physical geography in the United States is George Perkins March, *Man and Nature* (1864; repr. Cambridge: Belknap Press of Harvard University Press, 1965).

8. Eugen Warming, *Plantesamfund: Grundträk af den økologiske Plantegeografi* (1895) was translated by Knoblauch into German as *Lehrbuch der ökologischen Pflanzengeographie*

(1896) and then into English as *Oecology of Plants: An Introduction to the Study of Plant Communities* (Oxford: Clarendon Press, 1909).

9. William Coleman, "Evolution into Ecology? The Strategy of Warming's Ecological Plant Geography," *Journal of the History of Biology* 19:2 (June 1986): 181–96.

10. John M. Coulter, "Warming's Plant Geography," *Botanical Gazette* 22:2 (August 1896): 173.

11. An exhaustive account of Coulter's life and contribution to science is given in Andrew Denny Rodgers, *John Merle Coulter: Missionary in Science* (Princeton, N.J.: Princeton University Press, 1944). For a discussion of the influence of German botanical science on the Chicago Botany Department, see Eugene Cittadino, *Nature as the Laboratory: Darwinian Plant Ecology in the German Empire, 1880–1900* (Cambridge: Cambridge University Press, 1990), 151.

12. The dedication speech was given on July 2, 1897. William H. Welch, "Biology and Medicine," *American Naturalist* 31 (September 1897): 755, 766. Human life as it became understood through medical biology, urban ecology, and social psychology would later learn much from early work in botany and zoology. See Gregg Mitman, *The State of Nature: Ecology, Community, and American Social Thought, 1900–1950* (Chicago: University of Chicago Press, 1992).

13. Henry Ives Cobb (1859–1931), the architect of the Hull Complex, had just completed the Fisheries Building at the World Columbian Exposition that held live fish in ten different-sized aquaria. "In the salt and fresh-water aquaria, which are ten in number, are displayed nearly all the known varieties that people sea or river. As to the dimensions of these aquaria, it need only be said that their capacity ranges from 7,000 to 27,000 gallons, and with a total of 140,000 gallons, apart from reservoirs and water circulation." Hubert Howe Bancroft, *The Book of the Fair: An Historical and Descriptive Presentation of the World's Science, Art, and Industry, as Viewed through the Columbian Exposition at Chicago in 1893* (Chicago: Bancroft Co., 1895), 512.

14. Coulter's speech can be found in *The University Record*, vol. 1 (Chicago: University of Chicago Press, 1897), 287–88. Also quoted in Thomas Wakefield Goodspeed, *A History of the University of Chicago, Founded by John D. Rockefeller: The First Quarter-Century* (Chicago: University of Chicago Press, 1916), 304.

15. Robert E. Kohler, *Landscapes and Labscapes: Exploring the Lab-Field Border in Biology* (Chicago: University of Chicago Press, 2002). See also Sharon Kingsland, "The Role of Place in the History of Ecology," in *The Ecology of Place: Contributions of Place-based Research to Ecological and Evolutionary Understanding*, ed. Ian Billick and Mary Price (Chicago: University of Chicago Press, 2010), 15–39.

16. On the nineteenth-century definition of the laboratory in botanical science, see Cittadino, *Nature as the Laboratory*. The media coverage given to the laboratories seems disproportional to their actual value for the biological sciences in the United States; see "Plans for Splendid Buildings," *Chicago Tribune*, June 14, 1896, 43; "Students in a Squall," *Chicago Tribune*, July 3, 1897, 2. George L. Goodale, the Harvard botanical physiologist, gave an address at the laying of the cornerstone titled, "Some of the Relations of the New Natural History to Modern Thought and Modern Life," summarized in "News," *Botanical Gazette* 22:1 (July 1896): 78–79. For Coulter's early ideas regarding laboratory work in botanical education, see his "Laboratory Courses of Instruction," *Botanical*

Gazette 10:12 (December 1885): 417–21, and "Laboratory Appliances," *Botanical Gazette* 10:12 (December 1885): 409–13. For Coulter's later views, see *Plant Relations: A First Book of Botany* (New York: D. Appleton, 1900).

17. Eugene Cittadino, "Ecology and the Professionalization of Botany in America, 1890–1905," *Studies in History of Biology* 4 (1980): 171–98; Cittadino, "A 'Marvelous Cosmopolitan Preserve': The Dunes, Chicago, and the Dynamic Ecology of Henry Cowles," *Perspectives on Science* 1:3 (Fall 1993): 520–63.

18. Henry Chandler Cowles, "The Ecological Relations of the Vegetation on the Sand Dunes of Lake Michigan. Part I.—Geographical Relations of the Dune Floras," *Botanical Gazette* 27:2 (February 1899): 95–96. The entire dissertation was republished as Henry Chandler Cowles, *The Ecological Relations of the Vegetation on the Sand Dunes of Lake Michigan* (Chicago: University of Chicago Press, 1899).

19. Lorraine Daston, "Type Specimens and Scientific Memory," *Critical Inquiry* 31:1 (Autumn 2004): 153–82. On herbaria, see Edward Eigen, "Banking, Botany, and *Bibliothéconomie*: On the Science of Keeping the Books," *Aggregate* website, http://we-aggregate.org/piece/banking-botany-and-bibliotheconomie-on-the-science-of-keeping-the-books.

20. On the panorama, see Stephan Oettermann *The Panorama: History of a Mass Medium*, trans. Deborah Lucas Schneider (New York: Zone Books, 1997); Bernard Comment, *The Painted Panorama*, trans. Anne-Marie Glasheen (New York: H. N. Abrams, 2000). For an excellent analysis of reality effects related to the panorama, see Jonathan Crary, "Géricault, the Panorama, and Sites of Reality in the Early Nineteenth Century," *Grey Room* 9 (Fall 2002): 5–25.

21. He was given the title "Assistant in Botany," *University of Chicago Circular of Information* 7:2 (March 1907): 7. For the dissertation, see William Burnett McCallum, "Regeneration in Plants" (PhD diss., University of Chicago, 1905).

22. Edward Eigen, "Dark Space and the Early Days of Photography as a Medium," *Grey Room* 3 (Spring 2001): 91.

23. To compare with the picturesque, see Uvedale Price, *An Essay on the Picturesque: As Compared with the Sublime and the Beautiful; And, on the Use of Studying Pictures, for the Purpose of Improving Real Landscape* (London: J. Robson, 1796). On the role of photography and the picturesque, see James S. Ackerman, "The Photographic Picturesque," *Artibus et Historiae* 24:48 (2003): 73–94. Robert Smithson made the connection between ecological thought and picturesque aesthetics in "Frederick Law Olmsted and the Dialectical Landscape," in *The Writings of Robert Smithson: Essays with Illustrations*, ed. Nancy Holt (New York: New York University Press, 1979), 117–28.

24. In Cowles's words, "[we] have in this phenomenon a lagging of effects behind their cumulative causes, just as the climax of the heat in summer comes long after the solstice." Henry Chandler Cowles, *Plant Societies in the Chicago Region* (Chicago: University of Chicago Press, 1901), 9.

25. Ibid., 112.

26. Henry Chandler Cowles, "The Physiographic Ecology of Chicago and Vicinity: A Study of the Origin, Development, and Classification of Plant Societies," *Botanical Gazette* 31:3 (March 1901): 178.

27. See William Kerr Higley, "Historical Sketch of the Academy," *Chicago Academy of Sciences: Special Publication* 1 (January 1, 1902): 39–41. For another history of the academy, see Walter B. Hendrickson and William J. Beecher, "In the Service of Science: The History of the Chicago Academy of Sciences," *Bulletin of the Chicago Academy of Sciences* 11:7 (1972). See also Frank C. Baker, "The Chicago Academy of Sciences," *Science* 28:709 (July 31, 1908): 138–41.

28. Adolf Bernhard Meyer, *Studies of the Museums and Kindred Institutions of New York City, Albany, Buffalo, and Chicago: With Notes on Some European Institutions* (Washington, D.C.: U.S. Government Printing Office, 1905), 431–32.

29. Oscar Drude, "Position of Ecology in Modern Science," in *Congress of Arts and Sciences, Universal Exhibition, St. Louis, 1904* (Boston: Houghton Mifflin, 1906), 185.

30. For context, consider the changes instituted by George Goode at the Smithsonian, in "The Museums of the Future," in *Annual Report of the Regents of the Smithsonian Institution: Report of the U.S. National Museum, Pt. 2* (Washington, D.C.: Government Printing Office, 1891), 427–45. For the politics of museum reform, see Sally Gregory Kohlstedt, "Nature, Not Books: Scientists and the Origins of the Nature-Study Movement in the 1890s," *Isis* 96:3 (September 2005): 324–52; also by Kohlstedt, "'Thoughts in Things': Modernity, History, and North American Museums," *Isis* 96:4 (December 2005): 586–601. See also Victoria Cain and Karen Rader, *Life on Display: Education, Exhibition and Museums in the Twentieth-Century United States* (Chicago: University of Chicago Press, 2014).

31. Victoria Cain, "'Attraction, Attention, and Desire': Consumer Culture as Pedagogical Paradigm in Museums in the United States, 1900–1930," *Paedagogica Historica* 48:5 (October 2012): 745–69.

32. Frank M. Chapman, *The Habitat Groups of North American Birds in the American Museum of Natural History,* Guide Leaflet Series, American Museum of Natural History 28 (New York: American Museum of Natural History, 1909). See also the chapter on Cobb's Island in Chapman's *Camps and Cruises of an Ornithologist* (New York: D. Appleton, 1908), 63–75. J. A. Allen, "The Habitat Groups of North American Birds in the American Museum of Natural History," *Auk* 26 (April 1909): 166.

33. Karen Wonders has written several treatments of the habitat diorama including *Habitat Dioramas: Illusions of Wilderness in Museums of Natural History* (Uppsala: Almqvist and Wiksell, 1993). See also Carla Yanni, *Nature's Museums: Victorian Science and the Architecture of Display* (New York: Princeton Architectural Press, 2003).

34. The French physiologist Étienne-Jules Marey had invented photographic techniques to document the image of flight. The wide dissemination of his photographs and writings, as well as their influence on others at the end of the nineteenth century, served as the scientific basis for the artists who built the diorama. See Étienne-Jules Marey, *Animal Mechanism: A Treatise on Terrestrial and Aërial Locomotion* (New York: D. Appleton, 1874). On the reception of Marey, see Marta Braun, *Picturing Time: The Work of Étienne-Jules Marey, 1830–1904* (Chicago: University of Chicago Press, 1992).

35. W. W. Atwood, Sidereal Sphere, U.S. Patent 1,019,405 (issued March 5, 1912). Wallace W. Atwood, "The Atwood Celestial Sphere," *Bulletin of the Chicago Academy of Sciences* 4:2 (May 1913). See also "The Atwood Celestial Sphere at the Chicago Academy of Sciences,"

Proceedings of the American Association of Museums 7 (1913): 89–94; Richard Morrison, "Bringing the Stars to Earth," *Technical World Magazine* 19 (1913): 772–75.

36. See, for example, John Banvard's moving panorama shown in Louisville, Boston, New York, and London. John Banvard, *Description of Banvard's Panorama of the Mississippi River, Painted on Three Miles of Canvas Exhibiting a View of Country 1200 Miles in Length, Extending from the Mouth of the Missouri River to the City of New Orleans: Being by Far the Largest Picture ever Executed by Man* (Boston: J. Putnam, 1847).

37. Charles C. Adams, "Some of the Advantages of an Ecological Organization of a Natural History Museum," *Proceedings of the American Association of Museums* 1 (1907): 172–73. Adams defended his dissertation in zoology in 1908. During his time at the University of Chicago he participated in an excursion to the Cumberland Mountains in Tennessee with his advisor, Charles Davenport, and Henry Cowles. "Annual Report for the Year 1909," *Bulletin of the Chicago Academy of Sciences* 3:3 (February 1910): 7–8, 22–23. Henry J. Cox wrote an impressive book on *The Weather and Climate of Chicago* (Chicago: University of Chicago Press, 1914).

38. Wallace Atwood, "Annual Meeting, January 11, 1916," WA Box 1, Chicago Academy of Sciences Institutional Archives. See also Wallace Atwood, "Annual Meeting of the Chicago Academy of Sciences," *Science* 43:1104 (February 25, 1916): 284–85.

39. "Annual Reports for the Year 1910," *Bulletin of the Chicago Academy of Sciences* 3:5 (February 1911): 145.

40. "Make Photo 10 Feet High, 96 Feet Long," *Photographic Journal of America* 59 (1922): 495.

41. A letter from Woodruff is quoted, almost in full, by R. W. Shufeldt, of the Smithsonian, in "The Bird Groups of the Chicago Academy of Sciences," *Museum Work* 2:2 (November 1919): 62–63.

42. Ibid.

43. Letter from Woodruff to C. F. Hills, March 20, 1919, FW Box 1, Chicago Academy of Sciences Institutional Archives. Woodruff continued to be involved in collecting taxidermy specimens for the "Chicago Environs Series" at least through 1923; see his "Conditions of the Breeding Game Birds in North Dakota, Expedition of the Chicago Academy of Sciences," *Wilson Bulletin* 35:1 (March 1923): 4–20.

44. Frank Morley Woodruff, *Birds of the Chicago Area*, Bulletin of the Natural History Survey 6 ([Chicago: Jennings and Graham], 1907).

45. Peter Mortenson, "Contribution of Museums to Public School Education," *Museum Work* 2:8 (May 1920): 243. See also R. W. Shufeldt, "Combining Art and Museum Exhibits," *Bulletin of the Pan American Union* 48 (January–June 1919): 682–93.

46. Robert H. Wiebe, "The House of Morgan and the Executive, 1905–1913," *American Historical Review* 65:1 (October 1959): 49–60. See also Thomas K. McCraw and Forest Reinhardt, "Losing to Win: U.S. Steel's Pricing, Investment Decisions, and Market Share, 1901–1938," *Journal of Economic History* 49:3 (September 1989): 594.

47. "Gary: The Largest and Most Modern Steel Works in Existence," *Scientific American* 24 (December 11, 1909): 441.

48. Prairie Club members included Dwight Perkins, the founding architect of Perkins and Will and author of *Report of the Special Park Commission to the City Council of Chicago on the Subject of a Metropolitan Park System* (Chicago: W. J. Hartman, 1905); Jens Jensen, the

landscape architect, see Robert E. Grese, *Jens Jensen: Maker of Natural Parks and Gardens* (Baltimore: Johns Hopkins University Press, 1992); and Frank Dudley, the painter. On the conservation movement, see Samuel P. Hays, *Conservation and the Gospel of Efficiency: The Progressive Conservation Movement, 1890–1920* (Cambridge, Mass.: Harvard University Press, 1959).

49. Thomas Wood Stevens, *The Book of the Historical Pageant of the Dunes, Port Chester Indiana on Lake Michigan, May 30 and June 3, 1917* (Port Chester: Dunes Pageant Association, 1917), 8. Stevens was president of the American Pageant Association and head of the Department of Dramatic Art at Carnegie Institute of Technology.

50. Cittadino, "A 'Marvelous Cosmopolitan Preserve,'" 524–25.

51. Stephen Tyng Mather, *Report on the Proposed Sand Dunes National Park, Indiana* (Washington D.C.: Government Printing Office, 1917), 44, 45; see also "At Federal Hearing Chicago Pleads that Indiana's Matchless Sand Dunes Be Created National Park," *Chicago Commerce* 12 (November 3, 1916): 9–12.

52. Victor E. Shelford, "The Life-Histories and Larval Habits of Tiger Beetles" (PhD thesis, University of Chicago, 1907); Victor E. Shelford, "Preliminary Note on the Distribution of the Tiger Beetles (*Cicindela*) and Its Relation to Plant Succession," *Biological Bulletin* 14:1 (December 1907): 9–14. For Shelford's biography, see Robert A. Croker, *Pioneer Ecologist: The Life and Work of Victor Ernest Shelford, 1877–1968* (Washington, D.C.: Smithsonian Institution Press, 1991). Anecdotally, Shelford was also consulted on the choice of animal taxidermy for the dioramas at the Chicago Academy of Sciences.

53. For more on the influence of Child on Shelford, see Mitman, *The State of Nature*, 38.

54. In his analysis of the succession of animal life in streams and ponds, Shelford also applied physiographic methods to sketch out relations between the species living together to a body of water's geological age. See Victor E. Shelford, "Ecological Succession. I: Stream Fishes and the Method of Physiographic Analysis," *Biological Bulletin* 21:1 (June 1911): 9–35. Continued in Shelford, "Ecological Succession. II: Pond Fishes," *Biological Bulletin* 21:3 (August 1911): 127–51; "Ecological Succession III: A Reconnaissance of Its Causes in Ponds with Particular Reference to Fish," *Biological Bulletin* 22:1 (December 1911): 1–38. See also Kohler, *Landscapes and Labscapes*, 232–38.

55. Victor E. Shelford, *Animal Communities in Temperate America as Illustrated in the Chicago Region: A Study in Animal Ecology* (Chicago: University of Chicago Press, 1913), vi.

56. Shelford is referring to the experiments conducted by his student W. C. Allee. See their coauthored articles: "The Reactions of Fishes to Gradients of Dissolved Atmospheric Gases," *Journal of Experimental Zoology* 14 (1913): 207–66; and "Rapid Modification of the Behavior of Fishes by Contact with Abnormal Water," *Journal of Animal Behavior* 4 (1914): 1–30.

57. The first significant mention of animal communities in modern biology was by the German zoologist Karl Möbius in 1877 who called them *Biocœnosis*. See his "The Oyster and Oyster-Culture," in *US Commission of Fish and Fisheries, Report of Commissioner for 1880, Part VIII* (Washington, D.C.: Government Printing Office, 1883), 683–723. See also the foundational text by Stephen A. Forbes, "The Lake as a Microcosm," *Bulletin of the Scientific Association of Peoria, Illinois*, 1887, 77–87. For a good analysis of Shelford's turn

toward experimentation and return to the field, see Kohler, *Landscapes and Labscapes*, 157–63.

58. Shelford, *Animal Communities in Temperate America as Illustrated in the Chicago Region*, 8; emphasis added.

59. Victor E. Shelford, "An Experimental Study of the Behavior Agreement among the Animals of an Animal Community," *Biological Bulletin* 26:5 (May 1914): 294–315.

60. Victor E. Shelford, "A Comparison of the Responses of Sessile and Motile Plants and Animals," *American Naturalist* 48 (November 1914): 643; italics are in the original. Shelford's use of physiological terms to describe animal behavior derived from Child's work on regulation, a set of changes in the organism that helped it reestablish "functional equilibrium after such equilibrium has been disturbed." C. M. Child, "Contributions Toward a Theory of Regulation," *Archiv für Entwicklungsmechanik der Organismen* 20 (January 1906): 424. Child, following the work of the vitalist Hans Driesch on embryological development, studied the relations between the forms and functions of flatworms. Child's studies also include "The Regulatory Processes in Organisms," *Journal of Morphology* 22 (1911): 171–222.

61. Child, "Contributions Toward a Theory of Regulation," 424. For a discussion of this concept in biology, see Georges Canguilhem, "The Development of the Concept of Biological Regulation in the Eighteenth and Nineteenth Centuries," in *Ideology and Rationality in the History of the Life Sciences*, trans. Arthur Goldhammer (Cambridge, Mass.: MIT Press, 1988), 81–102.

62. Charles Zeleny, "Statement presented to Department of Zoology, University of Chicago, 1912: Research Facilities in Connection with the Vivarium in Behavior, Ecological Work, and Breeding Associated with the Same," Charles Zeleny Papers, Record Series 15/24/22, Box 6, University of Illinois at Urbana-Champaign Archives.

63. Ibid.

64. Charles Zeleny, "A Case of Compensatory Regulation in the Regeneration of Hydroides dianthus," *Archiv für Entwicklungsmechanik der Organismen* 13 (January 1902): 597–609. His dissertation was submitted on May 17, 1904, and published as "Compensatory Regulation," *Journal of Experimental Zoology* 2 (1905): 1–102. "Regeneration" was a common term used in the study of regulatory control; the chairman of the Zoology Department at Chicago, Frank R. Lillie, wrote the seminal texts in the American context: "Some Notes on Regeneration and Regulation in Planarians," *American Naturalist* 34 (March 1900): 173–77; "Notes on Regeneration and Regulation in Planarians (continued)," *American Journal of Physiology* 6:2 (October 1901): 129–41.

65. Charles Zeleny, "Preliminary Plan of Vivarium, January 23, 1911," "Preliminary Plan of Vivarium, June 12, 1913," and "Preliminary Plan of Vivarium, June 14, 1913, " Charles Zeleny Papers, Record Series 15/24/22, Box 6, University of Illinois at Urbana-Champaign Archives. The dimensions of the Vivarium increased between these sketches: the main building going from thirty to thirty-six feet square, and the glass houses from thirty-six to forty-two feet in length. The budget, which Zeleny estimated at $10,000 in 1913, was approved at $70,000 in 1915. See *28th Report of the Board of Trustees of the University of Illinois* (Springfield: Illinois State Journal Co., 1916), 300. Zeleny was appointed to be the "custodian" of the Vivarium after its completion.

66. James B. Dibelka, *Illinois Album of Public Buildings Erected during 1913–14–15–16* (Omaha: Pokrok Publishing, 1917).

67. Letter from Henry B. Ward to James M. White, August 8, 1914, quoting Shelford, Charles Zeleny Papers, Record Series 15/24/22, Box 6, University of Illinois at Urbana-Champaign Archives.

68. Compare to the comments given by Edwin G. Conklin on the University of Pennsylvania vivarium: "It is usual in building laboratories to provide an animal room in some small, dark corner of the cellar, while the whole of the building proper is devoted to lecture rooms, laboratories and museums. It is sad to think that such a disposition of space represents the popular view of the importance of the study of living animals. In a very important sense a vivarium is the most essential part of any laboratory of zoology, representing that for which all the rest exists." "Advances in Methods of Teaching Zoology," *Publications of the University of Pennsylvania: University Bulletin* 3 (1898): 150. In the mid-nineteenth century a vivarium was a glorified insect cage used by gentlemen entomologists. See H. Noel Humphries, *The Butterfly Home or Insect Home: Being an Account of a New Method of Observing the Curious Metamorphoses of Some of the Most Beautiful of Our Native Insects, Comprising also a Popular Description of the Habits and Instincts of Many of the Insects of the Various Classes Referred to, with Suggestions for the Successful Study of Entomology by Means of an Insect Vivarium* (London: William Lay, 1853).

69. Victor E. Shelford, *Laboratory and Field Ecology: The Responses of Animals as Indicators of Correct Working Methods* (Baltimore: Williams and Wilkins, 1929), 383–92, 400.

70. *28th Report of the Board of Trustees of the University of Illinois*, 289–90. For a short biography of James M. White (1869–1933), see "In the Illini Vineyard: A King Jim Version of James M. White, '90," *Alumni Quarterly and Fortnightly Notes of the University of Illinois* 3 (January 15, 1918): 145–46.

71. He wrote his senior thesis on the relative conductivity of heat through different insulation papers. See James M. White, "The Conductivity of Heat in Building Papers" (BS thesis, University of Illinois, 1890).

72. James M. White, "Farm House Architecture," *Annual Report of the Illinois Farmers' Institute with Reports of County Farmers' Institutes* 6 (1901): 125–28.

73. Ibid., 128.

74. "Advanced experimental research in zoology and entomology has never taken kindly to the natural history building because of the difficulty of control. . . . And lest Illinois which has long led in many aspects of scientific investigation, should lag behind in advanced sciences, the vivarium was built." "The Vivarium," *Alumni Quarterly and Fortnightly Notes* 1 (April 15, 1916), 294.

75. Shelford, *Laboratory and Field Ecology*, v. For a summary of Shelford's methods for teaching laboratory methods for ecology, see Victor E. Shelford, "Suggestions as to Field and Laboratory Instruction in the Behavior and Ecology of Animals, with Descriptions of Equipment," *School Science and Mathematics* 17:5 (May 1917): 388–409. For an early illustration of one large apparatus, see Victor E. Shelford, "Equipment for Maintaining a Flow of Oxygen-Tree Water, and for Controlling Gas Content," *Bulletin of the Illinois State Laboratory of Natural History* 11 (May 1918): 573–75.

76. Shelford, *Laboratory and Field Ecology*, 383–84.

77. Ibid., 385.

78. Victor E. Shelford, "A Comparison of the Responses of Animals in Gradients of Environmental Factors with Particular Reference to the Method of Reaction of Representatives of the Various Groups from Protozoa to Mammals," *Science* 48:1235 (August 30, 1918): 225–30. He wrote: "These graphs can not be made with mechanical exactitude but a high degree of accuracy can be attained. With a watch adjacent to the cage and a little practice there is no difficulty in making such record." And concludes: "The method of graphing has been found very useful in making accurate determinations of reaction where modification by environment has been attempted and where accurate determination of sensibility is necessary." Ibid., 226, 230.

79. Shelford still believed that plants could be subjects for physiological experiments in ecology. He was particularly interested in the laboratories of the Boyce Thompson Institute for Plant Research in Yonkers, New York. On the massive facility, see "Organization, Equipment, Dedication," *Contributions from Boyce Thompson Institute for Plant Research* 1 (January 1925): 3–58.

80. "Vivarium Pumping System," Letter from Charles Zeleny to James White, Charles Zeleny Papers, Record Series 15/24/22, Box 6, University of Illinois at Urbana-Champaign Archives.

81. Victor E. Shelford, "Physiological Problems in the Life-Histories of Animals with Particular Reference to Their Seasonal Appearance," *American Naturalist* 52 (February–March 1918): 129–54; "Physiological Life Histories of Terrestrial Animals and Modern Methods of Representing Climate," *Transactions of the Illinois State Academy of Science* 13 (1920): 257–71; "An Experimental Investigation of the Relations of the Codling Moth to Weather and Climate," *Bulletin of the Illinois State Natural History Survey* 16 (1927): 311–427.

82. Early air-conditioning patents were filed in 1906 by Willis Haviland Carrier. These machines were mainly applied to industrial and theater interiors until the 1930s. See Gail Cooper, *Air-Conditioning America: Engineers and the Controlled Environment, 1900–1960* (Baltimore: Johns Hopkins University Press, 2002). Shelford cites Carrier's publications extensively in *Laboratory and Field Ecology*. For publications by D. C. Lindsay, stationed in the Newark office, see "Manufactured Weather: An Aid to Modern Industry, Health, and Efficiency," *Industrial and Engineering Chemistry* 21:5 (May 1929): 502–5. See also D. C. Lindsay, ed., *Drying and Processing of Materials by Means of Conditioned Air; a Treatise for Manufacturers, Engineers and Students—an Illustrated Discussion of the Many Interesting Problems Involved in the Drying and Processing of Numerous Familiar Materials, under Controlled Conditions of Temperature, Humidity and Air Movement. Based on Investigations by the Research Department of Carrier Engineering Corporation* (Newark: Carrier Engineering Corporation, 1929).

83. Shelford, *Laboratory and Field Ecology*, 424.

84. Victor E. Shelford, *The Naturalist's Guide to the Americas* (Baltimore: Willliams and Wilkins, 1926).

85. See a long quotation in Kohler, *Landscapes and Labscapes*, 162. Taken from Victor E. Shelford, "Faith in the Results of Controlled Laboratory Experiments as Applied to Nature," *Ecological Monographs* 4 (1933): 491.

86. In fact, others assembled even more sophisticated mechanical instruments for experiments in animal and plant ecology, based on Shelford's early experiments. See Sharon E. Kingsland, "Frits Went's Atomic Age Greenhouse: The Changing Labscape on the Lab-Field Border," *Journal of the History of Biology* 42:2 (Summer 2009): 293–99.

87. Victor E. Shelford, "The Physical Environment," in *A Handbook of Social Psychology*, ed. Carl Murchison (Worcester: Clark University Press, 1935), 567.

88. The diagram was based on Shelford's reading of the naturalist Clinton Hart Merriam's *The Mammals of the Adirondack Region* (New York: Henry Holt, 1886). See V. E. Shelford, "Some Concepts of Bioecology," *Ecology* 7:3 (July 1931): 458. This was not the first such diagram used to describe the "food chain" in ecology; see, for example, Charles C. Adams, "An Ecological Study of Prairie and Forest Invertebrates," *Bulletin of the Illinois State Laboratory of Natural History* 11 (September 1915): 121. The form of the diagram is closer to those found in Charles Elton's *Animal Ecology* (London: Sidgwick and Jackson, 1927).

89. Shelford, "Some Concepts of Bioecology," 456. Bioecology was a term Shelford adopted from the work of Frederick Clements, a prominent plant ecologist who coined the term to include all living matter as part of ecological investigation rather than preserving the split between plant and animal ecology. It was employed to distinguish his work from the behaviorism that grew out of animal ecology. See Clements and Shelford, *Bioecology* (New York: J. Wiley and Sons, 1939).

90. Shelford, "The Physical Environment," 569.

91. Ibid., 573.

92. R. D. McKenzie, "The Ecological Approach to the Study of the Human Community," *American Journal of Sociology* 30:3 (November 1924): 287–301. Collected in Robert E. Park, Ernest W. Burgess, and Roderick D. McKenzie, eds., *The City* (Chicago: University of Chicago Press, 1925). On metaphorical borrowing, see Emanuel Gaziano, "Ecological Metaphors as Scientific Boundary Work: Innovation and Authority in Interwar Sociology and Biology," *American Journal of Sociology* 101:4 (January 1996): 874–907. Comparisons between human and nonhuman associations were already present in some American philosophical movements at the end of the nineteenth century. Perhaps this was most evident in the social psychological theories of George Herbert Mead, a professor in the Philosophy Department at the University of Chicago. Mead held that social forms were inherent in nature and claimed that societal interaction was a fundamental aspect of even the most basic forms of life. "All living organisms are bound up in a general social environment or situation," he wrote, "in a complex of social interrelations and interactions upon which their continued existence depends." The necessity of relations between organisms was fundamental to Mead's definition of the individual and his understanding of the organizational structure of institutions. George Herbert Mead, *Mind, Self, and Society from the Standpoint of a Social Behaviorist*, ed. Charles W. Morris (Chicago: University of Chicago Press, 1934), 227–28.

93. Ernest Burgess, "The Growth of the City: An Introduction to a Research Project," in Park, Burgess, and McKenzie, *The City*, 47–62. Consider also, as a prototypical example of the bull's-eye model applied to urban design in the City Beautiful movement, Daniel Burnham and Edward Bennett's *Plan of Chicago* (1909; repr. New York: Princeton Architectural Press, 1993).

94. William Cronon, *Nature's Metropolis: Chicago and the Great West* (New York: W. W. Norton, 1992).

95. "Committee on the Preservation of Natural Conditions for Ecological Study," *Bulletin of the Ecological Society of America* 1:6/9 (June–September 1917). See also Ecological Society of America, *Preservation of Natural Conditions* (Springfield, Ill., 1922).

96. For a history of planning in Gary, see Raymond A. Mohl and Neil Betten, "The Failure of Industrial City Planning: Gary, Indiana, 1906–1910," *Journal of the American Institute of Planners* 38:4 (1972): 203–14.

97. Johann Heinrich von Thünen's theory was not translated until 1966, *Von Thünen's Isolated State [The Isolated State in Its Relation to Agriculture and National Economy]*, trans. Carla M. Wartenberg, ed. Peter Hall (Oxford: Pergamon, 1966). For an excellent critique of the use of von Thünen's spatial economics for corporate purposes, see John Harwood, "Corporate Abstraction," *Perspecta* 46 (2013): 218–47. See also Alfred Weber, *Alfred Weber's Theory of the Location of Industries*, trans. Carl Joachim Friedrich (Chicago: University of Chicago Press, 1929).

4. IMAGING BRAINWORK

1. Ure's interest in this topic is addressed in chapter 1. Charles Babbage also wrote extensively on the topic, and regulation was equally central to his understanding of factory production. For example, "Regulating Power" was the third chapter of *On the Economy of Manufactures* (London: Charles Knight, 1832).

2. JoAnne Yates, *Control through Communication: The Rise of System in American Management* (Baltimore: Johns Hopkins University Press, 1989).

3. Taylor first used the term in *Principles of Scientific Management* (New York, 1911). Before that, the system was known as the "Taylor System." On the origin of the term, see Horace Bookwalter Drury, *Scientific Management: A History and Criticism* (New York: Columbia University Press, 1918). The scholarship on Taylor specifically and scientific management more generally is vast. Of the numerous fundamental texts, two have proved to be particularly useful in formulating this chapter: Hugh G. J. Aitken, *Scientific Management in Action: Taylorism at Watertown Arsenal, 1908–1915* (Princeton, N.J.: Princeton University Press, 1960), and Samuel Haber, *Efficiency and Uplift: Scientific Management in the Progressive Era* (Chicago: University of Chicago Press, 1964). An excellent history of the development of scientific management in relation to the factory system in the United States is Daniel Nelson, *Managers and Workers: Origins of the Twentieth-Century Factory System in the United States, 1880–1920* (Madison: University of Wisconsin Press, 1995). For a history of the transportation of Taylor's doctrine to several cultural contexts, see Judith A. Merkle, *Management and Ideology: The Legacy of the International Scientific Management Movement* (Berkeley: University of California Press, 1980).

4. Le Corbusier's interest in Taylorist thinking is treated in Mary McLeod, "'Architecture or Revolution': Taylorism, Technocracy, and Social Change," *Art Journal* 43 (Summer 1983): 132–47. Aphoristic allusion to Taylor's system is scattered throughout Le Corbusier's *The Decorative Art of Today*, trans. James Dunnett (Cambridge, Mass.: MIT Press, 1986). See also Alexandra Lange, "White Collar Corbusier: From the *Casier* to the *cités d'affaires*," *Grey Room* 9 (Fall 2002): 58–79.

5. The notion of "brainwork" comes from Frederick Winslow Taylor, "Shop Management," *Transactions of the American Society of Mechanical Engineers* 24 (1903): 1369. J. S. Mill had already noted the difference between physical and mental labor: "Labor is either bodily or mental; or, to express the distinction more comprehensively, either muscular or nervous; and it is necessary to include in the idea, not solely the exertion itself, but all feelings of a disagreeable kind, all bodily inconvenience or mental annoyance, connected with the employment of one's thoughts, or muscles, or both, in a particular occupation." See *Principles of Political Economy* (New York: D. Appleton, 1895), 55.

6. Anson Rabinbach, *The Human Motor: Energy, Fatigue, and the Origins of Modernity* (New York: Basic Books, 1990), 25. Rabinbach's quotations came from Charles Fremont, "Les mouvements de l'ouvrier dans le travail professionnel," *Le Monde Moderne* 1 (February 1895): 193.

7. Many articles and books dealt with this phenomenon that Rabinbach addresses in his intellectual history. One example among the many in the American context is "Sanitation—A Method of Improving Production," *Industrial Engineering and the Engineering Digest* 14 (January 1914): 1–9.

8. Beyond direct and indirect, Mill also made the distinction between productive and unproductive labor. Mill, *Principles of Political Economy*, 55, 60–64.

9. David F. Noble, *America by Design: Science, Technology, and the Rise of Corporate Capitalism* (Oxford: Oxford University Press, 1979), 258.

10. For an analysis of the application of time-based models to modern art and architecture, see the Eliot Norton Lectures given by Sigfried Giedion in 1941, "The New Space Conception: Space-Time," in *Space, Time and Architecture: The Growth of a New Tradition* (Cambridge, Mass.: Harvard University Press, 1982), 430–48. Building on the theory that art and architecture were directly influenced by changes in the management of industry, Giedion then wrote his famous sequel: *Mechanization Takes Command* (Oxford: Oxford University Press, 1948). Here, Giedion points to Frank and Lillian Gilbreth's motion studies in particular as a crossover point between art and industry. Motion study represents an important but eccentric practice in scientific management. Beyond this form of representation, many others exist that have yet to be addressed as part of the development of industrial management at the end of the nineteenth century. For more on the Gilbreths and the development of a discourse around the diagram, see Hyungmin Pai, *The Portfolio and the Diagram: Architecture, Discourse, and Modernity in America* (Cambridge, Mass.: MIT Press, 2002), 162–97.

11. The two books that developed from the collaboration between Frederick Winslow Taylor and Sanford Thompson were *A Treatise on Concrete, Plain and Reinforced: Materials, Construction, and Design of Concrete and Reinforced Concrete* (New York: J. Wiley and Sons, 1905) and *Concrete Costs: Tables and Recommendations for Estimating the Time and Cost of Labor Operations in Concrete Construction and for Introducing Economical Methods of Management* (New York: J. Wiley and Sons, 1912). For more on Thompson's time studies and their relationship to the history of management and architecture, see my "The Managerial Aesthetics of Concrete," *Perspecta* 45 (2012): 67–76.

12. Robert H. Thurston, a mechanical engineer who taught at the Stevens Institute, wrote: "The Useful and the Lost Work of a machine are, together, equal to the total amount of energy expended upon the machine, i.e., to the work done upon it by its 'driver.' The

Useful Work is that which the machine is designed to perform; the Lost Work is that which is absorbed by the friction and other prejudicial resistances of the mechanism, and which thus waste energy which might otherwise be usefully applied. These two quantities, together, constitute the Total Work or the Gross Work of a machine, or of a train of mechanism." *On Friction and Lost Work in Machinery and Millwork* (New York: John Wiley and Sons, 1885), 10. Thurston would later translate Nicolas Leonard Sadi Carnot's seminal paper of 1824, *Reflections on the Motive Power of Heat and on Machines Fitted to Develop that Power* (New York: John Wiley and Sons, 1890).

13. Sir William Fairbairn, *Treatise on Mills and Mill Work: On Machinery of Transmission and the Construction and Arrangement of Mills* (London: Longman, Green, Longman and Roberts, 1863). The most complete American treatise is John H. Cooper, *A Treatise on the Use of Belting for the Transmission of Power* (Philadelphia: Claxton, Remsen and Haffelfinger, 1878). Cooper translated Arthur Morin's 1834 "Experiments on the Tension of Belts" into English as the seventh chapter of his treatise. Here, Morin revised Charles-Augustin de Coulomb's equations to determine friction in each material. Constants were experimentally deduced as a material's coefficient of friction from empirically testing each on an experimental apparatus. For an excellent treatment of the relationship of work, friction, and political economic theory, see M. Norton Wise and Crosbie Smith, "Work and Waste: Political Economy and Natural Philosophy in Nineteenth Century Britain," *History of Science* 27:3 (September 1989): 263–301; 27:4 (December 1989): 391–449; 28:3 (September 1990): 221–61.

14. The etching is by James Nasmyth: Andrew Ure, *The Cotton Manufacture of Great Britain Investigated* (London: Charles Knight, 1836), 419. Ure also included a plan and a section through the same cotton mill. For an excellent collection of drawings that document the development of the factory in the nineteenth century, see Jennifer Tann, *The Development of the Factory* (London: Cornmarket Press, 1970).

15. See, for example, Gaetano Lanza, *Notes on Friction* (Boston: J. S. Cushing, 1896).

16. Frederick W. Taylor, "Notes on Belting," *Transactions of the American Society of Mechanical Engineers* 15 (1894): 213. A letter from Taylor to the president of the Bethlehem Iron Company, Robert P. Linderman, summarizes the "Rules Regarding the Use and Care of Belting, Pulleys and Counter-shafts." It can be found in folder "Belting: Taylor's Rules for Use and Care of-," in Carl and J. Christian Barth Collection, MS 708, Baker Library Historical Collections, Harvard University. Before Taylor's paper on belting, one paper by Wilfred Lewis dealt with the matter of tension through an experimental apparatus. The issue of power transmission in belting persisted as a point of conversation in the society meetings into the final years of the nineteenth century: "There are certain questions continually arising in engineering practice which do not seem to admit of settlement by either reason or experiment. Some of these ever-recurring questions relate to the transmission of power by belting. In what way are the belt tensions altered as the load is applied? What effect has the change of load on the sum of the belt tensions? Is there any relation between the belt tensions which does not involve time coefficient of friction?" William S. Aldrich, "The Variation of Belt Tensions with Power Transmitted," *Transactions of the American Society of Mechanical Engineers* 20 (1899): 136. See also Robert Thurston Kent, *Power Transmission by Leather Belting* (New York: John Wiley and Sons, 1916).

17. Taylor, "Notes on Belting," 218–19.

18. Frederick W. Taylor, "A Piece-Rate System: A Step Toward Partial Solution of the Labor Problem," *Transactions of the American Society of Mechanical Engineers* 16 (1895): 856–57. "The modern manufacturer, however, seeks not only to secure the best superintendents and workmen, but to surround each department of his manufacture with the most carefully woven network of system and method, which should render the business, for a considerable period, at least, independent of the loss of any one man, and frequently of any combination of men." Ibid., 860. Taylor was responding to the Towne-Halsey plan developed in two papers: Henry R. Towne, "Gain Sharing," *Transactions of the American Society of Mechanical Engineers* 10 (1889): 600; F. A. Halsey, "Premium Plan of Paying for Labor," *Transactions of the American Society of Mechanical Engineers* 12 (1891): 755. Their plan was specifically taken up as a point of discussion in Taylor's presentation; see "A Piece-Rate System," 864–65.

19. H. L. Gantt, "A Bonus System of Rewarding Labor," *Transactions of the American Society of Mechanical Engineers* 23 (1902): 341–72. Gantt would later formulate the "Gantt Chart" that is used for all varieties of project management including one that manages the schedule for constructing buildings.

20. For more on this hierarchical system, or what Taylor would call the "military type," see Daniel Nelson, "The Foreman's Empire," in *Managers and Workers*, 35–55.

21. These categories were outlined by Woodrow Wilson: "Bureaucracy can exist only where the whole service of the state is removed from the common political life of the people, its chiefs as well as its rank and file. Its motives, its objects, its policy, its standards, must be bureaucratic." See "The Study of Administration," *Political Science Quarterly* 2:2 (June 1887): 217.

22. Taylor, "Shop Management," 1369. Taylor believed that each task was a good fit for a particular man, clerical or otherwise; this goes beyond a mere analogy to Charles Darwin's evolutionary theory. Taylor has often been compared to the biologist; e.g. "More than one person has found a resemblance between Frederick Taylor, the engineer, and Charles Darwin, the naturalist": Frank Barkeley Copley, *Frederick W. Taylor: Father of Scientific Management* (New York: Harper and Brothers, 1923), 361. The reversal of Taylor's notion of "fitting the worker to the job" was largely the result of the discourse on "ergonomics." See John Harwood, "The Interface: Ergonomics and the Aesthetics of Survival," in *Governing by Design: Architecture and Economy in the Twentieth Century* (Pittsburgh: University of Pittsburgh Press, 2011), 70–94.

23. Notably, Sanford E. Thompson developed the first decimal stopwatch. See William O. Lichtner, "Time and Job Analysis in Management—II," *Factory and Industrial Management* 59 (May 1920): 361. For a history of a tenth of a second, see Jimena Canales, *A Tenth of a Second: A History* (Chicago: University of Chicago Press, 2009).

24. Taylor, "Shop Management," 1393.

25. The notion that the factory system was a community gathered for a common purpose is as old as political economic theory. In the American context, it can be found in Carroll D. Wright, "The Factory System as an Element in Civilization," *Journal of Social Science* 16:1 (1882): 101–26.

26. Taylor, "Shop Management," 1397.

27. H. K. Hathaway, "On the Technique of Manufacturing," *Annals of the American Academy of Political and Social Science* 85 (September 1919): 231–32.

28. For a history of slide rules, see Florian Cajori, "Notes on the History of the Slide Rule," *American Mathematical Monthly* 15 (January 1908): 1–5. See also his *A History of the Logarithmic Slide Rule and Allied Instruments* (New York: Engineering News Publishing, 1909); *On the History of Gunter's Scale and the Slide Rule during the Seventeenth Century* (Berkeley: University of California Press, 1920).

29. This was already evident in his first job as a draftsman after emigrating from Norway, working the drawing room of William Sellers and Company in Philadelphia for fourteen years and teaching evening mechanical drawing classes at the Franklin Institute. By the end of his time at the company he had been appointed the "chief designer." Drury, *Scientific Management*, 382.

30. See, for example, Carl Barth, "The Income Tax: An Engineer's Analysis with Suggestions," *Journal of the Engineers' Club of Philadelphia* 35:163 (June 1918): 280–97; 35:164 (July 1918): 342–45. Florence M. Manning, "Carl G. Barth, 1860–1939: A Sketch," *Norwegian-American Studies* 13 (1943): 114–32.

31. "An independent investigation and treatment of tangents that led to a presumably original method of establishing the fundamentals of the differential and integral calculus, by Carl G. Barth, Consulting Engineer, retired." Case 1, Folder "Calculus 1893–," Carl G. Barth Collection, Baker Library, Harvard Business School.

32. For a historical view of Taylor's work at Bethlehem, see Thomas J. Misa, *A Nation of Steel: The Making of Modern America, 1865–1925* (Baltimore: Johns Hopkins University Press, 1995), 174–209.

33. Carl G. Barth, "Supplement to Frederick W. Taylor's 'On the Art of Cutting Metals'–I," *Industrial Management: The Engineering Magazine* 58:3 (September 1919): 170–72. John May has theorized the active surfaces of managerial control; see "The Logic of the Managerial Surface," *Praxis* 13 (2012): 116–24.

34. Barth, "Supplement to Frederick W. Taylor's 'On the Art of Cutting Metals'–I," 170. For the patent on the slide rule, see C. G. Barth, H. L. Gantt, and F. W. Taylor, Slide Rule, U.S. Patent 753,840 (issued March 8, 1904). For a description of the use of these instruments, see Carl G. Barth, "Slide Rules for the Machine Shop as a Part of the Taylor System of Management," *Transactions of the American Society of Mechanical Engineers* 25 (1904): 49–62. See also Taylor's address, "On the Art of Cutting Metals," *Transactions of the American Society of Mechanical Engineers* 28 (1907): 31–432.

35. "To make the reason for this more clear it should be understood that the man with the aid of his slide rule is called upon to determine the effect which each of the twelve elements or variables given below has upon the choice of cutting speed and feed; and it will be evident that the mechanic, expert or mathematician does not live who, without the aid of a slide rule or its equivalent, can hold in his head these twelve variables and measure their joint effect upon the problem." Taylor, "On the Art of Cutting Metals," 32–33.

36. Barth, "Slide Rules for the Machine Shop," 51.

37. Carl G. Barth, "Standardization of Machine Tools: Some Suggestions Regarding Standards of Speed and Feed Series and Standardized Power for Machine Tools, Etc." *Transactions of the American Society of Mechanical Engineers* 38 (1917): 896.

38. This is selected from the testimony that Barth gave to Congress on April 14, 1914. Commission on Industrial Relations, *Industrial Relations: Final Report and Testimony*, vol. 1 (Washington, D.C.: Government Printing Office, 1916), 888. The revised testimony can be found in full in Case 1 of the Carl G. Barth Collection, MS 708, Baker Library Historical Collections, Harvard Business School.

39. Florence Myrtle Manning, "Carl G. Barth, a Sketch" (MA thesis, University of California, Berkeley, 1927).

40. Commission on Industrial Relations, *Industrial Relations*, 889.

41. Ibid., 863.

42. Taylor, "On the Art of Cutting Metals"; Misa, *A Nation of Steel*, 198.

43. The Link-Belt Company, *The Story of Link-Belt, 1875–1925* (Chicago, 1925). James M. Dodge, "A History of the Introduction of a System of Shop Management," *Transactions of the American Society of Mechanical Engineers* 27 (1906): 720–25. See also L. P. Alford, "Scientific Management in Use," *American Machinist* 36 (April 4, 1912): 548–50. Charles Piez, "Personal Reminiscences of James Mapes Dodge," *American Machinist* 44 (January 20 and February 3, 1916): 101–5 and 197–200. For a more extensive view of the stepwise process of the fabrication of a part at Link-Belt, see James M. Dodge, "Methods of Management that Made Money," *Industrial Engineering and the Engineering Digest* 9 (January 1911): 21–27. For a historical study of labor organization at Link-Belt, see Kathy Burgess, "Organized Production and Unorganized Labor: Management Strategy and Labor Activism at the Link-Belt Company, 1900–1940," in *A Mental Revolution: Scientific Management since Taylor*, ed. Daniel Nelson (Columbus: Ohio State University Press, 1992), 130–55. For a broader historical context, see Howell John Harris, *Bloodless Victories: The Rise and Fall of the Open Shop in the Philadelphia Metal Trades, 1890–1940* (Cambridge: Cambridge University Press, 2000).

44. C. Willis Adams, "Planning Work Ahead to Save Time," *Factory: The Magazine of Management* 2 (February, March, April 1909): 141–43.

45. A similar chart and description was published by C. Willis Adams as "How a Planning Department Works," in *How Scientific Management Is Applied* (New York: The System Company, 1911), 72.

46. Taylor suggested that clocks in machine shops be based on a decimal system; see "Shop Management."

47. There are numerous instances of Barth's influence both through direct supervision as in the case of H. K. Hathaway at Tabor and also in the application of his techniques. For an exhaustive description of one application at the Ferracute Machine Company in Bridgeton, N.J., see Frederic A. Parkhurst, *Applied Methods of Scientific Management* (New York: John Wiley and Sons, 1917).

48. Drury, *Scientific Management*, 418–22. For an extended treatment of the Tabor factory, see Rudolf Seubert, *Aus der Praxis des Taylor-Systems: mit eingehender Beschreibung seiner Anwendung bei der Tabor Manufacturing Company in Philadelphia* (Berlin: J. Springer, 1920).

49. A comprehensive analysis of the image is given in Hathaway's "Description of Photographs," February 23, 1915, Box 9, Folder 59, H. K. Hathaway Papers, 1907–1929, Special Collections JL011, Stanford University Libraries. Courtesy of the Department of Special Collections, Stanford University Libraries.

50. Hathaway, "On the Technique of Manufacturing," 232.

51. H. K. Hathaway, "The Planning Department, Its Organization and Function," *Industrial Engineering and the Engineering Digest* 12 (July–August 1912): 7–11, 53–55, 99–101. Hathaway also published articles that focused more on the problems associated with routing in *Industrial Management: The Engineering Magazine*: "Logical Steps in Installing the Taylor System of Management," 60:2 (August 1920): 89–96; "The Mnemonic System of Classification," 60:3 (September 1920): 173–83; "Routing Considered as a Function of Up-to-Date Management: How to Control the Flow of Production," 60:4 (October 1920): 278–86; "Routing Considered as a Function of Up-to-Date Management–II: How to Proceed when the Product Consists of Several Parts," 60:5 (November 1920): 353–61; "Routing Considered as a Function of Up-to-Date Management–III: How to Route an Assembled Multi-part Mechanism," 60:6 (December 1920): 445–51; "Routing Considered as a Function of Up-to-Date Management–IV: Evolution of the Progress Sheet," 61:3 (February 1921): 126–34.

52. "Keeping Track of Work in the Shop," *Industrial Engineering and the Engineering Digest* 13 (November 1913): 453–58. This is an excellent representation of the bulletin boards at the New England Butt Company, as managed by Frank and Lillian Gilbreth. See Jane Lancaster, "Scientifically Managing New England Butt," in *Making Time: Lillian Moller Gilbreth, a Life Beyond "Cheaper by the Dozen"* (Boston: Northeastern University Press, 2004), 133–42.

53. Hugh G. J. Aitken, "The Arsenal," in *Scientific Management in Action*, 85–134.

54. Fred H. Colvin, "Management at Watertown Arsenal," *American Machinist* 37 (September 12, 1912): 424–28.

55. Harry Braverman, *Labor and Monopoly Capital: The Degradation of Work in the Twentieth Century* (New York: Monthly Review Press, 1974), 124–51. The work that is referred to in the formulation "degradation of work" specifically refers to the work done by mechanics before the formulation of techniques for scientific management. Their accumulated knowledge and craft experience helped guide the work of manual laborers. For Braverman, craft knowledge is not a lower form of knowledge from that of the manager. He argued that the craftsmanship of the mechanic would always be "tied to the technical and scientific knowledge of his time." Ibid., 133.

56. A few years later the methods of graphic description were standardized. See C. E. Knoeppel, *Graphic Production Control* (New York: Engineering Magazine Company, 1920).

57. Aitken, *Scientific Management in Action*, 88.

58. It was known as the Walsh Commission after Frank P. Walsh, appointed chairman by President Woodrow Wilson. See also Commission on Industrial Relations, *The Taylor and Other Systems of Shop Management* (Washington, D.C.: Government Printing Office, 1912). On the history of the commission, see Graham Adams, *Age of Industrial Violence, 1910–1915: The Activities and Findings of the United States Commission on Industrial Relations* (New York: Columbia University Press, 1971), and Bruce E. Kaufman, *The Origins and Evolution of Industrial Relations in the United States* (Ithaca: Cornell University Press, 1992).

59. For a thorough treatment of the events that led up to the strike, see Hugh G. J. Aitken, "Conflicts," in *Scientific Management in Action*, 135–85.

60. Commission on Industrial Relations, *Industrial Relations*, 894. See also H. K. Hathaway,

"The Value of Non-Producers in Manufacturing Plants," *Machinery* 13 (November 1906): 133–34.

61. Thorstein Veblen, *The Engineers and the Price System* (New York: B. W. Huebsch, 1921). The essays were originally published in the journal *Dial* in the months immediately following the Armistice in 1919. Veblen closely aligns with Harry Braverman's later critique of Taylorism as the origin of the degradation of work in the twentieth century.

62. Ibid., 8.

63. Ibid., 47. See chapter 3.

64. Ibid., 50–51. For an excellent history of the events that led to the establishment of the Federal Reserve System, see James Livingston, *The Origins of the Federal Reserve System: Money, Class, and Corporate Capitalism, 1880–1913* (Ithaca: Cornell University Press, 1986).

65. Veblen, *The Engineers and the Price System*, 55.

66. Ibid., 51.

5. REGULATION THROUGH PAPERWORK IN ARCHITECTURAL PRACTICE

1. Hyungmin Pai, *The Portfolio and the Diagram: Architecture, Discourse, and Modernity in America* (Cambridge, Mass.: MIT Press, 2002). Pai's analysis relies on the detailed study of reforms to professional practices by Paul Bentel, "Modernism and Professionalism in American Modern Architecture, 1919–1933" (PhD diss., MIT, 1992).

2. For a broader view of this transformation in other professions, see Magali Lason, "Profession and Bureaucracy," in *The Rise of Professionalism: A Sociological Analysis* (Los Angeles: University of California Press, 1977), 178–207.

3. Louis Sullivan, *The Autobiography of an Idea* (New York: American Institute of Architects, 1924), 314. Thomas S. Hines has written: "Burnham approached . . . businessmen on businessmen's terms." *Burnham of Chicago: Architect & Planner* (Chicago: University of Chicago Press, 2009), 273. For a more recent essay on Burnham, see Jay Wickersham, "Learning From Burnham: The Origins of Modern Architectural Practice," *Harvard Design Magazine* 32 (Spring/Summer 2010): 18–27.

4. Dell Upton, "Pattern Books and Professionalism: Aspects of the Transformation of Domestic Architecture in America, 1800–1860," *Winterthur Portfolio* 19:2/3 (Summer–Autumn 1984): 107–50. Mary Woods, *From Craft to Profession* (Berkeley: University of California Press, 1995), esp. 82–137. See also Bernard Michael Boyle, "Architectural Practice in America, 1865–1965—Ideal and Reality," in *The Architect: Chapters in the History of the Profession* (Berkeley: University of California Press, 1977), 309–44. For a more current perspective, see Dana Cuff, *Architecture: The Story of a Practice* (Cambridge, Mass.: MIT Press, 1991). The history of the professions in America is a vast field of scholarship; one book that accounts for the simultaneity of the turn to management, including the architectural profession, is Kenneth S. Lynn, ed., *The Professions in America* (Boston: Beacon Press, 1967).

5. Julius F. Harder, "Architectural Practice—an Art and a Business," *The Brickbuilder* 11 (April 1902): 74.

6. Julius F. Harder, "Architecture,—American Aspect," *The Craftsman* 6:5 (August 1904): 424.

7. Cyrus Foss Springall, "The Business Organization of an Architectural Office" (BS thesis,

Massachusetts Institute of Technology, Department of Architecture, 1912). Earlier treatments of the subject exist. Those that precede Frederick Winslow Taylor are more apt to refer to the subdivision of labor in an office as "natural." For example, "The Management of an Architect's Office," *American Architect and Building News* 33 (August 15, September 5, and September 19, 1891): 97–99, 147–49, 178–80; and continued in *American Architect and Building News* 34 (October 10 and December 19, 1891): 27–29, 181–83. Immediately after *The Principles of Scientific Management* (New York, 1911) was published, there were a few instances in which it is mentioned in the architectural press. For example, Walter H. Kilham, "Some Phases of Modern Architectural Practice," *Architect and Engineer of California* 23 (June 1911): 52–56. For images of the architecture office from the turn of the twentieth century, see "Where Our Architects Work," *Architectural Record* 10 (July 1900): 76–83, 143–49, 238–44.

8. Springall, "The Business Organization of an Architectural Office," 7–8.

9. Ibid., 3–4.

10. Ibid., 4.

11. William Leffingwell, *Scientific Office Management* (New York: A. W. Shaw Company, 1917). See also his *Making the Office Pay: Tested Office Plans, Methods, and Systems that Make for Better Results from Everyday Routine* (New York: A. W. Shaw Company, 1918).

12. Lee Galloway, *Office Management: Its Principles and Practice* (New York: Ronald Press Company, 1918). The business literature on the value of air quality for office work during the 1910s is significant. For example, see Sidney G. Koon, "Fresh Air and Your Payroll," *System: The Magazine of Business* 23 (March 1913): 297–304; Kendall Banning, "Figures to Prove that Ventilation Pays," *System: The Magazine of Business* 30 (September 1916): 323–29.

13. George Twitmyer, "A Model Administration Building," *Businessman's Magazine* 19 (April 1907): 43. Reprinted without images in Jack Quinan, *Frank Lloyd Wright's Larkin Building: Myth and Fact* (Chicago: University of Chicago Press, 2006), 149. See also Joe Mitchell Chappele, "Common Sense—Just Common Sense," *National Magazine* 31 (November 1909): 195–98.

14. Frank Lloyd Wright, *An Autobiography* (New York: Duel, Sloan and Pearce, 1943), 270. For more on transformations in Wright's authorship, see my "American System Built Houses: Authorship and Mass Production," in *Frank Lloyd Wright: Unpacking the Archive*, ed. Barry Bergdoll and Jennifer Gray (New York: Museum of Modern Art, 2017), 148–55.

15. For a summary of the main tendencies in the development of office structure at the beginning of the twentieth century, see Elyse McBride, "The Development of Architectural Office Specialization as Evidenced by Professional Journals, 1890–1920" (MA thesis, University of Washington, 2009). See also *OfficeUS Manual*, ed. Eva Franch, Ana Miljački, Carlos Minguez Carrasco, Jacob Reidel, and Ashley Schafer (Zürick: Lars Müller Publishers, 2017).

16. Daniel Paul Higgins, "The 'Business' of Architecture," *Architectural Review* 4 (September 1916): 167. The next head of the design department at Pope's office, Howard Dwight Smith, continued the series. A summary of the relation between the architect and the draftsman in a scientifically managed office can be found in George Barnett Johnston,

Drafting Culture: A Social History of Architectural Graphic Standards (Cambridge, Mass.: MIT Press, 2008).

17. Daniel Paul Higgins, "The 'Business' of Architecture," *Architectural Review* 4 (November 1916): 193. A similar system was used in the office of Carrère and Hastings: D. Everett Waid, "How Architects Work," *The Brickbuilder* 21 (February 1912): 8–10. Later, Waid wrote a series of articles profiling various business practices in an architectural office entitled "The Business Side of an Architect's Office"; these included, "The Office of Mr. Donn Barber," *The Brickbuilder* 22 (September 1913): 197–98; "Descriptions of the Offices of Messrs. Henry Bacon; Ford, Butler & Oliver; Ludlow & Peabody; H. Van Buren Magonigle and Kenneth Murchison," *The Brickbuilder* 22 (November 1913): 253–54; "The Office of Messrs. Mann & MacNeille, New York," *The Brickbuilder* 23 (May 1914): 103–5.

18. Daniel Paul Higgins, "The 'Business' of Architecture," *Architectural Review* 6 (January 1918): 3.

19. Several authors have written on Kahn's office: Grant Hildebrand, *Designing for Industry: The Architecture of Albert Kahn* (Cambridge, Mass.: MIT Press, 1974); Federico Bucci, *Albert Kahn: Architect of Ford* (New York: Princeton Architectural Press, 1993); Terry Smith, *Making the Modern: Industry, Art, and Design in America* (Chicago: University of Chicago Press, 1993); Chris Meister, "Albert Kahn's Partners in Industrial Architecture," *Journal of the Society of Architectural Historians* 72:1 (March 2013): 78–95. More recently, Claire Zimmerman has taken on the size of Kahn's practice as a challenge to methods for conducting architectural history. See her "The Labor of Albert Kahn," *Aggregate* website (Not Peer Reviewed), http://we-aggregate.org/piece/the-labor-of-albert-kahn. Kahn's place in the broader context of factory architecture is addressed in Lindy Biggs, *The Rational Factory* (Baltimore: Johns Hopkins University Press, 1996), 100–160.

20. Smith, *Making the Modern*, 77. For an example of the comparison between Kahn's practice and the Ford Motor Company, see Charles K. Hyde, "Assembly-Line Architecture: Albert Kahn and the Evolution of the U.S. Auto Factory, 1905–1940," *Journal of the Society for Industrial Archeology* 22:2 (1996): 5–24. Another architect who adopted his clients' managerial systems was Cass Gilbert at the Woolworth Building. See Gail Fenske, *The Skyscraper and the City: The Woolworth Building and the Making of Modern New York* (Chicago: University of Chicago Press, 2008).

21. David Hounshell, *From the American System to Mass Production, 1800–1932* (Baltimore: Johns Hopkins University Press, 1984), 252–53.

22. George C. Baldwin, "The Offices of Albert Kahn, Architect, Detroit, Michigan," *Architectural Forum* 29:5 (November 1918): 125. For the twelve years that Kahn's office was in the Marquette Building, the drawings are collected as "Job Nos. 798, 798-D, F, G, K, L, O, P and Q," Drawer 14, Folder 1, Albert Kahn Papers, 1896–2011, Bentley Historical Library, University of Michigan. For an earlier treatment of the organization of a large architectural firm, see D. Everett Waid, "The Business Side of an Architect's Office: The Office of George B. Post & Sons," *The Brickbuilder* 23 (February 1914): 47–49. For more on Post, see Diana Balmori, "George B. Post: The Process of Design and the New American Architectural Office (1868–1913)," *Journal of the Society of Architectural Historians* 46:4 (December 1987): 350–54.

23. For a history of mass marketing of telecommunication, see Richard R. John, "Second

Nature," in *Network Nation: Inventing American Telecommunications* (Cambridge: Belknap Press of Harvard University Press, 2010), 269–310.

24. Ben Kafka, *The Demon of Writing: Powers and Failures of Paperwork* (New York: Zone Books, 2012). For a review of this emerging field, see also Ben Kafka, "Paperwork: The State of the Discipline," *Book History* 12 (2009): 340–53.

25. Peter Galison and Caroline A. Jones, "Factory, Laboratory, Studio: Dispersing Sites of Production," in *The Architecture of Science*, ed. Peter Galison and Emily Thompson (Cambridge, Mass.: MIT Press, 1999), 497–540.

26. The comparison of Wright to Kahn was the central opposition posed by Henry-Russell Hitchcock in his essay "The Architecture of Bureaucracy and the Architecture of Genius," *Architectural Review* 101 (January 1947): 3–6. Hitchcock elaborated a theory of anonymous production that he viewed as "organizational genius." As he wrote, "Kahn Inc." was a collective enterprise that produced a "fool-proof system of rapid and complete plan production." Ibid., 4–5. On the topic of corporate anonymity, see John Harwood, "Corporate Abstraction," *Perspecta* 46 (2013): 218–47. And on anonymity in architectural personhood more generally, see Timothy Hyde, "Notes on Architectural Persons," *Aggregate* website, http://www.we-aggregate.org/piece/notes-on-architectural-persons.

27. George Nelson, *Industrial Architecture of Albert Kahn, Inc.* (New York: Architectural Book Publishing Company, 1939), 7. See also his "Industrial Buildings: Albert Kahn," *Architectural Forum* 69:8 (August 1938): 87–141. Kahn's buildings were pictured in the publications of many European modernist architects from Walter Gropius to Le Corbusier, and then again in the histories of modernism from Adolf Behne to Sigfried Giedion.

28. Nelson, "Industrial Buildings: Albert Kahn," 89, 91. On the role of completeness in Ove Arup's corporate engineering firm, see Arindam Dutta, "Marginality and Meta-engineering: Keynes and Arup," in *Governing by Design: Architecture, Economy, and Politics in the Twentieth Century*, ed. Aggregate (Architectural History Collaborative) (Pittsburgh: University of Pittsburgh Press, 2012), 237–67. Consider the passage, quoted by Dutta, of Arup's view of the whole: "what we build is always a whole, an entity—a building, a precinct, a town with roads, etc.—and all these entities interact and influence each other." Ibid., 251.

29. Adolf Behne, *The Modern Functional Building* [1923], trans. Michael R. Robinson (Santa Monica, Calif.: Getty Research Institute, 1996).

30. *Machine Art, March 6 to April 30, 1934* (New York: Museum of Modern Art, 1995). For a thorough exegesis of the show in the context of modernist aesthetics and museology, see Jennifer Jane Marshall, *Machine Art, 1934* (Chicago: University of Chicago Press, 2012).

31. In the same year as the *Machine Art* exhibition, Lewis Mumford published *Technics and Civilization* (New York: Harcourt, 1934). He justified the "independent existence" of the machine, "apart from the user," as a transition away from viewing the machine merely as a means to a practical end: "The possibility that technics had become a creative force, carried on by its own momentum, that it was rapidly ordering a new kind of environment and was producing a third estate midway between nature and the humane arts, that it was not merely a quicker way of achieving old ends but an effective way of ex-

pressing new ends—the possibility in short that the machine furthered a new mode of *living.*" Ibid., 323.

32.   Hitchcock, "The Architecture of Bureaucracy," 5.

CONCLUSION

1.   Michel Aglietta, *A Theory of Capitalist Regulation: The US Experience* [1976], trans. David Fernback (New York: Verso, 2000), 19. Aglietta calls equilibrium theory "totalitarian." Ibid., 10.

2.   Most recently in Mauro Guillen, *The Taylorized Beauty of the Mechanical* (Princeton, N.J.: Princeton University Press, 2006).

3.   This term is often used to describe the processes of development in third-world nations, but social historians of the United States have used the term as well. One prominent example is Richard D. Brown's *Modernization: The Transformation of American Life, 1600–1865* (New York: Hill and Wang, 1976). Brown's view of the modernization process has been characterized as "neither a seamless web nor one-damn-thing-after-another, . . . but a coherent pattern of discontinuity. . . . The core of the modernization approach is based on the realization of a radical break in the historical record and the application of dichotomous ideal-types as a tool for explicating that discontinuity." Daniel Scott Smith, "'Modernization' and American Social History," *Social Science History* 2:3 (Spring 1978): 361. More recently, a similar language of modernization is used in Alfred D. Chandler Jr. and James Cortada, eds., *A Nation Transformed by Information: How Information Has Shaped the United States from Colonial Times to the Present* (New York: Oxford University Press, 2000).

4.   Robert H. Wiebe, *The Search for Order* (New York: Hill and Wang, 1967), xiv.

5.   Ibid., 164.

6.   For an excellent review of the historiography of Progressivism from the 1960s and 1970s, see Daniel T. Rodgers, "In Search of Progressivism," *Reviews in American History* 10:4 (December 1982): 113–32. Rodgers points to an essay by Samuel P. Hays to compare his methods to those of Wiebe, finding them both overly general due to their reliance—although largely unacknowledged—on the modernization thesis: "for those who persisted in asking what human intentions drove the great social engine, other than those bound up in the fashionable incantation 'modernization,' Hays's answers, still more than Wiebe's, seemed vexingly obscure." Ibid., 119. Research in this field is vast and expands daily, and numerous subsequent attempts have been made to reckon with the same issues addressed in Rodgers's essay.

Index

MICHAEL OSMAN is associate professor of architecture and urban design at the University of California, Los Angeles.